BELOVED ECONOMIES

BELOVED

JESS RIMINGTON
JOANNA L. CEA

ECONOMIES

TRANSFORMING
HOW WE WORK

PAGE TWO

Cataloguing in publication information is
available from Library and Archives Canada.
ISBN 978-1-989025-02-4 (paperback)
ISBN 978-1-77458-238-1 (ebook)
ISBN 978-1-77458-237-4 (audiobook)

Page Two
pagetwo.com

Authored by Jess Rimington and Joanna Levitt Cea
Co-created with a co-learning community
Book Doula, narrative, and writing support by Naomi McDougall Jones
Edited by Naomi McDougall Jones, Steve Woodward, and Amanda Lewis
Copyedited by Crissy Calhoun and Jenna Sofia
Research and supporting editors: M. Strickland and Nairuti Shastry
Fact checking by Emily Krieger and Carolyn A. Shea
Targeted research and editorial review by
Anke Ehlert, Lauren Ressler, and Fiona Teng
Interview support and targeted editorial review by Sonia Sarkar

The process of creating this book was profoundly collaborative.
Many of the individuals listed above made contributions that go far beyond
what these roles traditionally mean in a book development process. Learn more
in the section "A Window into the Research" and the acknowledgments.

Cover and interior design by Peter Cocking
Cover and interior illustrations by Jesse White

Printed and bound in Canada by Friesens
Distributed in Canada by Raincoast Books
Distributed in the US and internationally by Macmillan

22 23 24 25 26   5 4 3 2 1

"A beloved economy is induced, like your birth, and is born when ordinary people with extraordinary shared aims are tied in with things that create life and care for one another."

DR. VIRGIL A. WOOD

CONTENTS

CO-LEARNING COMMUNITY

THE RESEARCH and this book itself have been co-creatively shaped by more than one hundred people. The following sixty people stand out in the contributions each made to the research findings and analyses. Each person played a different role: some engaged during a particular phase of the research, while others continued to participate and shape the emerging analysis throughout all phases of the research. Together we formed a co-learning community.

The common thread among all members of this co-learning community is a commitment to, and strong practice of, changing how we work to embrace power-sharing ways that depart from business as usual. Each individual is listed below by name, along with an organization, initiative, or role with which they are currently affiliated or were previously affiliated during the course of their engagement in this research. Several of the individuals below are either no longer affiliated with the entity listed or are affiliated with multiple entities.

Many individuals listed below you will meet in the pages to come. Wherever someone's words, ideas, or stories are shared, they co-created this part of the content and had ultimate decision-making authority on what appears in these pages. Many of those featured read and informed the book's narrative, ideas, and structure, or had the opportunity to do so, through co-creation workbooks and prototyping of the research findings and draft content.

Throughout the book, wherever one of the following people is mentioned, we introduce them by first and last name and any titles. After that, we refer to them primarily by first name, as we invite the reader into community with us. The exception to this is Dr. Virgil A. Wood, who is referred to as Dr. Wood throughout the book.

Aisha Shillingford, Intelligent Mischief
Alfredo Cruz, Foundation for Louisiana
Andrew Delmonte, Cooperation Buffalo
Antionette D. Carroll, Creative Reaction Lab
Ashby Monk, Stanford Research Initiative on
    Long-Term Investing
Banks Benitez, Uncharted
Ben Joosten, Incourage Community Foundation
Beth Mount, Graphic Futures
Betsy Wood, Incourage Community Foundation
Bobbie Hill, Concordia
Brian McLaren, pastor
Brian Mikulencak, Blue Dot Advocates
Brooking Gatewood, The Emergence Collective
Bruce Campbell, Blue Dot Advocates
Bryana DiFonzo, PUSH Buffalo
Connor McManus, Concordia
Dawn Neuman, Incourage Community Foundation

Debbe McCall, Heart Research Alliance
Deborah Bidwell, Biomimicry for Social Innovation
Ed Whitfield, Seed Commons
Edgar Villanueva, Decolonizing Wealth Project
Enoch Elwell, CO.STARTERS
Eryn Wise, Standing Rock
Eugene Eric Kim, Faster Than 20
Farhad Ebrahimi, Chorus Foundation
Isabella Jean, independent consultant and
    organizational adviser
Jane Hwang, Social Accountability International
Jerome Segura III, regional economist
Jessamyn Shams-Lau, philanthropic consultant
Jessica Amon, Community Organizers Multiversity
Jessica Norwood, RUNWAY
Joe Terry, Incourage Community Foundation
John Ikerd, professor emeritus of agricultural economics,
    University of Missouri
Kalsoom Lakhani, Invest2Innovate
Kataraina Davis, Maurea Design
Katherine Tyler Scott, Ki ThoughtBridge
Kelley Buhles, Buhles Consulting
Kelly Ryan, Incourage Community Foundation
Kyle White, Thunder Valley Community
    Development Corporation
Lynn Cuny, Thunder Valley Community
    Development Corporation
Maggie Nichols, Innovation Engineering
Maile Keliʻipio-Acoba, Institute for Native Pacific
    Education and Culture
Marion Weber, Flow Funding
Markese Bryant, Remix: The Soul of Innovation
Maurice BP-Weeks, Action Center on Race & the Economy

McCall Langford, Biomimicry for Social Innovation
Melissa Lee, Concordia
Nancy Zamierowski, Yellow Seed
Nina Sol Robinson, RUNWAY
Paula Antoine, Standing Rock
Rahwa Ghirmatzion, PUSH Buffalo
Rebecca Petzel, The Emergence Collective
Serena Wales, Textizen
Sharon McIntyre, New Cottage Industries & Co.
Stephanie Wilson, Social Accountability International
Steven Bingler, Concordia
Tatewin Means, Thunder Valley Community
    Development Corporation
Toby Herzlich, Biomimicry for Social Innovation
Vera Triplett, Noble Minds Institute
Virgil A. Wood, educator and church leader

CHAPTER 1

WORK ISN'T WORKING

MORE AND more people have arrived at the same conclusion: our current ways of work are not working.

This book is about practices that transform work within our groups, businesses, and organizations—small and large—to provide a pathway out of what isn't working about work. It is based on our research on teams that are experiencing a particular form of success related to what makes life good—success that feels beloved.

We offer you seven specific practices that are a starting place for creating these changes in how you work. We also share how these deviations from the status quo are effective, and why such pathways into alternatives have been actively suppressed. Through this, we reveal uncomfortable truths about business as usual. And share how we came to uncover a way to generate innovation that audaciously prioritizes well-being, meaning, connection, and resilience alongside traditional metrics like quality and financial success. This book is a call to action: stop missing out on all that becomes possible when we change how we work, and instead step into our collective power for transformation.

IN WHAT HAS been called the Great Resignation, millions of people decided—for one reason or another—that their present work was neither sustainable nor worth it. More than nineteen million people in the United States quit their jobs over a five-month period in 2021,[1] and 40 percent of these people did so without having another lined up.[2]

Looking at the data, it's easy to see why more and more of us are fed up with and exhausted by the status quo of work. A staggering litany of statistics reveals how physical and psychological strains of the workplace are costing us our lives, while simultaneously leaving most people financially strapped—and often in debt.

It is no exaggeration to say work is killing us. In the United States, workplace-related illness and health issues may contribute to more than $200 billion in healthcare costs every year.[3] And according to research led by Stanford Graduate School of Business professor Jeffrey Pfeffer, the workplace may be the fifth leading cause of death in the United States,[4] over three times the number of deaths in 2020 from motor vehicle accidents.[5] For centuries, labor rights organizers have drawn our attention to the bodily harm that workers endure.

According to Dr. Pfeffer, workplace-related stress and illness are taking a growing toll on American workers and the healthcare system. As Dr. Pfeffer explains, "Seven percent of people in one survey were hospitalized—hospitalized!—because of workplace stress; 50% had missed time at work because of stress. People are quitting their jobs because of stress."[6]

Citing statistics that show as much as 75 percent of the disease burden in the US is chronic,[7] Dr. Pfeffer points out, "[T]here is a tremendous amount of epidemiological literature that suggests that [many chronic diseases such as] diabetes, cardiovascular disease, and metabolic syndrome... come from stress... [T]here is a large amount of data that suggests the biggest source of stress is the workplace."[8] In other words, researchers believe our workplaces are causing chronic disease. "I look out at the workplace and I see stress, layoffs, longer hours, work-family conflict, enormous amounts of economic insecurity," says Dr. Pfeffer. "I see a workplace that... [is] shockingly inhumane."[9]

Simultaneously, millions of people are finding it hard to obtain enough work hours to qualify for benefits and pay their bills. With hours fluctuating at the demand of their employers and sometimes customers, many working people are struggling to ensure a predictable and reliable schedule. The US Federal Reserve found in 2020 that 16 percent of American part-time and temporary workers' schedules fluctuated based on their employers' needs.[10] As summed up in a *New York Times* opinion piece by economic journalist Bryce Covert, "The people who suffer from just-in-time scheduling that never quite adds up to a normal 9 to 5 aren't spending their off hours on leisure. They're working second and third jobs. They are hovering over an app to find out if they're going to be called into work and are scrambling to piece childcare and transportation together if and when they are."[11] Even those who hold stable jobs are often struggling to make ends meet or build up savings.[12]

It's no wonder over half of workers in the United States report being burned out.[13] Many of us pour our life force into a week-to-week grind that leaves us feeling exhausted, unwell, and without the financial means to step off—or even take a break from—this frenetic conveyor belt.

To top it all off, not only is work failing us humans, it's also devastatingly evident that the predominant economic system, which our ways of work uphold, is endangering other forms of life on Earth. From the very real effects of climate change, such as wildfires and droughts of unprecedented scale, to the related great waves of extinction decimating countless species to depletion of our agricultural soils,[14] the living world is crying out, "This is not working!"

IT WAS A decade ago when we both started to recognize the depth of the problem with our current ways of work. Even though we had gone to work almost every day of our lives, we had not previously *examined* work. Sure, we had thought a lot about our jobs. After all, in our experience, when we introduced ourselves to a new person, one of the first questions asked was frequently "What do you do?"

When we first met, we surprised one another with how we answered that question. While we each shared what we did for work, we also talked about how we went about it. It was in that moment that we saw something kindred in each other: an unrelenting commitment to *how* things are done, not just *what* is being done. We met at a women's leadership training; we were both leaders of organizations at a young age—executive directors of small nonprofits with big dreams. Jess built new approaches to participatory youth-led education that inspired action in communities, and Joanna advocated for policy reform at international institutions, such as the World Bank, to make aid accountable to the people it's supposed to benefit. At the core of both our work was a dedication to aligning our ways of working with the values we believed in. Thus began a deep friendship that later turned into a close collaboration.

This collaboration began with a shared, burning question: Why are we trapped in exhausting, harmful modes of working, and what is possible when we innovate out of them?

As for many people, our jobs had become a cornerstone of how we perceived our context and identity, or how we fit in society. We had both started working in our teens and were part of a generation that took on student loans so we could go to college and learn how to work better. But it wasn't until we began our research endeavor in 2015, which eventually led to this book, that we took an in-depth look at how we work, why our current work patterns have us operating in unsupportive systems—and what else might be possible.

We began to see things with fresh eyes. We saw a hustle of survival and overachieving deeply embedded in ourselves and our peers. We observed that not only did the "reward" of moving to the next level only mean more work, we experienced it to also mean continuing to live paycheck to paycheck. More often than not—even when working within nonprofits— we felt we were participating in maintaining a status quo that was neither working for people nor our planet.

Our burning question eventually led to a seven-year research journey, including a shared short-term visiting scholar position at Stanford University and organizing to bring together multifaceted research collaborators. Each of these collaborators brought their own additional questions and insights to the table, which sharpened the emerging analyses through their input. Over time, sixty people from a wide array of teams and enterprises together formed a co-learning community that unearthed clear answers to our burning question.

Escaping business as usual

For the purpose of clarity, in this book, when we discuss current, harmful ways of work, we will use the term *business as usual*.[15] As you'll see, these ways of work are, at present, inextricably connected to the way that business and the economy operate. Building on the work of scholars before us, we define business as usual as ways of work oriented toward the maximization of monetary profit and growth at all costs and which shut down or narrow information that offers differing goals or strategies. Business as usual allows us to use the term *work* as neither an inherently positive nor negative thing but simply as a set of activities that can have positive or negative impacts, depending on the context.

In our research, we set out to determine whether we could find teams and groups who were already working together in ways distinct from business as usual, and if so, whether they were experiencing meaningful success. Was anyone out there managing to escape what isn't working about work?

Over the course of this research journey, we indeed found many such groups. They often achieved the kinds of success prioritized by business as usual, such as better quality products and services, lower levels of attrition, increased competency, reduced costs, and financial success. However, what the people in these groups emphasized most strongly were the other types of success they achieved: a greater sense of connection and belonging; feelings of peace, well-being, and confidence in their work; a newfound sense of purpose and satisfaction; and even feelings of happiness and hope. It seemed that these groups were finding success that felt like an antidote to what isn't working about work.

We define *work* as the modes in which groups of people imagine, design, and create something together—from products to processes to built structures to organizational systems and more. Work can be paid, for example, building a new offering to sell to customers, redesigning the way a company hires, or determining the most efficient way to assemble a product. Work can also be unpaid, for example, organizing a volunteer campaign for a social cause, designing a system for caregiving support within your family, or creating educational content as part of a volunteer community group.

When we use the word *work*, we refer to people devoting time toward a shared aim that requires them to create together and draw upon imagination. Imagination comes into play when what a team is creating either doesn't exist yet or is a revision of something that does. Through this lens, work encompasses a wide array of activities, which span white, blue, and pink collar; nonprofit and for profit; gig or traditionally employed; and across industries. Imagination and collaboration are used by groups of people in all these contexts—from those who provide value primarily by creating with their hands, to generating value via a computer, to providing outcomes through the facilitation, organizing, or coaching of groups, and from teams of just two or three people to whole companies of hundreds or more. This wide range of work requires (or holds the potential to benefit from) a certain kind of innovation: one based in imagining *together* the better, new, or different, and then—with one another—bringing these innovations to life.

We see most work as riddled with practices that prioritize and reinforce the way things are, even when that way isn't working. Within the business-as-usual culture that fails to serve most of us or our communities, we see an acceptance of innovation as just an upgraded version of what already exists. This contrasts with dreaming boldly into what could be—not only with the products and services we create but, perhaps most importantly, in how we relate to one another in the process of creating them.

After hundreds of conversations with many people and groups, we have come to believe that there is an escape hatch out of this state of affairs—out of business as usual.

We have found ways of work that unlock innovation from a wider, bolder vantage point. Such work breaks free from the status quo in a way that gives rise to stunning outcomes and more connection, vitality, and meaning along the way.

The escape hatch not only exists but there are people right now who—together with their team members, community groups, or whole enterprises—are already climbing out and into something wholly different.

Although we found and were inspired by groups around the world, we limited the scope of our research to those in the United States and narrowed our observations to the ways in which they were departing from business as usual within the US. And while there are many ways in which work is not working that are unique to the United States, the economic dynamics influencing, and reinforced by, business as usual are affected by actors across many nations and have impacts that span the globe. The practices offered in this book also reflect and complement strategies and technologies developed by people worldwide. Therefore, we believe, these ways out of business as usual are applicable across many geographic contexts.

It's been a long road from our research cubicles as visiting scholars at Stanford University. We've held down multiple jobs, at times moonlighting as researchers on this project in the evenings, and we've meticulously organized reams of notes and index cards from over a thousand pages of interview transcripts. Over time, we observed a growing ripple effect among the groups we were researching alongside. As these teams changed how they worked, something within the people involved also transformed, which they then carried to future spaces, circles of work, and communities. These changes added up to a larger web of economic transformation. It is a kind of transformation that makes not only work but life as a whole more beloved.

Learning this has been profoundly exciting and inspiring. At the same time, it raised a question: If work doesn't have to be locked in harmful, exhausting patterns for our endeavors to succeed, why aren't more of us adopting beloved ways of working?

As illustrated in the parable of the young fish who asks a wiser fish friend, "What is water?" we've learned we can be so thoroughly immersed in the present ways of work that it can be hard to perceive the rules and assumptions dictating how work should happen, and comprising the particular economic system within which we are working. This is the proverbial water in which we are swimming. Once we train our attention to recognize this water, however, it becomes easier to see that we are awash in a particular economic system, constructed through a series of specific decisions made by humans past and present. When we see that this system—like any other human-made system—is made through people's decisions, it becomes easier to realize that we could actually imagine and build different systems, based on different rules and assumptions, which could change how we work.

The business-as-usual economy functions exactly as it is intended: to create wealth, and—as a result of how it is designed—enable a small group of people to accumulate a whole lot of money.

Our ways of work are deeply influenced by how the present economy operates, and they serve to perpetuate this business as usual, day in and day out. The same forces that drive the economic system to consolidate wealth in the hands of a few, and lead many of us to be burned out, exhausted, and broke, also play a role in making many of us feel like the current ways of work are inevitable. But it doesn't have to be this way. Business as usual is the result of specific choices people have made over centuries, and continue to make today.

The current economy—in the United States and in most places globally—is rooted in the economic belief system of capitalism. There are many different varieties of capitalism that have existed over time and that exist today. For instance, in the United States, capitalism has shifted over the past decades and centuries to take different forms. Among the countries with capitalist economies worldwide, there is variety in how a nation's particular brand of capitalism operates—as governed by legislation—and therefore how people experience it.

It is important to understand that any number of economic ideologies—or isms—could perpetuate ways of work that exhaust and harm, depending on how they are designed. It's also important to remember that pointing out the problematic dynamics of current manifestations of capitalism does not imply that some other ism—such as socialism—is the automatic, only other option. The options for how an economy can operate are as broad as our capacity to imagine them. Since capitalism is presently a dominant paradigm, we are going to tease out some of its core mechanics—how the ways it is currently expressed influence how we work.

In a definitional sense, capitalism is based on private ownership with the use and allocation of resources determined by markets. As it relates to work, capitalism generally classifies the people who show up to the jobs, work the hours, create the things, etc. as workers. Similarly, capitalism tends to classify the people who front the capital—money and other assets (land, buildings, etc.)—to secure things required for workers to show up to the jobs, work the hours, and produce the things—as capitalists. According to the economic ideology of capitalism, the capitalists should be the ones to make the vast majority of critical decisions related to workers' day-to-day experiences of their jobs. The capitalists also receive the vast majority of the profits created by the workers, which are then distributed in some way among the capitalists involved in the effort—owners, lenders, venture capitalists, shareholders, etc.—but not typically to the workers.

Essentially, a pact has been made that those who own capital and are in a position to take risks with their assets (such as advancing funds to start a new business, purchasing a building, or buying out a company struggling with bankruptcy) will, in exchange for taking the up-front and interim risks of a given effort, receive the profits made by that venture. In other words, in capitalism, all the financial surplus—what's left after what's paid in wages and direct costs for production—goes to the few who were able to provide monetary or other assets to the venture.

In our current economy—because capitalists usually own both what is required to create things, such as our workplaces, and also the infrastructure for daily life from housing to grocery stores to cell phone networks—money generally flows in one direction: to the capitalists with the most monetary capital. This dominant economic paradigm is becoming more unequal over time as wealth accumulates in the hands of a few, and as those few with the most assets can afford to take the greatest risks with those assets, thus compounding the benefits. In this present system, as their wealth compounds, so, too, does their ability to set the rules and agenda.

Although ideologically capitalism makes a distinction between workers and capitalists, in the present context, many people move between being workers and small-scale capitalists (e.g., owning a small business, owning property, or making investments with retirement savings), sometimes acting as both at once. And while they may have more influence over how things work in their capacity as small-scale capitalists than they do in their roles as workers, they nonetheless experience many of the critical decisions related to their day-to-day work as often being out of their hands and their ability to receive or retain profits as limited. For instance, someone owning a corner store or running a hair salon is technically a capitalist, but they still might experience constraints determined by larger asset holders, such as the company to whom they pay rent or the bank setting the repayment terms on their business loan.

Money may pass through the hands of the workers or small business owners, but in this system, the money can become evermore consolidated in the hands of a few—unless there are, for instance, individual capitalists or worker collectives who act against the grain of business as usual, or rules and constraints from government that prescribe otherwise.

Compounding inequity

Since those with consolidated assets can currently wield huge influence over regulations, many people around the globe are experiencing an economy that is not oriented toward their well-being or the creation of wealth for their communities. How this has shaken out is, as described in 2019 by economic theorists and authors Marjorie Kelly and Ted Howard from the Democracy Collaborative, "a world in which 26 billionaires own as much wealth as half the planet's population. The three wealthiest men in the U.S… own more wealth than the bottom half of America combined, a total of 160 million people… Meanwhile, an alarming 47 percent of Americans cannot put together even $400 in the face of an emergency."[16]

"The extent to which inequality has grown is a symptom of an unhealthy system," points out Dr. Jerome Segura III, a regional economist based in central Wisconsin. We met Jerome in 2017 to discuss the economic questions arising from our research. At the time, Jerome was a professor at the University of Wisconsin at Stevens Point. A few years later, because of both economic and political factors at the university, his position ceased to exist, despite how much students loved Jerome's classes and his intellectual bravery. "A friend once referred to me as being a superhero economist," says Jerome with a laugh. "It made me blush and smile. But humbly the phrase does resonate with me because I am a renegade—specifically in that I understand economic growth and development are better achieved through the building of people within community and place." This understanding is something Jerome attributes to his Cajun heritage. He learned early in life the importance of investing in one's neighbors.

In the wake of job loss, Jerome decided to become a stay-at-home father while the mother of his children continued to build the small business she'd recently launched in town. In addition to caring for their two young sons, Jerome began a vertically integrated business growing and selling mushrooms to local restaurants and individuals. Even though he and his children's mother have been successful in their entrepreneurship, Jerome is still acutely aware of how broken the US economic system is, based on knowledge gained from his doctoral studies and his family's lived experience. "When you have a system that just doesn't seem to be working for the majority of people," argues Jerome, "you've got to start looking at what those inherent failures are."

Jerome points out that the growing levels of inequality reflect how the present economy disincentivizes ways of work that promote the retention of wealth by communities, the well-being of individuals, or the health of our ecosystems. Instead, our present economy orients work toward the consolidation of financial wealth into the hands of a few, time and again, creating an ever-widening chasm between the lives of those few and the lives of most.

The key word here is *financial*. Although we've been trained to think of financial wealth as an important end of its own, the glossed-over reality is that financial wealth is almost always a claim *against* real wealth. Real wealth is things like natural resources (such as rivers, trees, minerals in the Earth), physical assets (such as a paper mill or an apartment building), and even future wages, housing values, or projected company profits from selling real goods to real people. Translating real wealth into financial wealth can allow more choice in what we can obtain and do, and on what time frame. But in our current economy, this translation into financial wealth has spun out of balance.

Money isn't the only form of wealth to account for. In fact, money isn't much of anything on its own. It is nothing more than a stand-in for that which actually holds value—a tool to procure resources and services for well-being, in the form of things like shelter, food, clothes, and leisure activities. Money only has value because we give it value.

There are other forms of real wealth, which we often forget to consider, that directly contribute to our well-being as humans. A global study[17] on how people gauge their well-being pointed to a variety of other, nonfinancial forms: occupational (an enjoyment of what we do each day), social (having close, supportive personal relationships), community (being involved in the activities and happenings of our communities), physical (good health and a safe environment), and spiritual[18] (sense of purpose and connection to something greater than oneself).

Our business-as-usual economy has obscured the reality that money only matters insofar as it can be used to procure such well-being. The economy hides this fact so absolutely that it incentivizes destroying most other forms of real wealth and well-being in order to convert them into money. When our workplaces do pay attention to the well-being of workers, it is rarely as a legitimate end goal in itself. Worker well-being tends to get attention only as a key to productivity—which, in the way our current economy functions, translates as a way to more efficiently accumulate financial wealth.

Wealth extraction

Of course, generating financial wealth can also generate additional forms of real wealth in the process—such as knowledge or new types of technology. However, as author and public theologian Brian McLaren sums it up, "The current extractive economy has nothing to do with actual well-being. In fact, it now has almost everything to do with the loss of well-being." Brian became part of our research in 2018, when we reached out to him after coming across several of his writings on the nature of the current economy and how it is fueling a spiritual crisis of meaning among more and more people. He began his career as a college English professor, then pivoted to become a pastor in his late twenties, serving a congregation near Washington, DC, for twenty-four years. Brian's love of nature and literature, concern for social justice, and spiritual practice came together during those years, as he found his voice as a writer, public speaker, and activist.

"Gross domestic product," Brian comments, "is really just a measure of the speed by which we destroy the Earth and convert it into money. We destroy something real and turn it into a fiction, a fiction that's only held up by consensual agreements that we will give these little pieces of paper, these little numbers, value." The current economy is intensely focused on creating a certain type of wealth through extracting financial wealth from real wealth.

Extraction is the action of taking something, usually with effort or force, and not returning it. It's a one-way flow of resources. In order for our current economy to function (which is defined, in the present context, as capitalists receiving most of the benefit from productivity, and the wealthiest of society disproportionately so), we are compelled to operate in ways that make the majority of us and the Earth's resources possible to extract from. In today's dominant paradigm, this is how the economy grows.

This extractive dynamic is at the core of what isn't working about work.

What is taken is not adequately replenished, repaired, or made whole again—be it the labor of people or the trees of a forest. An extractive economy means that the generation of financial wealth *depletes* real wealth. To optimize financial wealth, the system incentivizes converting almost everything into money, one way or another, even as this makes it more and more difficult for most of us to access other forms of wealth—things like the social, physical, and cultural aspects of life we value.

Extraction happens to entire communities. Business as usual tends to perpetuate a pervasive phenomenon called community wealth extraction. This involves an entity, often a corporation in search of short-term profits, coming into a community and extracting the resources therein (labor, oil, trees, etc.). It simultaneously denies those who created the benefit (workers, long-time residents, and other stakeholders) and those affected by the effort from enjoying the profits.

We gained a deeper understanding of community wealth extraction from insights shared by members of the staff of Incourage Community Foundation, a small organization that serves the Wisconsin Rapids community in central Wisconsin and reimagines the role of community foundations as catalysts of local agency and action. As members of the co-learning community, they shared what transpired in their community when the town's former primary employer—a paper company and mill that had been at the center of the local economy for over a century—was sold in 2000. The sale resulted in significant reductions in staff and operations over time, relocation of corporate headquarters elsewhere, and related negative impacts on local businesses and suppliers as more and more operations were moved away from the community. With nearly 40 percent of total employment lost by 2005, the paper company and local mill subsequently changed hands multiple times, and the mill indefinitely idled in 2020.

Twice, the mill was purchased by a company that was controlled by a private equity firm—an investment entity that is essentially a pool of money used to buy and sell other companies. The investors of one of these companies made a series of moves that demonstrated their intent was to extract as much wealth as possible, rather than sustain the paper company.

In taking ownership, the company took out substantial loans, backed against what was left of the paper mill—including the projected future labor of its remaining employees. As Kelly Ryan, former CEO of Incourage Community Foundation, points out, the new company and its investors did not use the loan capital in ways that supported the paper company to adapt. "They didn't continue investments in R & D. They didn't do all the things that you would do to grow a sustainable business," explains Kelly.

Instead, the company downsized even further. Just over twelve months after acquiring the mill, it "declared bankruptcy after they had extracted resources," shares Kelly. The company left a trail of debt and unpaid invoices in the town, including from a local family-owned catering company, a printing company, and also to Incourage Community Foundation for workforce training programs. "They had also sold off incredible amounts of natural resources—timber lands, really unbeknownst to the community. Yes, some of the downsizing needed to happen, but the new owners took the mill operations down to the bone, past where it should have been. Our attorney looked at the proceedings, so we can say that with authenticity." The company emerged from bankruptcy with $2.4 billion in debt off its books.

In our current system, not only is everything that transpired arguably legal (although the financial transactions are currently under scrutiny[19]), but in the language of finance, what the new owning company did is termed *wealth creation*.

As community wealth extraction goes, what happened in Wisconsin Rapids is a highly visible example, but it can take many forms, some subtler but no less devastating. They all have one thing in common: capitalists siphon off resources from one place and consolidate them in another, without replenishing the place from which the resources were extracted.

The effects of community wealth extraction may look like a wave of small businesses closing in your community and never reopening, followed by dollar stores mushrooming[20] across your county and sending their profits to a corporate headquarters, while you now have no local grocery store. It may look like your hospitals closing down,[21] your children's school having to switch to a four-day week due to declining property taxes,[22] or property taxes increasing so much that you're forced out of your neighborhood (while also not seeing any of the benefits of that local wealth). It could look like your cash-strapped local authorities selling a local public park[23] to raise revenue. This extraction of natural, cultural, and labor resources leads to disinvestment, dispossession, and displacement.

There are also inequitable repercussions for individuals. For example, in recent years the United States has experienced a well-documented trend of decreasing financial wealth for Black and Latinx individuals and families. Wealth, as defined in the 2017 report *The Road to Zero Wealth*, "is the buffer families need when faced with unexpected economic shocks like a lost job or a broken-down car. Wealth is also the capital available to families to take advantage of economic opportunities, like buying a home, saving for college, or investing."[24] In other words, while you need income not to fall into poverty, you need wealth to stay out of it.[25] And while journalists, politicians, and researchers direct our attention to rising income inequality, wealth inequality is actually far more extreme.[26]

In the United States, racial disparities in wealth inequality are stark. Middle-income white households own nearly eight times as much wealth as middle-income Black households and ten times as much wealth as middle-income Latinx households.[27] Inequities also exist when it comes to disability[28] and across genders.[29] One recent US study, for instance, found that the median wealth of female respondents was just 55 cents for every dollar of male respondent wealth.[30]

The way the current economy is designed—and has operated for generations—leads to a disproportionate amount of the nation's wealth being held by people with intersecting identities of privilege. The cards are stacked disproportionally against entire groups of people—especially those with intersecting, historically marginalized identities.

Sometimes this can seem confusing to people with such privileges who are still struggling economically. If things are skewed in their favor, how can they be struggling? At scale, most of us are being cheated because the present economy is designed to extract wealth. But the differential in relative privilege can result in dramatic differences in lived experience.

Maurice BP-Weeks, co-executive director of Action Center on Race & the Economy (ACRE) and advocate for

corporate accountability, explains it best: "Because the country and our economic system was founded on a racist, sexist
vision, the economy impacts people differently the further
you are from white and male." Maurice lives with his wife and
young child in Detroit. Most weekday mornings around ten,
you can find him on his brisk walk to the office space he rents,
down the block from his home. Maurice is soon at his desk,
seated in front of two huge computer monitors as if he were a
computer programmer. The screens are filled with his calendar, email, the video meeting he just joined, a document with
a campaign planning template—and a tab with the sports
scores from last night. Here, you can find Maurice working on economic justice campaigns aimed to reveal harmful
practices of corporate actors, which disproportionately affect
communities of color and working-class communities, and
to secure accountability and change among those corporate
actors responsible. Maurice has devoted his life to this.

Growing up in north Jersey and experiencing poverty
and systemic economic neglect firsthand, he didn't know
that there was a way to change it. But something clicked for
Maurice in his early adult years, and he has not looked back.
His first phone call of the day is often a check-in with one of
the many campaign organizers, from various groups, whom
he advises. While this is not an official part of his role at
ACRE, he sees it as crucial to grow the number of organizers
and campaigners, especially fellow Black organizers and campaigners fighting for a better world.

"Corporations come into neighborhoods of color specifically to extract as much wealth as possible, offering almost
nothing in return," Maurice explains. "They come in, abuse
workers, force long-standing businesses to shut down, pol-
lute the area, and make money hand over fist." This dynamic
is as old as the US economy. From its start, colonizers

acquired land by violently displacing Indigenous Nations and extracted wealth with the forced labor of enslaved people, primarily from Africa. Racialized exploitation and extraction have long been central to the workings of the US economy.

Because the central tenet of the current extractive economy in the United States and in many places around the globe is the more money, the better—no matter what and at all costs—we tend to measure well-being only in terms of the accumulation of monetary wealth. We are told the more money we have, the better off we are. End of story. This leads to ways of work designed to maximize for only this variable, so money lands most often in the hands of the few.

As Maurice shares, "The rules of the economy make it so imperative that you maximize your money. Not only will businesses cut corners and hurt workers to do so, but people will literally sell their time down to the minute through app-based gig economy jobs." When the rules of the economy are designed to take from people, take from our natural resources, and take from our communities without replenishment, eventually that extraction weakens our personal security, which in turn weakens our well-being—that of our families, and ultimately that of our communities. As the current economic paradigm incentivizes continual extraction in many forms, over generations, entire human systems are weakened. "The truth is," offers Maurice, "the best most people can hope for is to just survive."

A beloved economy

The ramifications of wealth extraction are severe and can be overwhelming. As white, able-bodied, college-educated, cisgender women, we both benefit from a number of privileges.

And while our class backgrounds are different from one another, due to the pervasiveness and scope of wealth extraction, we each experienced challenging economic impacts in our families growing up. However, a key element of what drew us to this research was that we had also each had work and community experiences that showed us other ways are possible. We had witnessed examples of workplaces and groups that were oriented toward well-being and wealth retention for workers and for whole communities. Once we had seen it was possible, we couldn't unsee it.

Jess grew up in a blue-collar, small business family. Although they struggled economically at times, her family found ways to center human relationships and community building. In order to operate according to their own ethics, her family made choices that were not always in alignment with the rules that government prescribed about how the economy should function. This awakened Jess's imagination to dream beyond *what is* into *what could be*—a skill she later brought to her work building and leading global teams and enterprises that boldly shared decision-making power as a key strategy for social change. Her on-the-ground work later led Jess to join an international collective of people dedicated to changing the story about what is possible for the rules of our economy.

Joanna grew up in a middle-class family in Palo Alto, California, during the years when the community transformed from a quiet college town to a hub of the technology sector's Silicon Valley. While multiple family members and friends were part of this boom, she found herself questioning what all this "progress" meant and for whom. Joanna's parents and siblings were supportive when she followed these questions down a path that led her to learn from colleagues across Latin America, South Asia, and Southeast Asia. She collaborated with grassroots efforts in which community-led groups successfully stopped extractive "development" projects and instead built alternative pathways to economic flourishing. These included community systems for banking and lending in ways that supported local businesses. Joanna also worked with those of capital means to reimagine finance as something that could be nonextractive.

Together, we had both seen that audacious departures from business as usual were not only possible but that they could be extraordinarily successful, and in ways that mattered for the well-being and economic vitality of communities. We experienced firsthand that, even though the system is currently rigged in favor of those with consolidated wealth, it is also true that systemic change can be powerfully sparked at the grassroots level by individuals and enterprises joining together. Because of these experiences, we understood things didn't have to stay stuck in business as usual. We knew there was hope.

We also knew that although there are certainly bad actors doing horrific things intentionally, the lovelessness of the current economic system is perpetuated mostly by people who consider themselves to be playing by its rules. These people feel therefore that it's okay, and they often believe there is only one way this game can be played, that there are no other viable options.

We believe that a large part of what makes work feel so untenable goes beyond what is happening to us individually in a workplace to encompass the extractive dynamics underpinning our whole economy, which can make each of us, in our jobs, feel trapped in perpetuating such a system.

In this book, we call the kind of extractive capitalism that is dominant across and affecting so much of the globe the loveless economy. Visionary cultural critic and prolific Black feminist scholar bell hooks coined the term *lovelessness* to reflect the spiritual hunger and lack of true loving that is experienced and practiced across different dimensions of US society. "I awakened from my trance state," she wrote in *All About Love*, "and was stunned to find the world I was living in, the world of the present, was no longer a world open to love. And I noticed that all around me I heard testimony that lovelessness had become the order of the day."[31] In her writings, bell hooks points to the ways in which the underlying principles of our current economy are incompatible with an ethic of love.[32]

Through this research, we became acutely attuned to how participating in the current economy, day in and day out, doesn't feel like love. Our friends and family, at first, thought this insight was rather strange. Why *would* it feel like love? Why would you feel love from the economy?

What we asked each other was "But why *shouldn't* we?" Why shouldn't we have an economy that makes us feel valued and cared for? Makes us feel safe. Seen. Inspired.

These questions arose because of a dear collaborator, Dr. Virgil A. Wood, a pastor, educator, and someone who has been working for economic justice and transformation for more than seven decades. We first reached out to Dr. Wood three years into the research, after meeting him in an online seminar. We were struck by what he shared in the seminar about the nature of the economy, our role in it, and what is possible. He graciously agreed to a call with us. That call was the first of many conversations, which eventually brought us to spend time together in Houston, where Dr. Wood resides. Our dialogue with Dr. Wood continues to this day, and it has been a vital thread in weaving together the strands of this research journey.

Dr. Wood challenged us: "Who says we can't have and don't deserve a beloved economy? This deserves a serious conversation throughout the nation."

The phrase stopped us in our tracks. *Beloved economy.* What is a beloved economy? What would it be like to live and participate in a beloved economy? What would that feel like? Is it possible? We had spent a lot of time researching what *wasn't* working with work. The phrase beloved economy offered a dissonance that felt like a promise: lean in further and you'll find fertile soil to plant full-bellied futures.

Dr. Wood coined the term in 1975 at a convention of the Southern Christian Leadership Conference, when he and fellow civil rights leaders were focused on "the unfinished work" of economic transformation.[33] They recognized a different economy was necessary to realize the promise of a beloved community, articulated so powerfully by Dr. Martin Luther King Jr., of whom Dr. Wood was a friend and co-worker.[34] "I would say that the beloved economy and the beloved community are twins," Dr. Wood says. "They're two sides of the same coin."

Nearly fifty years later, now in his nineties, Dr. Wood advocates still for that beloved economy, dedicating his life to its realization through his work with church groups, multiple nonprofit organizations, and academic institutions. He has graciously bestowed the term upon our research to characterize and describe our findings.

The current economy, in its lovelessness, leaves communities carved out from extraction in search of financial profits, while compelling us to work in ways that make it harder for most of us to have time, energy, or resources to *be* together in ways that make life good. As financial wealth consolidates, it vacates a real place and takes with it sources of real wealth, without meaningfully replenishing them in return. We all feel these effects. And over time, this deprives people of the well-being present in a functional social fabric and in abundantly resourced communities. The loveless economy has caused many of us to believe that the devastating byproducts of such wealth extraction, and the hustle to continue it, are the only way. Many of us are tricked into believing business as usual is inevitable.

"I feel our nation's turning away from love," wrote bell hooks. "Turning away we risk moving into a wilderness of spirit so intense we may never find our way home again."[35] Brian McLaren echoes this sentiment, from what he witnesses in conversations with people in his congregation and who attend his speaking events across the United States and internationally. He believes that as an effect of our economy, there is an increasing crisis of meaning among people. He refers to it as a spiritual depletion that people experience— and struggle with—as they run so fast and hard to keep up. Even though we have seen that there is hope, we have also experienced this in our own lives and those of our families. Sometimes we or our loved ones have been overcome with a sense of "What am I doing this all for? Is this all there is?"

As returns on most people's efforts are disproportionately siphoned off, many of us are left without the physical or mental health, time, or privilege to access or partake in what feeds our well-being. We miss out on feeling part of a community, connecting with a higher purpose, engaging in play, or simply enjoying ample time to rest.

Scholar Dr. Nuria Chinchilla, whose work is summarized in Dr. Pfeffer's *Dying for a Paycheck*, describes how business as usual causes forms of social "pollution." This includes the breakup of couples, burdens on raising children, and a general disruption to wellness and social life.[36] Because the overburdens of corrosive ways of work lead to stress and then chronic illness, anxiety, and depression, which we spoke about earlier, they create a deterioration of our connections with one another and how we build and live in community.

In the rubble of all of this is *us*—the vast majority of people in this system, the exhausted majority,[37] feeling trapped in the clutches of ways of work and an economy that fails to serve our well-being.

When we realize that something is foundationally wrong with work, and even the broader economic system shaping our experience of work, as Brian explains, people "have to brush it aside like gnats, one hundred times a day, because their job requires them to not ever think about that." Spent, frustrated, disoriented, and stuck putting one foot in front of the other, it can be hard to confront the reality that we are largely working to benefit a small group of people, within a system that is destroying the very things that make life worth living in the first place.

A great many of us are spending most of our waking hours on work that fails to compensate us with the resources or assurance that we will be taken care of in our hour of need and also fails to engage us as the complex, insightful, soulful beings that we all are. Many of us have grown accustomed to a kind of precarious tightrope walk between options that all fall short in serving the health and well-being of ourselves, our families, and our communities.

Perhaps one has a sneaking suspicion that sacredness abounds, yet the unrelenting pings and dings from one's phone, the tangled web of highways and strip malls carved from former forests, the fluorescent glare of the supermarket lights all reverberate with a certain soullessness. To-do lists go unchecked, medical and utility bills accumulate, all while internal monologues pose mounting questions of "Is this it?"

Transforming how we work

What our research has confirmed—and what we share with you in this book—is that no, this most definitely doesn't have to be it. The growing circle of people we engaged with as part of this investigation share a conviction that *transforming how we work* can be a pathway to economies that work far better for all of us.

Dr. Wood emphasizes that in our daily lives, we all can effect economic change: "What I think about beloved economy is that it's not some grand, macro idea. Rather, I think a family, or a school, or a business, or a community group can be a beloved economic community. It is where there are certain values that help to shape the way people relate to each other, the way they help each other."

Throughout this research journey, an increasing number of people joined us to demonstrate that there are many reasons for hope. This co-learning community formed around our shared, burning question about work, and it has advised and informed our research ever since.

We call ourselves a co-learning community because our research methodology pushed beyond traditional research methods to fully embrace ways of creating, analyzing, and adapting the investigation together over time. In addition to participating in many interviews, this community stepped up to offer their deep insight and generosity of spirit to co-create evolving research inquiries and stress test our conclusions. (You can learn more about the research on page 357.) Throughout this book, we refer to those within the co-learning community as co-learners.

Our co-learner peers include people from startup enterprises and social movements, hospital departments and municipal governments, faith leaders and financial investors, and more. They have all belonged to a group or team achieving forms of success that contribute in standout ways to what makes life good, for everyone involved.

The seed of the co-learning community emerged organically during the first year of the research, from a series of conversations with diverse enterprises, community groups, teams, and organizations whose ways of work and forms of success stood out to us. Whether the group was a technology company, a youth-led social movement, or a hospital department, we noticed a common thread: those who worked differently enjoyed achievements that were distinct from business as usual. Over the years that followed, the circle of co-learners widened through referrals and continual research to include more groups expressing this common thread, and then later expanded to include individuals with expertise on select relevant themes.

Throughout the twists and turns of our research journey, this growing community has been our touchstone. This very book was co-created with its members in two ways. First, the insights mentioned throughout the book are a summary of our interview-based and dialogical qualitative research together. Second, many members of our co-learning community offered direct insight and feedback on evolving drafts of this book, with their responses substantially informing several iterations. Throughout the process, this community of people has contributed richly to what we have come to see and believe about work, whether on a group Zoom call, spending time in a team's offices and community, or simply calling to hear a co-learner's thoughts on an emerging research question or conclusion.

In the pages to come, you will hear from many of these co-learners directly. This book chronicles the journeys of everyday individuals and groups who have managed to step out of business as usual, which is draining and killing us, and into life-affirming alternatives for how we work. We introduce you to real-life organizations and businesses that have discarded what is damaging about the status quo, and we provide guidance on how you can find your own pathway out.

This book is for anyone looking—or longing—for ways to pull open the escape hatch and guide themselves and their teams toward a more beloved way of working. It is for anyone exhausted and fed up with what's not working about work and who has the will and latitude to make a change as an individual within a team or as a whole team, department, community group, or business reading this book together.

The economy—and its impacts on our everyday lives and the planet—is shaped by factors like the laws and policies that guide how it operates, which prohibit certain behaviors and actions and incentivize others; these laws and policies are inextricable from the political system that puts them in place. We are therefore operating within an economic system in dire need of change at all levels, from all places—such as policy reform, collective worker organizing, and new legal precedents. As you'll read more about in Chapter 12, we have come to believe that transforming how we work is one of the most underused yet powerful ways to bring about economic change. All forms of change are vital, and changing how we work is one lever of several that we can add to the toolbox of strategies to get ourselves out of the loveless economy.

This book offers findings alongside seven concrete, actionable practices that our research has found can activate the potential of our groups, organizations, and enterprises to turn into a powerful lever for economic change. It is also a love letter to the people we have learned alongside on this journey—and to you, dear reader. This book admires our collective power to step out of business as usual into audacious, healing futures. It asks you to join us in dreaming and building ways of work that bring to life beloved economies.

It is our hope and firm conviction that as more groups reimagine and enact different ways of working, there will be more and more living examples of teams that nourish what makes life good. We believe such examples can expand our collective imagination of what is possible, inspire what we build in our communities, and spark shifts that foundationally change how our economy functions.

These shifts invite us into the promise of Dr. Wood's concept of a beloved economy, into a world where our economy no longer drains us, leaving us starving for power, agency, and connection. This mode of work is one in which each person matters, and it centers on what makes life good. Where we not only imagine and build bold new futures, but we also prioritize repairing and replenishing what is unwell from harms of the past, where we keep balance, and where our days are awash in abundance. Where our modes of work make our inherent connectedness feel like a sweet space of possibility and resilience. Where our business practices express love like prayers in recognition of what it takes for life to thrive. Where we all feel like we belong.

Where we bring into being an economy that feels like love.

CHAPTER 2

RECLAIMING OUR RIGHTS TO DESIGN

IN ORDER to find our co-learning community members, we scoured roughly two hundred cases for groups that had innovated out of business-as-usual modes of working and were achieving notable forms of success. Prospective groups came through referrals, online research, cold calls, and the networks we had formed through years of pushing beyond business as usual in our own work. After initial interviews, sometimes we would visit in person or reach out for conversations with other stakeholders involved to understand their work more fully. The more of these teams we met and spoke with, the more inspired we became by the particular type of success they were experiencing.

Participants' outcomes were uniquely visionary in the way they prioritized the things most meaningful to them and their communities, clients, and other stakeholders instead of exclusively valuing the traditional metrics of business as usual. In one case, in an economically struggling small town, the idea arose for a brewpub that would sell beer from local microbreweries with a community space next door offering equipment, classes, and training for all aspects of the brewing process.

Interviewees also shared how enthusiastically their projects, processes, or products had been embraced. For example, a campaign to protect a sacred water source grew from a local effort involving a few dozen people into a global movement that made international headlines and inspired over 25,000 supporters to join the advocacy.

In transforming how they operated, interviewees emphasized that the ways in which they and their colleagues approached work had fundamentally and permanently shifted. The co-founder and CTO of a tech startup was so compelled by her company's distinct approach to work that she has walked away from subsequent opportunities that didn't engage the same ethos.

These specific ways of working have also created lasting, positive effects in other areas of interviewees' lives. One staff member of a local municipal government shared how his work experiences inspired him to adapt his parenting style.

We began noticing patterns among the case study research and interviews. There was a particular form of success each of these groups was experiencing. We came to call such groups, and the individuals within them, breakout actors.

What distinguishes breakout actors from business-as-usual actors is that the innovations they produce don't just make an intolerable state of affairs marginally better; they break out of business as usual by working together in ways that meaningfully prioritize diverse forms of well-being neglected within the loveless economy. The particular kind of success they experience is one we have come to call breakout innovation.

Breakout innovation

Breakout innovation is transformative change that is far-reaching, enduring, and imaginative in its departure from the lovelessness of the status quo. The plans, processes, and/or products that emerge from breakout innovation share three key qualities.

1. Such ideas are bold reimaginings that support what makes life good

They go beyond tweaking the details of existing approaches. Breakout innovation offers deep imagination on what could be, often moving beyond the usual, assumed constraints of a particular field. Such bold departures value ways to enhance and retain diverse forms of wealth and well-being across a system, breaking free from the lovelessness of the current economy.

One example is the work of breakout actor RUNWAY, a financial innovation firm that you'll learn about in the pages to come. In business as usual, investment in early stage companies tends to be focused on preventing financial risks to the investor by requiring enterprises to run through a harrowing gauntlet of applications, pitch sessions, and capacity-proving steps. Only if they measure up to the bar set by investors do they have a chance of receiving financial partnership. RUNWAY has completely reimagined the investment experience so that it strengthens early stage companies and makes the entire experience emotionally supportive, and even joyful, for the founders and teams involved. In the process, RUNWAY's community of investors and entrepreneurs has innovated new investment approaches and products that eliminate traditional barriers for BIPOC businesses and create opportunities where they never previously existed.

2. These ideas achieve widespread adoption

Many innovations don't receive the support needed to be fully realized. But breakout innovations are embraced in ways that enable far-reaching implementation—across whole organizations, communities, or fields of work. This robust uptake is often characterized by people not only using or accessing the innovation but also taking initiative to make it better or expand its reach.

A key example of this is the Unified New Orleans Plan, a municipal recovery plan facilitated by breakout actor Concordia, a community-centered planning, design, and architecture company whose team you'll meet in upcoming chapters. In the wake of Hurricane Katrina in New Orleans, several disaster recovery plans failed to win city-wide approval. Concordia facilitated an alternative approach—one that boldly departed from how such plans are usually made. The resulting Unified New Orleans Plan directly engaged over nine thousand residents in its creation and was the only recovery plan to gain the widespread support and subsequent official approval required to unlock urgently needed federal relief funds.

3. The process awakens a deep sense of agency to innovate

Among the stakeholders involved, the process of generating and implementing the new ideas sparks lasting shifts. This leads to greater numbers of people within a community, enterprise, or industry taking initiative and continuing to improve the current endeavor, as well as bringing new or different approaches to their future work.

Consider, for example, the breakout case of Heart Research Alliance, which opened the doors of medical research to patients and their family members, doctors, nurses, and hospital administration staff. Through this initiative, those with a stake in the outcomes of medical research collaborated as peers with researchers to determine the topics and questions to be investigated. Years after the time-bound project wrapped up, the collaborative experience continues to activate the people who had been involved. In new spaces and interactions, many of the patients who participated continue to contribute to research questions vital to improving many people's quality of life.

ALTHOUGH WE were able to identify these three commonalities in breakout actors' success, it was initially more difficult to figure out what it was that such disparate groups were doing that linked to outcomes with these same qualities. On the surface, there was little that could explain it. The breakout actors we followed came from a wide variety of industries, all doing very different things. They also used vastly differing terminology to describe their ways of work. But when we decided to assemble as a co-learning community to explore these outcomes more deeply, upon meeting, it was as though they shared a secret, instantaneously recognizable in one another.

Something kindred bonded them.

We had a hunch that if we could get to the bottom of what linked their ways of work, we could discover the secret to their breakout success.

As we explored this hunch, we also noticed a different phenomenon that initially seemed unrelated: something about what breakout actors were doing sometimes triggered a reaction from people operating in business as usual. We watched some breakout actors—who were achieving extraordinary things—face extraordinary levels of resistance. It was confusing. We could understand why those benefiting most from the status quo might want to thwart efforts that boldly departed from what they were used to. What felt strange was that some of the resistance seemed automatic—like an involuntary impulse—and often came from collaborators who were not particularly benefiting from the current system. Something was triggering people to act in protection of consolidations of wealth and influence, even if doing so didn't benefit them in any way.

We'll examine this phenomenon more in Chapter 11. For now, what matters is this: we found that the ways of work connected to breakout innovation are often in direct opposition to what business as usual deems to be viable and effective. The path to achieving breakout innovation can include facing a chorus of naysayers, convinced that what you are choosing to do and how you are choosing to do it—whether it's how your group spends time or resources, who you invite into the room to make decisions, or how boldly your group dares to imagine—will lead to the ruin of your enterprise. Breakout actors are often told to be more realistic, to accept that the dog-eat-dog dynamics of the "real world" won't let their efforts thrive, particularly when it comes to monetary profits.

However, from what we've observed, breakout innovation does *not* come at the expense of financial success. Instead, breakout actors often thrive financially, attracting significant investment, an abundance of clients and customers, or grant funding. Also, when conditions become difficult—for example, the economic impacts of the COVID-19 pandemic— breakout actors demonstrate incredible resilience.[1]

From what we've seen, the skepticism about breakout actors is unfounded. Instead the push from naysayers to be realistic is most often code for "This is not acceptable only because it opposes what business as usual is designed to do: to stockpile wealth and power in the hands of a few." We've learned that naysayers' assumptions about inefficacy are often unconsciously myopic. Innovation does not need to be limited to the confines of that which is currently most accepted within the status quo. If we intend to break out of what isn't working, then stepping into the so-called impossible or improbable might mean we're on the right path.

We wondered if what connected the breakout actors was related to these triggered reactions from business-as-usual skeptics. Were the breakout actors' ways of work activating something in direct opposition to the core of what keeps business as usual ticking? Could it be that this particular element was the key to their success?

The answer, it turned out, was yes.

As we unpacked the roots and histories of business as usual, we saw the bedrock forces at play. Together with our co-learning community, we came to understand that our loveless ways of work actively suppress a connection to the rich contexts, information, and insight available when more of us sit around the decision-making table. And that there has been a systematic effort to disconnect us from a certain type of power by separating us from one another and the larger web of life.

In our conversations with breakout actors, we often talked about how they were "tapping into" or "unlocking" something. After much investigation, we realized that the breakout actors were each, often unknowingly, unleashing a particular type of power—the same power that business as usual incentivizes our disconnection from. We came to call this power our rights to design.

Our rights to design

Rights to design are what we exercise when we imagine, decide, and build together—when we hold the designer's pen and sketch our individual and collective futures. These rights are rooted in our universal ability to generate insight into what is (the circumstances around us), imagine possibilities for what could be (potential circumstances that do not yet exist), and play a role in determining and taking ownership of how to bring such possibilities to life.

We understand rights to design to be linked with internationally recognized rights,[2] and primarily, they allow one to engage in imagining, deciding, and building the circumstances of our everyday lives.

Rights to design might look like shaping how an enterprise's profits are used and by whom, or contributing to the vision and decisions for a product's development—keeping in mind the impact on the greater community. Or they may be as simple as having the flexibility to create our own schedule and work hours within an organization.

To uphold our rights to design, we must each be able, freely and fully, to contribute our unique insights and ideas and to share in the responsibility of deciding how to implement those ideas so that we may find a way forward together.

In business as usual, however, these rights to design are highly consolidated. As we learned in Chapter 1, relatively few people have accumulated the power to exert outsized influence—and all of them have, are connected to, or are bolstered by extreme wealth. This reveals something vital: in business as usual, only a small percentage of people are fully able to express their rights to design when it comes to shaping the economy. In loveless ways of work, such rights are consolidated rather than distributed across a given system, as is evident in most workplaces. This is the consolidation of rights to design.

The consolidation of rights to design could occur as investors, top executives, and board members having the only say in what an enterprise will prioritize; an organization asking community members for feedback while failing to engage them in actual decision-making; or a company pursuing a plan that will directly impact the lives of many without meaningfully including those stakeholders in the process, let alone putting the designer's pen in their hands.

In the loveless economy, wealth and rights to design tend to be consolidated together because of a bias underpinning business as usual—a bias so pervasive many barely notice it. Economic theorist Marjorie Kelly calls this *capital bias*, defined as "attitudes and institutions that favor those who have money."[3] Capital bias ties into how the loveless economy compels us to deprioritize anything not directly related to optimizing financial profit for capitalists.

Sometimes, this bias is built into the very structure of a company or organization, as in a decision-making arrangement that only includes financial investors and highly paid executives. Capital bias can also show up culturally in informal ways. For example, if someone speaks in a meeting in a way that associates them with capital or knowledge of finance, others may automatically value that person's opinions more than those of someone who suggests priorities unrelated to capital accumulation.

So, as the loveless economy consolidates wealth, it simultaneously consolidates agency to imagine, decide, and build to the same few people. Our workplaces normalize this inequality, usually in the name of efficiency or because it's deemed unfeasible to do otherwise.

Even though this inequality is accepted in the loveless economy, it is not inevitable or natural. It has been actively created. Vast inequitable accumulations of capital or influence do not occur naturally. The ugly truth is that much of what we consider normal practice in our workplaces is actually derived from techniques developed explicitly to conquer, enslave, oppress, and subjugate people, as a means to violently extract wealth and consolidate rights to design along with it.

This is not hyperbole. Here's one critical example: many present-day tactics and customs of business as usual have roots that trace directly back to large-scale plantations of the US South, were developed by those responsible for enslaving people, and are linked to the brutality of forced labor. The use of spreadsheets, ways of thinking about scale, modes of employee supervision, cost accounting, ways of interacting with commodity markets, concepts of depreciation, and notions of collateral were all developed as a part of slavery in the American plantation economy.[4]

Business as usual replicates tactics that reinforce supremacist notions that some people should be able to exercise rights of design and others shouldn't, and that wealth should accumulate in the hands of those with consolidated influence. A whole range of attributes has been used to otherize, divide, and exploit—such as those based on race, class, gender, sexual orientation, and physical and mental ability.

"Every possible division between people was utilized to weaken our ability to resist this exploitation," emphasizes Ed Whitfield, a member of the co-learning community. A social critic, writer, and community activist, Ed has thought deeply—and written prolifically—about how exploitation in the United States is deeply intertwined with the building of its early and current economy.

Originally from Little Rock, Arkansas, Ed began his political activism as a teenager, doing antiwar work while attending Little Rock Central High School. After being involved in the Black studies movement at Cornell University, he moved to North Carolina, first to teach at Malcolm X Liberation University and then to continue doing community and labor organizing. After thirty years working at a unionized tobacco plant in Greensboro, he retired to co-found and co-direct the Fund for Democratic Communities, a small private foundation that focused its work on economic democracy and cooperative development in marginalized communities in the US South. He focused on studying, thinking, and writing about the roots of economic injustice in the United States and organized alternative economic models for economic and racial justice—through a number of other groundbreaking initiatives, including the Seed Commons, a community wealth cooperative. Ed now resides in Mississippi, where he is committed to continuing this work and sharing it with youth, in particular.

"While the most obvious and dramatic division has been race, the distinctions between hill people and valley people, woods people and swamp people have all been used to tighten the grips of exploitation," says Ed in an interview. "The poorest parts of the USA are poor now due to historical patterns of oppression and exploitation that date back to the seizure of this land from its original inhabitants, the importation of Africans who were forced into chattel slavery, the immigration of indentured servants, the settling of Europeans fleeing various oppressions and seeking opportunities, and more recently the immigration of our neighbors."

Although techniques have changed over time, much of business as usual still requires—and thereby replicates—approaches that seek to dehumanize. These are ways of working that implicitly consider certain people, beings, and places as separate and less consequential—as other. Many things celebrated in business as usual—such as exponential financial returns and endless capital growth—are only possible with ways of work that increasingly cast human and nonhuman life as *other*. This way of treating people, and life at large, can even get disguised as a kind of cool, collected rationalism—or "professionalism."

When we see companies achieve revered hockey-stick growth curves, we might well wonder whether this meteoric financial rise occurred as a result of applying nonhuman work expectations to human workers. For instance, Amazon's rise to such tremendous levels of financial success is arguably enabled by a context in which it's legal—and even encouraged—to demand inhumane levels of productivity from workers. Amazon has been reported to transfer and even fire workers when they underperform on efficiency standards, such as picking four hundred items off shelves within an hour (that's seven seconds per item) or inspecting and scanning at a mandated rate of 1,800 packages an hour (that's thirty packages per minute).[5] Such metrics usually require exploitation of some kind, and that exploitation is made more possible by creating cognitive separations between people—in this case, between Amazon's investors or executives and Amazon's warehouse workers.

Business as usual includes the intentional creation of these separations, not only as ways to enable the violence of extraction but also to ensure that we, the majority, do not unite to reclaim our rights to design and build a better economy. Nowhere is this truer than in the intentional creation of whiteness. As incisively described by Dr. Vilna Bashi Treitler, professor of sociology at Northwestern University, "Whiteness was a fiction created by elites who wished to protect their own class position of extreme wealth." Her award-winning 2013 book, *The Ethnic Project*, examines in detail the creation of the construct of whiteness in the United States:

> The English developed slave codes and applied them to
> an invented black race in an attempt to "squeeze out class

similarities between blacks and whites by bringing racial distinctions to bear against the former." Elites purposefully created whiteness to suppress, disquiet, and pacify poor Europeans and their Euro-descendants by racially raising the status of the poor without having to share any of the wealth.[6]

The loveless economy is designed so that most of us are less likely to "see where the wealth and power... has gone," explains former Secretary of Labor Robert Reich. "[We'll] cling to the meritocratic myth that [we're] paid what [we're] 'worth' in the market and that the obstacles [we] face are of [our] own making... Racism reduces the odds [we] will join together to threaten that system."[7]

Today, capital bias and white supremacy intermingle, creating compounding inequities. The co-learning community helped deepen our understanding of how these intermingling forces are inextricably linked with the loveless economy, creating a racialized capitalism that foments divisions.

Co-learner Maurice BP-Weeks offered a clear analysis on this issue: "At Action Center on Race & the Economy, we believe that race and class are intrinsically linked and that it is not possible to fix the structural problems in our economy in a race-neutral way. The financial and corporate elite use structural racism, targeting Black and Latinx communities in particular, to divide us and pit us against each other while they destroy our livelihoods." ACRE's work spotlights these dynamics and demands accountability from specific corporate actors perpetuating them. "We cannot achieve economic, environmental, or educational justice until we confront structural racism and take our demands directly to the financial elite profiting off the crises in our communities," explains Maurice.

To build systems that work for all, we have to move beyond what is accepted in the loveless economy as progress or innovation. As we mentioned in Chapter 1, what often passes as innovation only marginally improves the state of affairs, tweaking things within the constraints of what is. It's like adding a shiny new part to a hopelessly broken machine. The underlying mythology that an other exists continues to justify and maintain the extraction and consolidation of wealth and influence. Ironically, it is often those pushing most strongly for innovation within the loveless economy that are most entrenched in these subpar dynamics of business as usual, which in turn prevent them from achieving the success of breakout actors.

In contrast, breakout actors disrupt this limiting bedrock dynamic by choosing not to replicate practices that reinforce the social construct of an other. They do this by broadly distributing rights to design. Since most of us are acculturated in business as usual and trained to keep rights to design consolidated in alignment with capital bias, at first this can trigger an impulse of resistance. It can feel new and unexpected. But unleashing the power associated with distributed rights to design is the key to unlocking breakout innovation.

The secret of breakout innovation

This was the secret thread that linked breakout actors' work together across industries. They had all figured out how to deconsolidate rights to design. Deconsolidating rights to design means redistributing them broadly across a system. By doing so, breakout actors work to dismantle the social constructs of supremacy, such as white supremacy and patriarchy, that underpin dehumanization in the loveless economy. They start to mend the separations wrought by business as usual.

How do teams work in ways that deconsolidate rights to design? It may look like a small company assembling everyone involved as peers—founders, new staff, buyers, end-users of the company's offerings—to share experiences and decide together what direction the company will take. It may look like a school-district-wide planning process, in which hundreds of teachers, administrators, families, and students—as young as five years old—reimagine how their school looks and how it could best serve as a center of community life. It may even be as simple as a team with a decision-making protocol that enables its members to learn from one another's lived experiences as part of deciding upon a path forward.

Such shifts in how we work could seem subtle, but reclaiming our rights to design represents a profound change in how we work.

When people engage in activities like planning and problem-solving within the supremacist dynamics of the loveless economy, they usually make decisions based only on the limited insight available. When rights to design are consolidated into the hands of a few, ideas are formed and decisions are made without access to the benefit of the knowledge and wisdom of the many. In that exclusion, our communities lose out on volumes of accessible insight and creative genius.

In contrast, when our ways of work deconsolidate rights to design, a vastly richer informational field becomes available. This is because our design and decision-making tables have many more seats than business as usual trains us to believe are available.

There is a transformative power unlocked by deconsolidating the rights to design and it reflects what makes living systems best function. Life exists in complex adaptive systems, in which many independent elements interact and lead to difficult-to-predict emergent outcomes. For example, a forest is a complex adaptive system. So is a human neighborhood, a business, or an economy. Healthy and resilient complex adaptive systems have many interconnected checks and balances to make sure that as circumstances change, they adapt to orient the entire system toward survival. These checks and balances come in the form of feedback loops.

There are two kinds: correcting feedback loops and reinforcing feedback loops.[8] A correcting feedback loop limits imbalances that start to occur, such as runaway exponential growth. This is a built-in feature in nature and observable in our own bodies: when we overheat, for example, sensors in our skin and other organs send signals to a part of our brain that regulates our temperature by cooling us through sweat production and skin flushing; our temperature lowers to levels tolerable for our systems to function properly. A reinforcing feedback loop strengthens an existing direction of change that is occurring in the system, suggesting more of it occur. It is rarer in nature, but observable in, for example, the case of childbirth, when oxytocin stimulates uterine contractions and the production of more oxytocin and prostaglandins, which both stimulate more contractions and more oxytocin until birth breaks the cycle.

When complex adaptive systems have a balance of correcting and reinforcing loops, information updates constantly allow for adjustments; tweaks and corrections maintain the health of the system. When feedback loops are nonfunctional or work suboptimally, then unbalanced exponential growth can occur, creating instability that can make the system vulnerable to collapse. We can see that in both ecological and social systems. In a complex adaptive system like a business, widely distributed rights to design allow for correcting and reinforcing information to flow freely, allowing the system as a whole to adapt in response. When rights to design are consolidated, however, the range of available information is limited, and necessary tweaks and corrections to the system may not occur.

The capital bias incentivizes business-as-usual practices that aim to perpetually shield enterprises and the wealthy from a balanced circulation of information. The potential for correcting feedback is seen as a risk to capital accumulation, instead of as a vital contributor to the health of a system. For example, one study found that a shocking 57 percent of US workers are bound by nondisclosure agreements,[9] which can function to restrict their ability to offer vital correcting feedback.

Crucial information that could help our systems adapt is suppressed out of a sweeping interpretation that such information (e.g., dissenting voices or ideas coming from varied ways of work) could impede short-term profit maximization. Impediments to short-term profit maximization could include pausing production for a month to fix a safety issue, adjusting development plans to avoid destroying a local estuary, creating ramps and handrails for accessibility even if not legally required, or sharing decision-making with workers.

In place of what could be healthy circulation of feedback, business as usual promotes the unchecked expanse of one type of information: reinforcing feedback, specifically information, evidence, ideas, and decisions that affirm the extraction and consolidation of financial wealth. The problem is that systems without a regular circulation of both reinforcing and correcting feedback are unhealthy. They can become quite fragile—even brittle. Systems that reinforce only what is already happening, and from the perspective of a small group, encourage the continuation of what is over the prioritization of what could be. Put simply, they do not adapt effectively.

When breakout actors instead deconsolidate rights to design, they tap into what enables systems to evolve and thrive. They effectively reopen channels of correcting feedback across a system, thereby receiving a much richer, fuller breadth of information. Ways of work that deconsolidate rights to design offer wisdom for the long run and sound discernment for our collective well-being. Wise plans, processes, and products contribute to designs that nourish rather than extract, which sets them apart from the status quo.

The success of this information-enriching dynamic is supported by a number of studies. For example, James Surowiecki's influential 2004 book, *The Wisdom of Crowds*, explains that the judgment of a crowd can be more effective than the judgment of even the most expert consultant.[10] In his book, Surowiecki suggests that when a sufficiently large and diverse group of people is asked to make independent predictions, the errors and biases that each brings will cancel each other out, leaving the most accurate information. Studies on businesses and industry trends also show that when enterprises engage in what business scholars Dr. Venkat Ramaswamy and Francis Gouillart call a co-creation paradigm—in which a variety of stakeholders and clients gather to share insights and shape key decisions facing the enterprise— the results tend to be rich, including high financial returns.[11]

Breakout actors create paths forward that have been carefully considered, honed, and embraced by diverse, numerous groups—a far cry from the select few invited to the table by business as usual to exercise rights to design. *This* is the secret to breakout innovation.

Practices for breakout innovation

As we studied the ways in which breakout actors transformed their work, we came to understand that there was a clear pattern in what they did that led to deconsolidating rights to design. This pattern is the seven practices we share with you in this book. The seven practices are a way you can deconsolidate rights to design and set yourself on paths away from the loveless economy and toward breakout innovation.

Early in the research journey, we gathered with co-learners in New Orleans, and after three packed days and many late-into-the-night conversations, we had together identified a set of specific ways in which they transformed work. There were twelve practices they all had in common. We had an intuition that this first draft of pattern identification needed further refinement. To stress-test it across a wider number of practitioners, we partnered with an organization called Feedback Labs to lead several virtual prototyping sessions to test and hone the practices.

The sessions included some people from our own co-learning community as well as additional breakout actors that Feedback Labs pointed us to. Through this prototyping, we were able to group and condense the twelve practices into five, which over fifty practitioners across diverse industries—ranging from healthcare to high technology to community planning and design and more—could affirm. We then expanded our research pool again to independently test and verify the practices outside of the cases identified in our first phase. Once again, the practices checked out. We published our first article sharing the results[12] and started to hear from people around the world who were implementing the practices in their workplaces.

We began our research to learn how, as practitioners, we could move beyond loveless ways of work. So, we were eager to roll up our sleeves to intentionally implement the practices. We wanted to support organizations and companies in adopting the practices. Over the course of two years, we supported three enterprises in incorporating the practices into large-scale projects from the start: a socially minded technology startup in the for-profit sector, a nonprofit advocacy network, and a philanthropic community foundation.

In this process, we came to believe that there were two key practices missing from our initial pattern identification. With fresh eyes from active implementation, we could see these practices had actually been embedded within our interviews and desk research from the start. As we incorporated the two additional practices into our work, outcomes deepened. After experiencing the positive effects firsthand, we returned to our co-learning community members to discuss the two additional practices. During another round of interviews, we learned that many of the co-learners had seen the same.

By 2019, a clear pattern of seven practices had emerged and been vigorously tested, refined, and confirmed by the co-learning community:

1　Share decision-making power
2　Prioritize relationships
3　Reckon with history
4　Seek difference
5　Source from multiple ways of knowing
6　Trust there is time
7　Prototype early and often

Across the wide range of co-learners, everyone affirmed these practices were an accurate distillation of their foundational ways of working. This far surpassed what we had ever dared to hope would come from our research journey. We had uncovered a pathway to breakout innovation.

CHAPTER 3

THE SEVEN PRACTICES

I N THE FINAL years of our research, we observed that transforming how we work through deconsolidating rights to design was not only linked to breakout innovation but also seemed to meaningfully contribute to shifts that could affect whole systems, changes across a geographic region, industry, or the economy itself. You'll learn more details about these changes in Chapter 12.

Noticing these shifts presented a conundrum: since one of the primary features of the loveless economy is the consolidation of influence, how could it also be possible that shifts in how people worked within organizations and groups ignite expanding circles of change strong enough to affect even the economy at large? We were initially skeptical that transforming how we work could be a lever for change of this magnitude. However, in conversation with our co-learning community, we came to understand the truth within these seemingly contradictory phenomena.

The loveless economy continues to exist, in part, because a substantial number of us replicate it every day with our belief that things have to operate according to business as usual. The status quo, as we discussed in Chapter 1, is most often reinforced by people who feel they are simply playing by the rules, assuming there are no alternatives to business as usual, or by people who feel trapped and unable to make different decisions due to the extractive dynamics of the loveless economy. To varying degrees, we are all complicit in upholding business as usual when we do not actively choose something different and instead renew what is, rather than what could be.

The answer to the conundrum is that our shared complicity is actually a reason for hope. Because we are entangled in many daily opportunities to uphold and reinforce the loveless economy in our places of work, transforming *how* we work can actually begin to move us into a different economy.

We are rarely taught about this lever for economic change. The messaging most of us receive—in classrooms, on the news, from our peers—is that economies shift only because of governments, legislative rules, and the actions of massive multinational corporations. But the reality is that economic transformation can also ignite from the grassroots, from groups of individuals within their workplaces and communities.

This is because, at its core, an economy is simply a shared set of decisions created by people to manage the collective resources available. "Economics," shares Dr. Valerie Luzadis, a State University of New York economics professor and the past president of the US Society for Ecological Economics, "is a way of considering how we provide for ourselves" and ideally "how we organize ourselves to sustain life and enhance its quality."[1] Economies are necessary because we are interdependent; they are among the primary ways we negotiate that interdependence—how it will work, how we will manage resources, and what priorities will guide us. The economy of any specific society is a created construct reflecting how it operates, day to day.

As explained by J.K. Gibson-Graham (the pen name of Katherine Gibson and Julie Graham, economic geographers and co-authors of numerous groundbreaking books and articles on the nature of economy), we "build the economies we live in."[2] As such, economies are an expression of our ethics: they're built on what we decide to value, what we deem essential, and how we care for one another. An economy is affected and created by the everyday decisions we make in the places where we work—whether the work happens in a business, a government agency, or a volunteer neighborhood association.

An economy is a framework created by us—all of the people in our various teams and groups. We make economies real by behaving according to our belief that they exist. Given this, how we choose to work matters in that it affects, and *is*, what makes up the economy at large. Economies are not abstract things separate from us. Economies *are* us. *We* are the economy.

And because we are the economy, the way we work can either contribute toward remaking the existing economy or creating different ones, perhaps ones we want more. But it cannot ever be neutral. Also, you don't have to work inside a team in a business to participate in these economic shifts. The fertile spaces for change within the decisions we make exist within families, gig work, volunteer groups, or organizations. From how we run a meeting, to the way we structure a family business, to the way we organize shared resources in our neighborhoods, to the ways we interact when selling and buying, all of us shape the economy.

Even though an economy is a social construct, its effects are undeniably tangible and can be devastating. We exist in a present-day context that was built through the decisions of many yesterdays. As co-learner Brian McLaren explains, there is an "accumulation of a million small decisions... with 900,000 of them going in the same direction," which add up to create our current context.

While transforming how we work is a powerful tool, the weight of these accumulated decisions means creating such changes is often difficult. The latitude people have to make these changes varies because of inequitably distributed barriers and ramifications. A person's position, social identities, socioeconomic status, and a whole host of other factors affect the potential severity of costs they face if they dare to challenge the way things work. In our research, co-learners pointed out that for many people, speaking up to advocate for change in how their workplace functions could risk their job.

And yet co-learners also talked about how they have been surprised by the degree to which it can be possible to enact alternatives, once they have worked together in collaboration to build a vision for such changes. They pointed out that a single successful effort in changing ways of work can spark a domino effect of other shifts. Our research shows that, although there are risks, people also sometimes have more latitude than they at first assume, and this latitude can exist across various positions within an enterprise.

A 2019 article in *Harvard Business Review* entitled "How One Person Can Change the Conscience of an Organization" supports what we've seen. Authors Nicholas Eyrich, Robert Quinn, and David Fessell argue, "[W]hile corporate transformations are almost universally assumed to be top-down processes, in reality, middle managers, and first-line supervisors can make significant change when they have the right mindset."[3] Their research chronicled dozens of professionals who succeeded in making change within large organizations. "In one example, a woman in a Fortune 50 company... noted that challenging the status quo is a skill that one can develop, and it applies at every level." Whether you lead a team, play a supporting role in your organization, or are a participant within a complex community ecosystem, you may still hold some power over the how of your workplace.

Indigenous writer and bestselling author, activist, and self-described "angelic troublemaker," Edgar Villanueva emphasizes this: "There are choice points in our daily lives that we as individuals in community, and we as professionals in an organization, have—and thus actions we can take." Edgar joined the co-learning community in 2018. His people—in his own words—are the Lumbee, Southern, and hard-working people of faith who do not have financial wealth but are rich in relationship, love, and community. For the past eighteen years, Edgar has worked in the space of philanthropy, advising national and global philanthropic foundations as well as corporations on social impact strategies to return wealth to communities of color. He also considers himself a healer, and he believes that money can be medicine if it's used for a sacred purpose: to restore balance and heal the communities that have been marginalized and harmed by exploitative economic systems. Edgar says, "I think people often don't understand the power they have, because we get locked into institutional mindsets and ways of being often inside governments, organizations, corporations."

It is that locked mindset, we believe, that keeps so many of us participating in business as usual—the feeling, perhaps even the conviction, that nothing else is possible. The consolidation of rights to design contributes to a feeling of futility, which can lead us to not exercise the influence we do have (however small), thus further entrenching the status quo by stifling us from imagining what else could be.

"The power of one's economic system to limit one's imagination has become staggering in its importance to me," shares Brian McLaren. "I'm seeing in new ways the degree to which my brain is formed and framed and limited and brainwashed by economic assumptions. I'm feeling these days that the way our economic system has worked, it's like a cult, and it has so much influence over the framing and shaping of our minds." When the definitions of *realistic* and *possible* are narrowed to whatever keeps the current paradigm churning, our ability to imagine different ways, worlds, and tomorrows is limited.

This topic of imagination was brought up with striking frequency by co-learners in our conversations. We often talked about how deconsolidated rights to design nourish the inherent diversity of imagination as more people can contribute their visionary insights with ease. We came to understand that, to breakout actors, imagination is something with real teeth—a powerful tool. Many breakout actors see imagination as essential to transforming how we work. They speak to a point that poet Lucille Clifton sums up: "We cannot create what we can't imagine."

The act of breaking out of business as usual requires vision and, in many cases, creative invention. When groups boldly imagine what's possible with work—what we call economic imagination—they can affect the bedrock constructs upon which business as usual is continually recreated. Across the coming pages of this book, we share what these changes can look like.

The importance of imagination was often part of our conversations with co-learner Antionette D. Carroll. Antionette is the founder, president, and CEO of Creative Reaction Lab, where she has pioneered an award-winning form of creative problem-solving called Equity-Centered Community Design. Bringing this approach to life, Creative Reaction Lab educates and deploys youth to challenge racial and health inequities impacting Black and Latinx populations in St. Louis, Missouri—the organization's home base—and throughout the United States. Antionette is a mover and shaker within the field of human-centered design, sometimes referred to as design thinking, and now expanding into a new field she co-created called equity design. In recent years, she has won numerous international awards and fellowships; she's also been invited to speak and facilitate around the world. Antionette has been a mentor and inspiration to many aspiring designers and cultivates a growing network of "Redesigners for Justice," a leadership model she developed.

"We can't imagine what a different economy can look like because we've been taught to lose our imagination," shares Antionette. "We've been taught to only think one way. For people that don't think the way we want them to think, we devalue them. We push them out." Antionette has a passion for working in ways that enable everyone to boldly imagine. It comes from her own lived experience—especially from the communities that have shaped her. Describing herself as a Black woman who centers her identities and living knowledge in her "day-to-day actions of being a serial social entrepreneur; specialist in equity, diversity, and inclusion; mom; wife; daughter; sister; and Redesigner for Justice," she cares deeply about changing the economy. She cares because historically her family has been erased from it. From the history of slavery's erasure of a connection to her cultural home to the erasure of her family's all-Black neighborhood that no longer "exists" (though her people are still there and displaced), Antionette is rooted in her recent ancestry of being a St. Louis native who, she quips, understands the nuance, bias, and stereotyping embedded in St. Louis residents' favorite question: "What high school did you attend?"

Antionette shares that when it comes to reimagining how we work, she often thinks of an example from education that was shared at a talk she attended:

In school, we are taught to answer a question such as, What does two plus two equal? And when we get the question, we are told that there's one answer. There's no imagination. You're told this is the one answer; you stick to that. I equate that in my mind to the status quo. But what we actually should be teaching people is to be able to answer the question, What equals four? If you ask *that* question, you would receive an infinite amount of answers.

And that to me is the epitome of the imagination that we need in all of our settings, but particularly the work setting. When we are trying to build a business or an educational lesson or a policy, or whatever it may be, it requires us—especially if we're redesigning through the lens of challenging the status quo of harm—it requires us to be imaginative. It requires us to try things that have never been experienced before.

To transform how we work, we have to cultivate imagination as an active stance that leans into what could be for our work and asks the big, hard, improbable-sounding questions. We must be up for, as Antionette says, trying things we have never experienced before. Just as the past and current realities of work, and our economy at large, were drawn forth into existence through imagination, we can imagine and build different ways of work.

By returning the designer's pen to the hands of more people, breakout actors unleash wild and vibrant imagination. When we repair the connective channels between us, allowing us all to learn and grow from what others contribute, transformative ideas arise. When we deconsolidate rights to design, we welcome all our imaginations to dream daringly.

The seven practices therefore expand what teams dream as possible about work—almost like strengthening an imagination muscle. As a part of navigating the path to breakout innovation, we believe the seven practices cultivate economic imagination by enabling groups to dream with evermore visionary boldness about how they work or their whole enterprise functions. The more you practice along the edges of your imagination, contributing to and building on the visions of collaborators, the more your group or team can imagine what else is possible[4]—whether it's changes to your organization or a broader vision of economies. As our imaginations expand, what was once audacious becomes expected, practical, even habitual. By awakening the imagination in our own bodies—in our nervous systems, guts, and minds—and practicing feeling the future there, we awaken to an ever-evolving set of possibilities.

IN THE FOLLOWING chapters, we explore each of the seven practices—what they are, how and why each one works, stories of the practices in action, and tips for how you might begin or deepen your own practice.

The chapters about each practice draw upon the voices and experiences of many people who helped shape the information and advice shared.[5] You will hear directly from breakout actors within the co-learning community who offer firsthand experience in applying the practices. They share examples from their own work, insights on how to avoid common pitfalls, and tips for how to implement the practices in ways that create a solid foundation for breakout innovation. We also share our own takeaways and analysis grounded in what we've learned throughout our research journey as well as from applying the practices in our own work in teams.

Interspersed between each of the coming chapters are profiles of particular breakout actors and their ways of work. These profiles offer glimpses into everyday ways that different breakout actors deconsolidate rights to design, sparking imagination and building beloved economies through their work. In each glimpse, we see multiple of the seven practices at play. We hope these windows into the workplaces of breakout actors spark your imagination about what might be possible.

Before diving in, there are a few important things to note.

We invite you to add practices

First, we would like to be clear that while our research has shown these seven practices to be an effective foundation for teams to achieve breakout innovation, we do not see these practices as all-encompassing. Our sense is that these seven are likely a subset within a wider universe of possible practices that can support teams to build beloved economies by embodying wise ways of work.

Co-learning community member Katherine Tyler Scott says it best: "I think this book will help us ask the right *questions*, which is far more important than having the right answers. Because soon there are going to be many, many different ways of approaching the practices that will help us be the beloved community that we seek."

Katherine leaves us feeling reflective whenever we speak with her. She has worked for many decades supporting adaptive leadership development and organizational change with groups all across the United States. Her clients include community organizations, corporations, universities, and some of the largest philanthropic foundations in the country. She is a writer, educator, and poet whose work is, as she says, "infused with wisdom gained from clients and colleagues." We've twice witnessed people she worked with years ago letting Katherine know how singularly transformative her guidance had been—making them better colleagues, leaders, and even family members. We, too, feel grateful for the many insights we have gained through our conversations with Katherine over the years.

This is about continual practice

There is one point of advice that Katherine often shares, a point that many co-learners wanted to emphasize in presenting the seven practices we have illuminated together: learning to apply and embody these practices "isn't just a one-time thing," as Katherine sums up. "It's something you do over time." They are, in fact, a *practice*.

Breakout actors learn, adapt, and build their capabilities in these seven areas through practice. The seven practices are not activities you can do once and consider them done—like a checked box. Instead, they are about continual commitment to trying, learning, and growing. Practice provides an opportunity to get comfortable with messing up. This is how learning happens. As Antionette explains, "if we are not continually growing, then honestly we're not going anywhere. Let go of perfection because perfection does not exist."

Becoming highly attuned to the seven practices is about accepting that you will continually be learning by not always getting them right. Like training in a sport or artistic discipline, this work is about returning to your practice, again and again, to continually grow and improve. And "for someone that's starting brand new, guess what? Everyone always starts their journeys and learning brand new," offers Antionette. "That's the process of everything you've ever done, everything in your life... This is just another natural part of life."

The practices are not new

While breakout innovation is about the possible and emergent *not yet*, it is crucial to note that the seven practices are not new. Elements of these practices have long been an important part of many Indigenous Peoples' lifeways and the work of grassroots social movements around the globe. It thus makes sense that, over the years, numerous people we interviewed mentioned that following these practices often felt to them like remembering.

The practices exist on a spectrum

The seven practices are not binary characteristics that a process either does or does not have. Each practice is about continually striving to strike the right balance—feeling into what might be too much or too little.

Because business as usual does not actively prioritize these practices, co-learners tend to speak about incorporating them as a correcting action. This is to compensate for the tidal pull of the loveless economy in directions *away* from these practices. But even these practices can be overdone. Ultimately, we are seeking to continually find balance in each practice.

Don't pick and choose

The seven practices are not offered in any particular order. This is not a recipe in which things should happen in a certain linear sequence.

Additionally, while each practice is covered in its own chapter, the seven practices function as an interconnected set. They do not function as successfully without one another because of how deeply interrelated they are. Breakout innovation happens when we strive to do *all* of them, as part of a holistic shift in how we go about our work.

It is vital not to pick and choose one or a handful to begin practicing but instead to approach them all. If in reading, you find yourself feeling that a particular practice or two may be too difficult, and you are tempted to skip them, we invite you to notice that feeling. It is possible that the practices that feel most challenging to you are the ones that reflect the shifts you and your team need to make most, which may generate some of the most meaningful outcomes. And remember, as Antionette emphasizes, it's not about getting it perfect, it's just about getting started. With time and commitment, you and your group's capacities in each realm will strengthen.

AS WE LEARNED about the ways breakout actors were deconsolidating rights to design, we noticed something striking: breakout actors reported that their ways of work undid certain things. Practicing seemed to also be about *undoing*.

We have to come to believe that breakout actors deconsolidate rights to design through the seven practices in ways that also inherently unravel a part of what Katherine calls "the unconscious part of a culture, the part that people can't explicitly talk about." In this case, what they unravel are the unconscious parts of the loveless dynamics of business as usual that keep so much imagination locked up.

As Katherine explains, examining and making sense of history together can "reveal patterns and trends—and even values that you're not always aware of—that people just take for granted, or make assumptions about, without questioning them." Again and again, the idea of undoing came up in close association with breakout innovation, with words like *unlearning, untraining,* and *deprogramming.*

Loveless ways of work have history and context. The choices we make within work about how we relate to one another are not neutral. These choices are inherently political—in that they reflect values and priorities and worldviews we accept. When groups practice with this awareness, it can support their ability to achieve breakout innovation. As Katherine says,

> When done well, looking back on history surfaces what people can't always talk about comfortably and makes it conscious, and makes it able to change, especially if it needs to change. What's going on now in the country is a lot of unconscious stuff that people have not wanted to face about their bigotry and their biases about particular groups. And it fuels their behavior. It affects your attitude, your behavior. It affects everything. It's very connected to understanding culture. And culture's very powerful—particularly unconscious aspects of it.

Breakout actors cultivate an awareness of the past and of our present-day possibility for choice to undo harmful behaviors that have been normalized in the loveless economy.

In the coming pages, you will hear insights from members of the co-learning community about what they have found each practice undoes about business as usual, and how engaging with the practice may require a shift in one's understanding of key concepts. We've found that groups and teams can often be most clear and committed in their practice when they can bring mindful attention to what they are choosing *not* to replicate in their work.

Together we have what we need to make wise plans that break out of what isn't working about work. The beautiful thing about the seven practices is that every single one contributes to building a rich web of authentic, meaningful relationships around the person practicing. When we all share the designer's pen, we are not alone. As co-learner Dr. Wood says about getting started, "The first thing is to understand that I'm not trapped. It looks like there's nothing going for me, but wait a minute: I got me. I got you. We got each other, see?"

Together we invite you to climb through the escape hatch and up and away from loveless ways of work—into economies that prioritize what makes life good.

. . .

RUNWAY

IN SPRING 2020, with the world in the throes of a global pandemic and business as usual grinding to a halt, RUNWAY—a groundbreaking financial innovation firm committed to dismantling systemic barriers and reimagining financial policies and practices in the name of Black liberation[1]—held a "family meeting" with the community of entrepreneurs in which they were invested. Just like family, they asked one another what was needed to get through this unprecedented time. Many were struggling with temporary shutdowns of their operations, worried about feeding their families and keeping their households safe. Others were working to get their businesses COVID compliant, and all were doing so amid a backdrop of ongoing state-sanctioned violence against Black people in the news and in their own communities.

RUNWAY's staff were deeply moved by the care and love their entrepreneurs were demonstrating for their colleagues, employees, and communities. They also had brilliant ideas for how their offerings could provide much-needed services during this time. However, the reality of unstable and unpredictable income due to the impacts of the COVID-19 pandemic, on top of layers of racial inequities in access to funding that Black entrepreneurs and families face on a daily basis, was making it nearly impossible for the entrepreneurs to keep their businesses afloat or to mobilize them in support of community needs.

During that first community call, a simple truth became clear: in order for RUNWAY's business partners to truly unlock their brilliance and be of service to their communities in this critical time, they needed a predictable and steady flow of income. Only then could they take a breath, clearly see the opportunities for their offerings, and creatively respond to the shifting realities of pandemic life. "Realizing... our entrepreneurs needed us more than ever, we determined that Universal Basic Income (UBI) was the single most impactful thing we could provide in support of their desire for peace of mind," wrote staff in a 2021 RUNWAY publication. "We moved to action to swiftly raise funds for an emergency relief fund, and created RUNWAY's Universal Basic Income Pilot—the first of UBI initiatives expressly dedicated to Black entrepreneurs."[2]

RUNWAY's UBI pilot program—rooted in trust in the wisdom of Black entrepreneurs to determine how best to spend critical funds to keep their families, businesses, and communities afloat—had a powerful impact. Not only are 100 percent of RUNWAY's business partners still operating after over two years of pandemic life, but 87 percent also received a forgivable loan from the federal government's Paycheck Protection Program, compared to only 1.9 percent of Black-owned businesses nationally.[3] Without having to worry about how to get food on the table, the entrepreneurs supported by RUNWAY's UBI program were able to keep their businesses running *and* make meaningful contributions to their communities with, for instance, free masks, immunity-boosting food and drinks for healthcare workers, and strengthened safety protocols for their employees and vendors.[4]

The launch of RUNWAY's UBI pilot program and the monthly community calls also catalyzed the inception of a new governing body of entrepreneurs that continues to play a critical role in deciding how emergency funds are used. Its creation was a natural extension of RUNWAY's belief in collective wisdom and the importance of sharing decision-making power with the communities and individuals most impacted—and historically marginalized—by the financial sector. "That is how our RUNWAY family was born," reflects Nina Sol Robinson, fund director at RUNWAY. "We didn't have a formal governing group of entrepreneurs until the pandemic. Because we started having these monthly community calls to hear what was going on, once we secured the funds, we started turning to this group as more of a governing body."

Placing decision-making power in the hands of their community of entrepreneurs is one part of RUNWAY's larger mission of boldly rewriting the rules of how investment happens. Since its founding in 2016 by Jessica Norwood, RUNWAY has turned heads across the startup investment field with its commitment to reimagining a "friends and family" approach to capital investment rooted in love for Black entrepreneurs and communities.

Jessica's determination to approach startup investment in a profoundly different way from the mainstream was born in the aftermath of Hurricane Katrina: "This was the first time in my life where I saw all of the systems that were supposed to be there for folks *really* fail." Born and raised in Alabama, Jessica was acutely aware that "there was a racialized component to what failure looked like, and what the ability to recover from a disaster looked like." She saw with increasing clarity that for so many Black people, families, and communities, Black-owned small businesses could play a central role in recovery and thriving. And yet far too few of these businesses had access to the kind of initial, flexible financial support needed to get off the ground, flourish, and weather unexpected challenges—the kind of financing that the investment world calls "friends and family" capital. "So, if you didn't have the kinds of friends and family that had that kind of capital, then guess what?" asks Jessica. "In a disaster, you don't have the kinds of friends and family that can get you out of that disaster." The glaring racial inequities in access to business funding that Jessica witnessed in the wake of Hurricane Katrina reflect a larger racial wealth gap that pervades every layer of how wealth accumulates in our current business-as-usual economy.

When Jessica launched RUNWAY, she did so with a bold vision for making friends and family investment widely available to Black entrepreneurs and for redefining what investment looks like in the first place. In enacting this approach, RUNWAY does far more than write checks; their investment is about "people really showing up for you, being there for you in a deep way, around the success of your business and your life," explains Jessica.

Jessica and the RUNWAY team trust and respect their portfolio entrepreneurs as thought leaders and decision partners in all aspects of their investment work. This reverence for the brilliance of community-based Black entrepreneurs is reflected in RUNWAY's 2019 impact report:

> Every day we are inspired by the folks that, despite the odds, dare to dream bigger for themselves and communities. They dare to bet on themselves. We are honored to

provide that critical gap capital, that early stage, "friends and family" funding that signals a deeply profound notion: "I believe in you." That belief is love in action. That belief is a requirement to shift our status quo. When we believe in one another, we believe the world can be transformed.[5]

RUNWAY's boldly different approach to friends and family capital has yielded far-reaching results. With a twelve-person team and support from select strategic partners, RUNWAY invested in forty-three businesses over four years to not only achieve financial success but also bring artful, healing, and essential products and offerings to their communities. These range from plant-based food and natural hair and skincare products, to graphic design and strategic marketing services, to healing beauty products and gathering spaces.

In supporting these businesses, RUNWAY itself has deployed hundreds of thousands of dollars, but the volume of capital it has influenced is far higher. RUNWAY has inspired changes in practice, terms, and culture at major financial institutions, including banks, community development financial institutions, and family investment offices. And Jessica is now frequently called upon as a thought leader in the sector.[6]

"The fact that we are getting banks and institutions to provide friends and family style capital—*that* in itself is revolutionary," emphasizes Nina. Her years of work in small business investment and capacity-building have made her appreciate all the more just how revolutionary RUNWAY's approach is. At RUNWAY, Nina draws on her experience in small business finance, as well as the bold artfulness and creativity that she brings to her other realm of work—as a DJ, well loved in Oakland, where she lives, and other locations she is invited to spin. For Nina, both realms of work—being a DJ and being part of a one-of-a-kind financial innovation firm—are fundamentally about moving people in mind and heart.

"So, yes, at RUNWAY, we are moving money," Nina says. "But the impressive thing is that we are getting banks and institutions to operate as if they were friends and family of the groups they are supporting—to show that kind of flexibility, care, love, relationship. All of the things that, if you're lending money to a family member, it's based on those things—not collateral or credit score. It's bringing that spirit and way of operating into institutional funding for early stage and small businesses—and we want to see this across the board."

The central spirit of RUNWAY's approach is one of right relationship. In Jessica's words, being in right relationship is when "it doesn't feel like an imbalance of power. It feels like we're collaborating and working together and creating these really spacious and thoughtful agreements that allow us to show up fully whole with our entrepreneurs." For RUNWAY, part of being in right relationship is robust transparency—sharing openly about their processes and decisions—as well as sharing decision-making power on how RUNWAY will operate and best serve its entrepreneur family. Through embodying this ethos of care, respect, and believing in one another, RUNWAY creates conditions for imagination to flourish.

"There is an imagination that does not accept the circumstances of today, but will believe so deeply that it will manifest what it is tomorrow," emphasizes Jessica. She continues,

I think about that imagination, particularly Black imagination. I love it so much. Because it really calls on making a way out of no way. Entrepreneurs are world makers. And they are literally taking something out of their imagination, and then giving it to you in the world, and then you get to be in their film, or their fashion, or their vision of something. And I think that kind of creativity and imagination is essential to what we're trying to get back into. I think it's one of the ingredients of what it means to repair.

Through profoundly changing the way that investment works, RUNWAY is reimagining how finance can be a force for repair, resilience, and joy.

CHAPTER 4

SHARE DECISION-MAKING POWER

RUNWAY'S SPIRIT of power-sharing is a major ingredient in the special sauce behind its groundbreaking
innovation, as it is for all the breakout actors in our
co-learning community. When decision-making power is
shared through a thoughtful and deliberate process, the practice can elevate a team from feeling like a set of disjointed
individuals at work to operating as a tight-knit community. It
inspires each of us to bring our A game, to pool creativity and
initiative in order to build something in which we all truly
have a stake. A practice of sharing decision-making power lies
at the very heart of what can enable work to break free from
business as usual and spark breakout innovation.

Yet sharing decision-making power is the practice that,
when we bring it up with friends or colleagues, can most
often induce groans of concern. What usually follows is
venting about the botched attempts at consensus-building
they've participated in; fears about long, unwieldy meetings;
and visions of a chaotic, leaderless free-for-all.

While many people may have had negative experiences
with attempts at sharing decision-making power, such experiences are often only a reflection of how such a process can

unfold when poorly managed. It is absolutely possible to share decision-making power without such challenges. This chapter offers guidance to help avoid common pitfalls.

Breakout actors emphasize that sharing decision-making power is neither simple nor easy, but that it is an essential pathway to breakout innovation and, often, unexpectedly fun along the way.

> **Sharing decision-making power** is the practice of operating as peers across teams and groups—trusting one another to hold responsibility, impart insight, and shoulder the risks and consequences of our decisions. Sharing decision-making power means distributing the functions of agenda-setting, visioning, implementing, creative problem-solving, and evaluating among all involved. It means dissolving binaries of business as usual—such as designer and consumer, expert and beneficiary, manager and worker—and instead creating thoughtful ways for everyone involved, or impacted, to contribute and steer while designating clear decision-making protocols for each area of shared work. At its most robust, shared decision-making power can significantly challenge the status quo, resulting in shared ownership and financial returns.

Shifting how we understand power

To begin sharing decision-making power, many of us first have to shift how we understand the concept of power. "[T]he right question is not 'How can everyone have equal power?'" explains author, researcher, and former business coach Frederic Laloux. "It is rather 'How can everyone be powerful?'" Laloux's influential 2014 book, *Reinventing Organizations*, speaks to this reconceptualization of power:

"Power is not viewed as a zero-sum game, where the power I have is necessarily power taken away from you. Instead, if we acknowledge that we are all interconnected, the more powerful you are, the more powerful I can become... Here we stumble upon a beautiful paradox: people can hold different levels of power, and yet everyone can be powerful."[1]

Laloux's framework for understanding power—while revelatory for scores of his readers—is nothing new for many Indigenous Peoples and other communities that hold worldviews distinct from business as usual. As co-learner Kataraina Davis points out, in her Māori community, this understanding of power is age-old knowledge—and common sense.

Kataraina is a leading practitioner in the field of social design. Internationally and in her home country of New Zealand, she has designed and facilitated co-creative processes that have engaged scores of residents working together to generate breakthrough policy changes and new social programs. Sharing decision-making power, she says, is not only central to effective social design but also aligns with a core Māori value. "There is a value that is very big for us," she explains. "It's a concept called manaakitanga, and basically, if you break that word down, *manaaki* means to build mana-enhancing relationships. And *mana* means power or strength. Authority. Solidarity. Respect."

Kataraina continues, "Manaakitanga is about enhancing someone else's mana. So the idea is that through hospitality, through making things accessible, through making processes accessible, this enhances mana." She emphasizes how fundamental this value is to Māori lifeways. "Through many of the protocols and processes that we have within Te Ao Māori, the main purpose of those things is to enhance the other person's mana. And through doing that, you enhance your own as well."

Similarly, many breakout actors talk about the distinction of prioritizing a power-with ethos, rather than power-over ways of operating. They note that when groups direct their understanding of power away from a zero-sum analysis, they begin to shift from a mindset of scarcity to one of trust in an abundance of power—in which everyone can share. This shift can alert groups to unnecessarily hierarchical structures rooted in practices of othering and designed to enable wealth consolidation. A power-with mindset can help realize ways of operating that enhance the power and authority of all involved.

What does sharing decision-making power look like?

While there is no set formula for how to share decision-making power, there are several common elements we observed and discussed with co-learning community members. Standout among these are:

- Customized decision-making protocols;
- Full and accessible information-sharing; and
- Shared leadership, shared responsibility, and shared rewards.

Customized decision-making protocols

One of the most resounding findings of our research is that sharing decision-making power is *not* unwieldy chaos. Instead, it is about deliberate and carefully defined responsibilities, structures, and processes for each kind of decision. The goal is to create decision-making protocols that, on the one hand, empower individuals and subgroups to make everyday decisions while, on the other hand, clarify which situations should trigger broader deliberation. Broader deliberation might involve calling in a full team, entire orga-nization, or even stakeholders and community members impacted by the decision. Rather than hierarchical or one-size-fits-all approaches—such as a senior management team that automatically makes all the key decisions—breakout actors recognize that different situations require different combinations of people to provide ideas and feedback and to determine together how to integrate that feedback into a sound decision.

Through working together to craft protocols for the spe-cific kinds of decisions that need to be made across their shared work, and by being thoughtful about the *who* and the *how* for each type of decision, breakout actors collaborate in ways that are both agile and wise.

Mindfully created, customized decision-making pro-tocols are key to preventing what some call the tyranny of structurelessness—a term inspired by political scientist Dr. Jo Freeman's 1972 essay of the same name.[2] This tyranny occurs when a lack of clear structures and protocols enables the most dominant voices in the group to wield dispropor-tionate decision-making power; the result is often a replica of existing societal power structures, even when a group may have set out to model nonhierarchical leadership. In her essay, Freeman points out that for groups to avoid such structure-lessness and its unintended consolidations of power, they can follow principles of "democratic structuring" to build decision-making protocols and organizational structures that align with their values. Such protocols and structures create accountability among group members and enable a team to be "free to develop those forms of organization best suited to its healthy functioning."[3]

Although all breakout actors point to the importance of establishing clear lines of decision-making, they also emphasize not following a set formula while engaging in this practice. Every group arrives at the precise system for power-sharing that best serves their context and aims at that time. What is universal across the breakout teams and enterprises is this: groups engage in intentional, team-wide processes to regularly question and reimagine together precisely how decision-making power is shared.

> **Tip: Try an existing decision-making framework.** In creating decision-making protocols, there is no need to start from scratch. You could consider using toolkits such as Community-Rule[4] or decision-making frameworks such as DARCI, RACI,[5] or MOCHA,[6] which clarify who is responsible for shaping, making, and implementing different kinds of decisions. Breakout actors emphasize the value of decision-making frameworks like the RACI matrix of roles and responsibilities, in which teams designate who is responsible, accountable, consulted, and informed for any given decision. Such tools can help groups move away from, on the one hand, having the same few leaders decide everything or, on the other hand, unwieldy consensus-building in which everyone has equal say on everything.

Decision-making frameworks are also often used in business-as-usual workplaces; something that sets breakout actors apart is the wider range of stakeholders their protocols involve. That greater range of stakeholders also assesses and actually decides, rather than only informs decisions. A practice of sharing decision-making power can mean the people making a decision are a combination of those whose lives will be most impacted by the decision; those who will be implementing the decision; and/or those who have critical experience, expertise, and perspective required to make a wise decision.

While clear protocols and expectations are essential, the practice of sharing decision-making power is also about creating together through emergent adaptation. Breakout actors sometimes refer to it as an art. Steven Bingler, co-learning community member and founder and principal of the New Orleans–based community-centered planning, design, and architecture firm Concordia, points out the importance of keeping this practice in balance. He emphasizes not allowing our structures and protocols to become too rigid, especially when signs point to a change being needed. "Rather than robotically following protocols, treat them as a compass," Steven advises, "while staying attuned to what may need to evolve as we go. A wise teacher once said that they could tell when learning was happening when they walked into a classroom by listening to the buzz. When a process is out of balance, a room full of people can feel like a morgue. When the process is in balance, the buzz is collaborative, active, and alive with imagination." And while Steven is a nationally acclaimed architect, he's equally passionate about music. Steven likens Concordia's ways of work to Wynton Marsalis's conception of swing in jazz:

> No one person can control the ebb and flow. Swing demands three things. It requires extreme coordination, because it is a dance with other people who are inventing steps as they go. It requires intelligent decision-making, because what's best for you is not necessarily best for the group or for the moment. And it requires good intentions, because you have to trust that you and the other musicians are equally interested in making great music and are not guided by ego or musical shortcomings that haven't been addressed... As with other wonderful human activities, swinging is a matter of equilibrium, of balance—of knowing when, how, and how much.[7]

In their practice of sharing decision-making power, breakout actors embrace the art required to effectively work together through decision-making protocols. Doing so elevates such tools into nuanced, responsive channels through which each individual in a group, whether small or large, can fully express their rights to design.

Full and accessible information-sharing

Breakout actors emphasize that sharing decision-making power only works if everyone has access to accurate information about the context within which they are operating. Information needs to flow to and from multiple sources, so everyone understands the big picture. Without equal access to relevant information, people cannot bring their best to decision-making.

Co-learner John Ikerd eloquently distills an array of points about information-sharing made by breakout actors. "You involve everybody, and you're honest and fair," he explains. "If there are restraints on what you can do, you need to tell everyone up front: 'These are the constraints. Within these boundaries, we can do whatever we want to.' You just have to be honest in terms of that."

John recently began his eighth decade on Earth. He and his wife live in Fairfield, Iowa, where they moved ten years ago because they—in John's words—wanted to finish what good years they may have left in a small town. Prior to retiring in his sixties from the University of Missouri, he had a thirty-year academic career as an agricultural economist. While he started out with a business-as-usual approach, during the 1980s and the farm crises of that era, John experienced the failures of the policies he had been advocating to farmers. He became convinced that what he had been taught and was teaching about economics wasn't working.

"It wasn't sustainable ecologically, socially, or even economically," reflects John. "It was making most people's lives worse, not better." He walked away from professional opportunities that were prestigious but no longer in line with his deeply held sense of what was right, and he refocused on supporting community-driven, innovative approaches to sustainable farming and resource-sharing. He did this work through the US Department of Agriculture's agricultural research and extension initiatives, as well as initiatives with state and local agricultural groups. He also began speaking and writing about the changes needed in agriculture and the economy to reach sustainability. A practice of sharing decision-making power is something John believes to be central to revitalizing farming communities and linked to a needed reimagination of our broader economic and food systems.

This practice only works, he points out, when critical information is openly shared with everyone involved, including information about any constraints. "In most cases where there's money involved," he notes, "there are some boundaries. There are some things you've promised to do, and you just need to tell everyone." Breakout actors point out that it's not enough to simply make information available. To enable the practice of sharing decision-making power to reach its full potential, information-sharing needs to happen in proactive ways that ensure the information can be accessed by all involved.

"I've seen that information can be shared in ways that disempower people," explains co-learner Isabella Jean, drawing on her experiences around the globe documenting lessons from humanitarian aid efforts. A member of our co-learning community since its initial year, Isabella shares insights from the many initiatives she has evaluated. Isabella and her fellow co-authors of the acclaimed book *Time to Listen*[8] have witnessed, and been a part of, programs that successfully included stakeholders receiving aid in determining how such aid could be most effective. A key element that led to these successes was the effort group members made to share information in accessible ways with all stakeholders. "Since knowledge is power," points out Isabella, "information kept in the hands of gatekeepers, or information shared in ways that only a few can access or work with, can be a tool for maintaining consolidated power," sometimes even when groups are intending to share decision-making power.

> **Tip: Share information in truly accessible ways.** Actively reach out with information, and present it in ways that are accessible to, and therefore inclusive of, everyone involved. Co-learner Isabella suggests considering steps such as translation into multiple languages, removing jargon with which only some people may be familiar, and engaging people who can serve as info intermediaries with key stakeholders to support everyone to digest and understand the relevant information, so it can fully inform the decisions a group will make together.

Whether with a broad group of stakeholders or within a small team, the ways we share information matter. This includes seemingly small details, like sending a document ahead of time for review and then using a meeting to discuss it, rather than waiting until the meeting to bring up the document and ask for feedback on the spot. As with decision-making protocols, each group of people can collaboratively craft what it means to them for information to be accessible and supportive of sharing decision-making power.

Shared leadership, shared responsibility, and shared rewards

The practice of sharing decision-making power doesn't end the moment a decision is made; to the contrary, the practice is equally about sharing in all that arises from these decisions. "In my experience," shares Steven Bingler, "this practice takes into account two conditions. First, sharing decision-making rewards when things go well, and second, sharing decision-making responsibility and risk when they don't." This means distributing the burden of devising and implementing solutions—as well as sharing in the successes and benefits that result from decisions.

Several breakout actors point out that when groups extend the practice of sharing decision-making power into the realm of financial returns and ownership—reimagining together how financial decisions are made, and how profits are distributed—the benefits of this practice deepen. Co-learner Ed Whitfield strongly emphasizes the importance of shared decisions in financial returns and ownership. If sharing decision-making power doesn't extend into these realms, "if there hasn't been some shift in who owns what and consequently who is in a position of power to create with or not," explains Ed, "then it's not transformational." He adds,

> If you start the day at a big table with someone on one end loaded with money and people begging them for money on the other end, and at the end of the day, you still have a big table with someone loaded with money on one end and people begging for money on the other end, then whether co-creation has taken place or not in the meantime, nothing transformative has happened. So, at the end of the day, something structurally transformative needs to happen. And that's not just for individuals... Because this is not an individual problem.

Given that in the loveless economy, consolidations of wealth and rights to design are tightly linked, it makes sense that breakout innovation has the best chance of arising when groups of people reimagine together both how decisions are made and how financial returns resulting from these decisions are shared.

Bruce Campbell, a member of our co-learning community and the founding attorney of the law firm Blue Dot Advocates, reflects on how his team's transition to becoming a worker-owned cooperative has reinforced the quality and creativity of their work. Blue Dot is a unique firm whose small team of attorneys innovate beyond typical legal and financial structures to best serve clients working for positive change. Blue Dot has done precedent-setting work creating nonextractive lending agreements, collaborative ownership structures, and governing bylaws to enable enterprises to embody structuring that is truly aligned with their values.

Blue Dot started out as a typically structured enterprise, with founder Bruce as the sole owner. But through the profound learning experiences of accompanying clients as they transformed beyond an enterprise's traditional rules and bounds, the Blue Dot team was inspired to do the same. "I didn't want to be the only owner anymore. It felt uncomfortable for me, and it probably felt uncomfortable for other folks," reflects Bruce. "So, we started a process of coming together and talking about what it would look like as a multiowner firm." Even for this team of attorneys with expertise on alternative ownership and governance structures, it wasn't a simple change to make. "It took us a long time to come up with the ultimate form of the new organization and work through how governance would work," notes Bruce. "But in the end, we came up with something that reflected our values and that was really unique." As a cooperative and certified

B Corporation, the Blue Dot team shares decision-making power by sharing financial responsibilities as well as returns.

Brian Mikulencak, a partner at Blue Dot, reflects on the benefits of the team now operating within this structure: "There's definitely a responsibility uptick; there's a shared feeling of trust." Bruce sees change happen when business owners ask themselves profound questions about the consolidated power they may hold: "To me, ultimately there is a spiritual component." Bruce reflects,

> It's about right relationship. Concentrated power and financial resources are mistakes of history. They don't reflect right relationship with the world. And so it's not that I'm giving something up by sharing those things, it's that I'm actually going back to a more natural way of being.

Many breakout actors express this sentiment. They offer that while a practice of sharing decision-making is not easy, once a group shifts into power-sharing ways of working, the experiences that individuals report are immensely positive. In addition to team members enjoying the benefits of more agency over their work, the most common descriptions of the experience of sharing decision-making power are "relief," "more fun," "exhilarating," and "alive."

Like Bruce, many people express that the experience sparks a newfound sense of connection—with the people around them, with life itself, and even with the divine. Our research has revealed this to be true, even for those who have amassed or inherited consolidations of monetary wealth. For example, wealth inheritor and co-learner Marion Weber views her shift to sharing decision-making power as a turning point in her work as a philanthropist and in her life at large. Marion made a lifelong commitment to give away the wealth she continued to inherit, but she found that doing so was wearing her down. She felt increasingly overwhelmed and paralyzed. "My work with money was exhausting, depleting, depressing, and not creative at all," Marion says. Eventually, she came to develop an approach to grant-making that she calls flow funding.

Flow funding centers on circles of grassroots activists and artists who each identify people and groups to receive grant funding. The donor brings together a circle of eight flow funders to serve for three years. The circle members come together each year to share about their selection processes, what moves them about the groups and people they are supporting, and their learnings. After a three-year circle is complete, the individual who initiated the circle invites an enthusiastic member to start their own new circle, and a decentralized web of grant-makers grows, based on networks of trust across communities and sectors. Once Marion started divesting her wealth through flow funding, her work became "relationship-based, inspiring, full of surprises, full of freshness and adventure," she reflects. She also healed from burnout. "If you divide up one person into a thousand people, it's quite a difference," says Marion. "It's like it's more attuned to working with the immune system of the Earth, different cells working with the needs of life."

Breakout actors from across diverse industries affirm a newfound sense of connection can arise from the practice of sharing decision-making power. This can, in turn, fuel group members to effectively navigate the art of working in a power-with frame.

Tip: Remember that effective leadership requires inner work. If you find yourself feeling nervous or fearful at the prospect of sharing decision-making power—and specifically if you are worried it may result in you *losing* power—we invite you to turn your attention inward. Breakout actors note that by mindfully observing your own reactions, you can better discern if a reaction is coming from what you may have been taught about power as a zero-sum game. Groups that are successful at sharing decision-making power involve members who individually take responsibility for the personal growth needed to show up for this practice. This might look like assessing when fear arises in you: What about your reaction could point to issues that are important to trouble-shoot with your team? What about your reaction may point to a belief that you want to unlearn? Consider: What would it look like for everyone in your team, organization, and/or community to be powerful?

Sharing decision-making power in action

Breakout actor Concordia exemplifies broadening who is involved in decision-making in ways that break far out of the confines of business as usual. While a power-with ethos was central to the founding mission of the company, the way Concordia's team practices sharing decision-making power significantly deepened through the role they played in New Orleans's recovery from the devastation of Hurricane Katrina.

A year after Katrina, New Orleans was still struggling to rebuild. Two city-led planning processes had failed. These top-down efforts had resulted in plans that were fiercely opposed by civic groups who felt that these plans were based on overly simplistic and discriminatory fixes to the complex challenges of rebuilding neighborhoods in New Orleans. Concordia stepped up to lead a third effort with an approach that defied conventional planning processes—and which resulted in a plan that was widely embraced by residents and approved by the city, finally unlocking desperately needed federal funds for recovery and rebuilding.

Concordia's success was rooted in their team's approach: residents were decision-makers in every step of the process. According to Bobbie Hill, a principal of Concordia, "We have found through the years that if people have good information, they make level-headed decisions. And when you're planning at a very large scale, we believe you can't ever have too many people at the table, because then everyone has access to better information since each person offers an important perspective based on their lived experience."

This belief has been a formative force in Bobbie's life. As one of the most active members of our co-learning community, Bobbie has taught us a great deal about how possible it is to increase the number of seats at the decision-making table far beyond what business as usual says is feasible or prudent. She also shares how to do so in ways that are both exceptionally well organized and deeply human. "I am the oldest of seven children growing up in Louisiana with aunts, uncles, and cousins all around," shares Bobbie. "I am all about relationships and creating community. This has driven everything along my life's journey." Over several decades, Bobbie has made her life's work about designing and supporting authentic engagement. "I believe that whoever is impacted by any decisions being made deserves a seat at the table," says Bobbie firmly.

It was this spirit, shared by all members of the Concordia team, that underpinned a planning process in the wake of Hurricane Katrina that was unlike any planning process the city had seen. Concordia hired residents to conduct an extensive grassroots community engagement process that resulted in more than nine thousand New Orleans residents serving as researchers, designers, and decision-makers. For every city district, regular planning meetings were held, along with multiple city-wide Community Congress meetings at the convention center. These meetings hosted almost two thousand residents in attendance, alongside simultaneous, two-way broadcasts, which brought the event to parallel meetings in Houston, Baton Rouge, Jackson, Atlanta, and sixteen other cities where large numbers of New Orleanians had found refuge after fleeing from the storm.

When it came down to determining how the co-created recovery plans were to be implemented, the Concordia team held an election process in which residents of each neighborhood voted for their top-choice planning firm, with whom they'd work on a recovery plan specific to their neighborhood. In order for residents to make an informed choice, Concordia organized an event at which dozens of planning and development firms from across the country each presented a ten-minute pitch about their approach. Residents then voted for the firms they liked best. It turned out that every single neighborhood was able to work with their first or second choice firm.

The Concordia team had initially felt nervous about how the outcome of the election event might unfold: Would it be possible for every neighborhood to work with a top-choice firm? However, despite their worries, Bobbie explains, they never questioned that residents needed to be the ones to choose their planners: "If residents didn't continually have a seat at the table for every single aspect of this process, then it all could have fallen apart. And the people who participated in this were the ones that had the intimate knowledge of the condition of their neighborhood; they knew what was important to bring back and what was important to redo. They were the experts."

Throughout the process that led to the enthusiastically approved Unified New Orleans Plan, the Concordia team practiced sharing decision-making power in a whole host of ways—from small groups making recommendations to large groups in which everyone voted to inviting people who had stepped up as community fellows or "table hosts" to decide the best next step for their group, and more. Concordia's approach demonstrated that investing in a shared decision-making process can ultimately save time and money, as well as create new connections among everyone involved.

How does sharing decision-making power unlock breakout innovation?

Sharing decision-making power distributes rights to design by involving more people in the workings of an enterprise than are involved in business as usual. Whether in a law firm determining its structure or a neighborhood charting a course toward its recovery, when many people are influencing a group's trajectory, they encourage an increase in responsive, course-correcting actions, steering the group toward wiser decisions. "In cases where I have been able to get teams I have worked with to share power," reflects John Ikerd, "the results have been far more impressive than in cases where I had to make the decisions." Whatever the context of our shared work, a practice of sharing decision-making power unlocks the full potential of each person involved. People can feel inspired to give their best because they have authentic ownership in what they're building.

This practice is not easy; it frequently requires navigating conflict, dealing with the baggage of past experiences that we may carry into our present work, and continual inner work to face inherited patterns. "The reality is that this is not only the right way to go, but also some of the hardest work that any of us will take on in our lifetimes," admits Steven. When groups stay the course with this practice, they can nurture teams in which everyone cares about what is being designed and feels accountable to the processes and protocols created together. When there is a power-with ethos, individuals within groups also tend to readily take initiative when something goes wrong. As in the example of RUNWAY's response to the first wave of economic impacts from the pandemic, when individuals are nourished by the benefits of their group's successes, they are better resourced to bring their best as challenges arise—and even to turn these challenges into opportunities for further breakout innovation.

When decision-making power changes from something we shoulder alone or fight to access into something we approach creatively together, each of us becomes more powerful.

· · ·

HEART RESEARCH ALLIANCE

DEBBE MCCALL still remembers how she felt when she was first diagnosed with atrial fibrillation (AFib). "I was devastated. No, I wasn't devastated; I was pissed. I was at my absolute healthiest when AFib hit and I was so angry," recalls Debbe. "My mother had four heart attacks before she died, and her first one was before she was fifty. I knew what my genetics were going to bring to me, and I had busted my butt to not have that happen." While the diagnosis was shocking and upsetting, Debbe resolved to find community with other people navigating the same health condition. Debbe soon connected with a group of fellow AFib patients, and the newfound sense of connection, hope, and solidarity—as well as new relationships that deepened into friendships—made a world of difference in her life. She has been an active member of patient advocacy groups and networks ever since.

From her own experience and by hearing from fellow patients, Debbe understands that "in any patient community, the first thing, when anybody gets a diagnosis, is suddenly 'I feel alone and isolated.' And that's why they reach out to support groups." Once they do, Debbe explains, many find that "yes, there's information that we can share; yes, there's learning about the science. But it's more about 'You are not alone.'" Debbe has found that it's that sense of solidarity and community that makes an immediate positive difference in people's lives. "When I welcome new members, that's one of the first things I say: '*Breathe.* Just breathe and know that you're not alone. We're all here, we've all been in your spot.'"

In the wake of her AFib diagnosis, and grounded by the power of these new relationships, Debbe became one of the founding participants of a "patient-powered" research initiative called Heart Research Alliance.[1] It was a collaborative research initiative coordinated by the University of California San Francisco Medical Center, in partnership with multiple heart health advocacy organizations and made possible by grant funding from a federal initiative. Based on an organizing principle of recognizing the value of patient voices, Heart Research Alliance worked to improve the quality of health-care systems and interventions from a patient perspective, as well as promote deeper research on heart disease—including on how to meaningfully improve quality of life for people living with AFib.

"The grant required that patients be involved in the design process of how researchers determine what to study," Brooking Gatewood shares. Brooking and her colleague Rebecca Petzel were hired by the UCSF to design and facilitate the creation of a patient-powered research network that would identify research questions. Brooking is a self-described "network nerd" and someone who, from a young age, has been working on and thinking deeply about systemic change. She is also a poet and writer, and she recognizes that artistry is an essential element of collaborative social change. Brooking and Rebecca bring this spirit of both art and science to their facilitation work, which is centered on redistributing power to foster both individual agency and collective intelligence. This orientation made them exceptionally well positioned to support UCSF in making Heart Research Alliance truly patient powered from its inception to its final decisions and research recommendations. According to Brooking,

> We put together a steering committee and there was a thorough go-slow-to-move-fast kickoff process designed to enable participants to build trust and relationships—to actually get to know each other as humans and be able to work together as peers. And then we all designed, with a lot of patient input, an initial event that brought together doctors, researchers, and patients to explore project ideas. In designing the event, participants decided to set very specific ground rules where the patients got one set of invitations and the doctors and researchers got another set, and each was invited to step into an edge of discomfort to challenge their usual ways of operating. And so for the patients, it was "please speak," and for the doctors, it was "please listen."

Kathi Sigona, a patient participant, reflects on how this approach that Brooking, Rebecca, and all the participants co-created was key to Heart Research Alliance's success: "I think what really helped drive the success of the group was the fact that we didn't have a hierarchy. Sometimes patients working with doctors on a different level can be somewhat intimidating. But we became colleagues; we all put our pants on the same way."

The facilitators of Heart Research Alliance created the conditions for trusting relationships, which allowed patients to truly drive much of the conversations and process. "It was a huge shift that way," Debbe shares. "And it showed because there were more of us patients than there were of the researchers. We drove the conversations, not them. And every time they tried to use big words, we called them on it, and that would never happen anywhere else." Debbe emphasizes that the process of having patients "lay the groundwork" for how Heart Research Alliance would operate "had given us the confidence that this was *our* conference, and we were there to bring researchers into our world, not the other way around, which is the way research has been for hundreds of years."

Another unique aspect of the Heart Research Alliance initiative was that it paid stipends to all involved—researchers and patient participants. "That made a big difference," Debbe affirms. "And because of that, most of us who were interested in being in research, like I was, were able to use that as a stepping-stone." Being paid enabled Debbe and others to spend more time participating and learning with fellow participants, researchers, and doctors without having to worry about missed income from spending time away from their usual work. As a result of the substantial experience Debbe gained in designing research questions and methodologies, she has been able to build a consulting business serving as a patient PI (principal investigator) on federally funded research initiatives—and is even paid to attend and do social media coverage of medical conferences. Kathi also found that participation in the Heart Research Alliance initiative "provided so many of us citizen scientists the opportunity to lead and participate in the planning and execution of clinical trials and research. This model has been very successful."

After the inaugural event, the Heart Research Alliance was firmly established and kept growing. Although the initial project was time-bound and wound down in 2019, the results continue to reverberate today. Dr. Mark Pletcher of the UCSF epidemiology and biostatistics department was one of the founding members of the project. He shares that the Heart Research Alliance "continues to support deep patient engagement for research studies." It set a new bar for how patients can participate as peers and leading experts in the shaping of meaningful medical research. For instance, he points to a recent research initiative called BP Home, a randomized trial of home blood-pressure monitoring, which "used the Heart Research Alliance to assemble and support a patient advisory board that helped develop participant onboarding, surveys, and instructional materials." When results of the BP Home study were ready to share, "they hosted a webinar where results of the study were presented to study participants," says Dr. Pletcher, "with patient advisory board members and the principal investigator of the study as panelists." It was the influence of Heart Research Alliance's approach and former participants, explains Dr. Pletcher, that inspired BP Home to turn the tables on how research results are usually presented and to whom.

As facilitators, Brooking and Rebecca were also deeply affected by the experience and by the powerful results that unfolded from the foundation of authentic, caring relationships patients formed with one another. This focus on relationship-building is something they carried into their subsequent work together with The Emergence Collective, the collaborative consulting experiment they formed after Heart Research Alliance to continue practicing and fostering collective leadership with future colleagues and client collaborators. The relational, power-shifting, and participatory design principles from the Heart Research Alliance project have informed all of their subsequent projects.

Brooking reflects that what most impacted her about Heart Research Alliance was experiencing the ways that members of the patient community "really show up for each other," and how patients brought this spirit of care and solidarity to everything that the Alliance members did together. As a result of being welcomed into this community, Brooking experienced a shift in perspective. She recalls one moment, early in the process, when this shift started to occur for her.

> One of the patients invited me to a 5k walk supporting one of the foundations. That's the kind of thing that, in the past, I would have thought, "Oh, that's not exactly work, that's not on the clock." But I went and did the walk and wore my Heart Research Alliance shirt, and I remember meeting all these people, and realizing that for so many of the people in the patient communities, these were their best friends in life. Many of these people had known each other for decades and had seen each other through scary near-death moments and surgeries and the loss of friends, and they were all sharing information about what they're learning about how to live well with their conditions, and it was really powerful. And I remember realizing in that experience, "Oh, *this* is real relationship."

Like Brooking, many of the people involved in Heart Research Alliance—patients, doctors, and researchers alike— emphasize the strength of relationships that characterized their work together. This is evident in the continuing collaborations among members today, several years after the formal completion of the Heart Research Alliance. Former participants continue to look out for one another, share new research opportunities and information, and reach out to one another as thought partners and peers when it comes to new medical research questions. The power of their relationships has kept the Alliance alive in spirit—and is at the heart of its continuing influence on reimagining medical research.

CHAPTER 5

PRIORITIZE RELATIONSHIPS

A DEFINING characteristic of the Heart Research Alliance was the care and respect with which everyone involved treated one another, regardless of whether the person was a patient, doctor, or researcher. Operating with a focus on relationships is something strongly emphasized by all the breakout actors with whom we learned. They brought this ethos to our co-learning community from the start. We'll never forget the first evening of the co-learner gathering in New Orleans. Co-learners had driven from Baton Rouge, bussed from Atlanta, and flew in from various corners of the country to gather. After a dinner of home-cooked food, we congregated in a big circle, sitting on folding chairs, sofa arms, even a piano bench. Everyone briefly introduced themselves by sharing their response to a single question: What made you say yes to this gathering?

People spoke about the nature of their work; they shared that the research questions aligned with questions they, too, had been holding; they shared their interest in meeting and learning from one another. One of the last people in the circle to speak was co-learner Eugene Eric Kim, who had arrived that day from San Francisco, where his consultancy,

Faster Than 20, is based. We'd learned about Eugene's work through our research interviews: two different interviewees had raved about his brilliant approach to "high-performance collaboration" and how it had led their enterprise to major breakthroughs in effectiveness.

"I resonate with a lot of what you all have shared," Eugene began. "And also in terms of why I'm here: I have never met Jess and Joanna in person before. We've literally only had two phone calls. I get a lot of phone calls and emails inviting me to things that I say no to. A big part of why I traveled here is because Jess and Joanna were *kind*." Eugene paused; you could have heard a pin drop. "That stuff *matters*. Being kind and genuine matters. My guess is that's a big part of why all of us are here."

Prior to that moment, to be frank, we had both considered ourselves people who needed to work on making our emails more concise—fewer exclamation points and smiley faces, perhaps. We had not linked our tendencies to care to our efficacy as professionals. Eugene's comment shifted that. Later in the evening, sweeping up crawfish shells in the backyard, we overheard Eugene and co-learner Steven Bingler having an animated conversation about indicators of success, as they stacked folding chairs. Eugene mentioned one of his personal favorites: the number of hugs exchanged at a multistakeholder meeting. He and Steven agreed: you could tell how successful the final outcome would be based on the number of hugs.

While we didn't know it at the time, Eugene was speaking to something we now recognize as a bedrock foundation of ways of work that spark breakout innovation—something that is both a practice unto itself as well as woven into every one of the other six practices: prioritizing relationships.

Prioritizing relationships is the practice of bringing a spirit of care to everyday interactions with team members and people in the broader community whom our work affects. It is caring about these relationships for their intrinsic sake, rather than for transactional purposes. The primary focus is not on getting value from a person for the task at hand. Instead, it is on caring for the quality of our relationships with one another, apart from any additional aim, by caring about that individual as a whole person. This involves staying curious about and tuning in to whatever may arise from the connections we build together. To prioritize relationships is to recognize that being in right relationship with ourselves, one another, and our planet is core to unlocking possibilities for breakout innovation.

Shifting how we understand relationships

Business as usual teaches that relationships matter: it's *who* you know, not what you know. There is a clear distinction between the business-as-usual view of work relationships and the breakout actors' view. Whether conscious or not, those in business as usual often teach that people must leverage their relationships toward a predetermined aim and steer all interactions toward that specific outcome. In the loveless economy, we are taught to view relationships primarily as a means to an end. When interactions unfold in ways that don't clearly have something to do with advancing agendas, many people may feel uncomfortable. Or they may even feel guilty about it—if, for example, they take time on a business call to talk to a colleague about how they're doing, leaving scheduled agenda items undone. The teachings of business as usual have trained us over generations to feel that such relational moments are supposed to take place outside of our paid time, outside of work.

In contrast, breakout actors recognize that truly successful work cannot happen without authentic, caring relationships among the people involved. Quite simply, breakout actors have found a transactional approach to work to be less effective.

There is a paradox in play here: when we stop focusing only on what we can get from someone to achieve a goal and start caring about our connection for its own sake, the people around us rapidly become the greatest blessing to the task at hand. The heartfelt quality of our connections with one another vaults our shared potential far beyond what was possible to imagine or plan for. Grounded in authentic relationships, group members are inspired to give their best effort, and they feel safer to share their sharpest thinking.

At the same time, this practice does not mean that a person should feel pressured to open up or share all dimensions of themselves at work. Sometimes we don't want to do so, which is perfectly okay. Sometimes it may also feel unsafe to do so. Prioritizing relationships is not about demanding or expecting a level of intimate sharing or familiarity. Our work teams are different from a family or a friend group.[1] And while there are often overlaps between friendships and professional relationships in our collaborations, how we express our whole person through the creative energy we inject into our work may look and be different from how we express our whole selves within friendships or family relationships. These various expressions of ourselves are all *us*. They are all authentic. And we each decide for ourselves how much they overlap.

The practice of prioritizing authentic relationships honors each of us as a whole person in our work—the humanity in our creativity, insight, and effort that we each bring to our work. It is about remembering that who we are when we're at work is a full self, is human. Business as usual seldom leaves space for us to learn about, show up for, or tend to our relationships in that spirit. Yet, as in all other realms of our lives, if we cultivate only transactional relationships, we miss out on so much.

What does prioritizing relationships look like?

Breakout actors demonstrate this practice in their work in ways both big and small. Several common elements stand out in how they prioritize relationships:

- Building a culture of care,
- Welcoming brave conversations, and
- Cultivating a relational worldview.

There is a key dynamic across all these elements that is central to unlocking breakout innovation, which we discuss in Chapter 7 on seeking difference. For breakout actors, the practice of prioritizing relationships is about building caring, strong relationships across differences. Without meaningful forms of difference and diversity among those with whom we cultivate strong relationships, a practice of prioritizing relationships can swing far out of balance and create or reinforce insular or discriminatory ways of working. Breakout actors operate with an ethic of care and connection across difference, intentionally departing from the insular dynamics in which business as usual can keep people.

Building a culture of care

At its essence, a practice of prioritizing relationships comes down to caring about one another and expressing this care in our day-to-day actions. Co-learner Kataraina Davis speaks about the Māori value of kaitiakitanga—a concept of unity that is deeply tied to relational ways of being and an ethic of care. "Basically, to tiaki someone," she explains, "is to care and make someone feel comfortable."

Kataraina shared that kaitiakitanga can work in many different ways: sometimes it's about helping someone to feel supported when they are struggling; other times, it may call us to be unflinchingly honest when asked for feedback. In our everyday work together, she pointed out, this approach of care and responsibility extends to ensuring we also operate as kaitiaki—guardians or caretakers—of each other's stories and knowledge. It is only when we operate with this spirit of deep respect that we enable one another to share our most powerful insights and offerings—to, as Kataraina describes it, "hear the deep stories."

There are many different ways that breakout actors foster an ethic of care. This might look like starting a gathering with delicious food and music, not necessarily for a special occasion but simply to nourish one another's bodies and spirits. It could look like taking extra steps to support a group member when a hardship occurs in that person's life. And in everyday meetings or tasks, it can look like simply taking time to ask how one another is doing and to listen deeply to the answer.

Tip: Start meetings with a check-in. This simple practice is one that just about every breakout actor we learned from does regularly. At the start of a meeting—whether between two people or many more—before diving into the agenda, begin by sharing a prompt or question that invites everyone to share in ways that can build further connection with one another, to whatever extent each person desires in the moment. There are endless possibilities for check-in questions. They aim to connect us and share in ways that go beyond baseline exchanges like "Fine. And you?" A check-in question could be: What was a highlight of your weekend? Or they can inspire us to share less serious sides of ourselves, such as: What song do you know every single word of? They can also help ground us in the seriousness of what is at stake in the conversation we are about to have, for example: Who in your life inspired you to do this work? Whether they spark laughter or poignant sharing, check-ins can help team members deepen connections and trust.

Breakout actors emphasize the importance of creating times for care and connection that are intentionally not about "getting things done." Their many ways of doing this range from calling a few minutes early into an online meeting to catch up with colleagues to taking the time to visit collaborators in-person to hosting seasonal celebratory events. Another example is coming together "to talk about big-picture work stuff—the visions and connections you wish for," explains Bryana DiFonzo, a member of our co-learning community and the director of new economy for PUSH Buffalo, a grassroots organization in Buffalo, New York, leading groundbreaking work in affordable housing as part of vibrant neighborhood economies. She emphasizes that making time to be together outside of getting tasks done doesn't have to be limited to things like a happy hour or holiday party, but can include creating opportunities to share our deeply held hopes for the work we do together. Bryana is passionate about the behind-the-scenes effort that goes into quality work—the infrastructure and relationships that sustain a group's success. Bryana reflects that creating opportunities to share big-picture visions and questions with our colleagues "lets people bond over things they feel very passionate about and proud of, and often sparks creative ideas, leaving people feeling more spacious or energized."

It's important, she noted—on a phone call from her neighborhood community garden where she'd come to take a moment to pause from her other tasks that day—that you don't go in with an outcome in mind, "other than connecting about the stuff that stokes your fires."

Welcoming brave conversations

Breakout actors clarify that prioritizing relationships does not mean avoiding conflict. As Eugene emphasizes, kindness is different from superficial politeness. Prioritizing relationships means we invest the time and care needed to be real with each other. Breakout actors build resilient relationships in which they are willing to challenge one another's thinking and to be challenged; group members feel a sense of responsibility to call attention to ways of work that may be detrimental to their collective aim.

Co-learning community member Jessamyn Shams-Lau relates this element of the practice to the concept of radical candor,[2] which she sums up as "a way of communicating that challenges directly whilst caring personally." Jessamyn herself embodies this ethos—whether she's speaking on a panel at a large conference or in the office with her team. This approach has been vital to the breakout initiatives that Jessamyn has been a part of in the philanthropic sector, which change the norms and rules of how grants are awarded and by whom. She notes that the changes she's worked toward are only possible when there are direct and open conversations about what is not working.

In a recent team that Jessamyn led, the group designed its own unique approach to 360 reviews. Each team member had a time when they would do their annual review, and all other team members would provide feedback. The person being reviewed had the option to read the feedback in advance, which most did, but all the feedback—both positive and negative—was still delivered verbally on the day of their review. "This gave our team the chance to practice both giving and receiving feedback face-to-face, within the context of a shared belief that doing so demonstrated our care and investment in the success of each other. It took courage and significant trust for all involved," explains Jessamyn. Yet the process became something team members deeply valued and even looked forward to. Each person's annual review was framed as a celebration—of them, their growth, and also of *all* the feedback, that which was positive as well as that which identified areas for change and further growth.

> **Tip: Co-create containers for honest conversations.** Brave conversations involve asking in advance to exchange feedback—and mutually agreeing to do so—before the feedback is shared. This can look like co-creating a system for peer feedback among team members. It can involve a regular evaluation and reflection step after any major event or milestone, which invites everyone involved to respond to questions about what didn't work and how it could be better. As with decision-making protocols, these containers and customs can be co-created by group members to align with their specific aims and values. As co-learner Katherine Tyler Scott describes it, prioritizing relationships looks like being tough on systems as opposed to tough on people. Whatever systems we design together, the key is to first create a container where people feel safe to share feedback, so that tough feedback or vented frustration doesn't come out of the blue when someone is not ready to receive it. When information is exchanged in this thoughtful way, there's a better chance it will be accepted and absorbed by all involved and lead to the necessary course corrections.

In the loveless economy, radical candor can be hard to practice; depending on one's positional power, social identities, and other factors, such honest sharing can lead to inequitable consequences. This can prevent a team from accessing information that could serve as correcting feedback, which is vital for the health and optimal functioning of a system. Because most people have spent years impacted by and participating in loveless ways of work that consolidate rights to design, breakout actors recognize it is crucial to work together to proactively create spaces where it is safe to offer authentic feedback. By inviting one another into these spaces and upholding care and respect, we serve our shared work. Co-creating intentional spaces for approaching one another to address ruptures or to share feedback can help give us the push we need to be courageous and kind.

Cultivating a relational worldview

In the loveless economy, transactional ways of being in relationships form such a big part of how people see and engage with the world; it can be hard to conceive that anything else is possible. However, there are other ways of being rooted in what is sometimes referred to as a relational worldview. A relational worldview means different things to different people; one definition that strikes us is "an embodied understanding of the interdependent relationship that exists between self, Earth, community, and the numinous (mystery, awe, wonder)."[3] We've observed that breakout actors cultivate this kind of relational worldview, rooting their work in the vast interconnectedness of all beings and forces.

Co-learner Paula Antoine, program coordinator at the Rosebud Sioux Tribe's Sicangu Oyate Land Office and an organizer of the Standing Rock movement, reflects that this concept is foundational for her Lakota people:

In our way of life, being respectful, being a good relative is one of the highest things you can be, and that means to totally give of yourself, be generous, be honest, be trustworthy, have a concept that whatever you do is going to affect the next seven generations in your life. So you try to live every day with that concept. Your actions show how you are as part of the collective—of the Lakota people. So then it contributes to the health and well-being of the... entire Lakota people because you are living that way. So that encourages people beside you to do that same thing.

Examining what is required to move away from business-as-usual mindsets and toward a relational worldview, co-learning community member Ben Joosten describes this shift as "breaking out of main-character syndrome." A former volunteer with breakout actor Incourage Community Foundation, Ben started this shift in high school through his participation in a community planning process organized by Incourage. In the years since, he has deepened the ways he operates with a relational approach. "If you go through your life thinking your life and worldview is the only thing that matters," points out Ben, "then you'll think making strong relationships doesn't really matter, unless they are deeply personal or intimate relationships with people you directly surround yourself with. Why would you put in any effort to be kind to, say, a service worker you interact with or someone you find yourself around for a brief moment in time?"

In contrast, reflects Ben, "if you're able to break out of that mindset and realize that everyone is living their life, those little moments and relationships you share seem to start carrying a lot more value." For Ben, such moments of connection in his own life have led him to some of his biggest learnings and to even reconsider his path. Ben shares that his participation in a community planning process facilitated by Incourage instilled in him a new approach to forming relationships. In the process, he formed friendships with people across differences, and this deepened his sense of connection to the place where he had been born and raised. This was a big part of what made Ben ultimately decide not to move far away to attend college, but rather to study close to home and be able to continue to enjoy and deepen these connections. "That interconnectivity of how small relationships can have incredible outcomes is a part of why I think they're so important." Today, Ben brings a relational approach to the classrooms he has worked in as an instructor and to the team of a small business he is helping expand into new markets.

Kataraina also speaks about interconnectivity and about how the Māori value of kaitiakitanga, caring for those around us, applies to the broader web of relationships in which we live and work. "In a Māori worldview, it's not just your mom and dad, your brother and sister," she notes. "It's your mom, your dad, your brother and sister, your grandparents, your ancestors that have gone before you; it's your aunties and uncles; it's your friends that you choose, your family that you choose. It's your hapū, which is a subtribe, it's your iwi, which is your greater collective tribe."

Furthermore, she explains, this concept extends beyond people: "Māori here in New Zealand act as kaitiaki, as guardians, of our land. We're kaitiaki of our water. So, what do we do to make sure that we share information with people when they come to our land here in Auckland to take care of it as well and act as kaitiaki of our space?" Acting with a relational worldview means awakening to the interconnections we share with the people and living world around us and stepping up to help care for the living web of which we are a part. When we do so, these many connections guide our shared work to breakout innovations that can protect and nourish life and community.

> **Tip: Don't forget nonhuman relationships.** With a relational worldview, opportunities abound for extending the practice of prioritizing relationships in your work to include nonhuman relationships as well. Is there a part of the surrounding land that is particularly important to your work? Do you have non-human stakeholders that you may not have thought about yet, such as trees, animals, or whole ecosystems? For example, Incourage Community Foundation supports and encourages holding events that center the community's relationship with the local river, honoring the life energy it brings to their region.

Prioritizing relationships in action

Incourage has made prioritizing relationships a keystone of its work in the community of Wisconsin Rapids, the small city in central Wisconsin where the organization is based. Incourage's focus on relationship-building was demonstrated in the creation of a different approach to the city's Community Picnic, an event that Incourage first catalyzed more than a decade ago in order to foster relationships and build trust among residents. Thanks to an outpouring of community support and enthusiasm over its seven-year run, what started as a foundation-supported event to promote community building and celebration for Wisconsin Rapids' natural resources, food, and businesses grew into a local event that attracted over seven thousand people—nearly 40 percent of the population of the city—with food and supplies donated annually from dozens of vendors and community members.

And the price of admission? Committing to meet at least one new person, a requirement that Incourage staff and residents took seriously. "The Community Picnic is more than a free meal," emphasized co-learner Kelly Ryan, former CEO of Incourage and continuing supporter of the organization. "It's designed to intentionally celebrate and foster appreciation for local assets—and the dignity and worth of every person who lives in our community."

Local farmer Harold Altenburg remembers when he heard about the event in its initial year and called up the Incourage office to ask, "What can I bring to the picnic?" He showed up with one thousand ears of corn, a roasting machine, and volunteer help. The next year, he brought more than double that amount. And in the years since, Harold donated and served literally tens of thousands of ears of corn.[4] Harold shares,

> Why do I participate in the Community Picnic? To make something happen! To help people make something happen. Do it! Let's have a little excitement. A little fun. *Enjoy* the area. The water skiing. The river! People! We got it! This community needs a little more movement, action, doing more things. So when somebody comes up with an idea, my suggestion is to say, "How can I help?" Don't "but" it to death! ... Help make it happen!

The spirit that Harold brought to the event each year, alongside many other residents also bringing their enthusiasm to share and volunteer and make new connections, made the simple idea of the Community Picnic into a powerful force for deepening a spirit of connection and care across the community and resulted in other events in the city, including a music festival, taking more inclusive approaches. In Kelly's words, "Every community in the nation would be better off if the people who live there appreciated the fact that their neighbors are the most important resource in building a community. At the picnic, our residents demonstrate what it means to be in a community together. At the end of the day, it's the people who matter most."

How prioritizing relationships unlocks breakout innovation

In business-as-usual workplaces, if frustration builds up or one team member feels wronged by another, too often people are taught or told to bottle up their feelings and keep moving. But these kinds of ruptures, even if relatively minor, can block the channels of feedback and information that need to flow freely. When we affirm the importance of open conversations, and when we care for our relationships and attend to the inevitable blockages and rifts that arise, our shared work becomes full of both wisdom and heart.

The importance of nurturing caring, authentic relationships as the foundation for good outcomes has been at the heart of many Indigenous Peoples' teachings and lifeways for millennia. Only in recent years have business studies come to the same common-sense conclusion. For instance, one major study on effective teams conducted by Google found that psychological safety—when members of a team feel safe enough with each other to take risks—plays a singularly powerful role in creating conditions for a group to achieve standout success.[5] It turns out that authentic relationships are the ultimate high technology and that fostering care among teams is an investment that generates great value.

Co-learning community member Aisha Shillingford emphasizes how strong interpersonal relationships spark optimal functioning of team processes. Aisha describes herself as an artist, writer, and experience designer from Kalinago/Warao land (Trinidad and Tobago) currently living in Lenapehoking, unceded territory of the Lenape people (Brooklyn, New York)—and as the daughter of Brenda, the granddaughter of Ena and Eileen, and the great-granddaughter of Mary and Henry. Aisha is also the artistic director and co-principal of Intelligent Mischief, a creative studio "unleashing Black imagination to shape the future." Before founding Intelligent Mischief, Aisha worked as a facilitator with two leading consulting organizations to guide teams at companies, public agencies, and nonprofits through processes to transform dysfunctional dynamics into strong relationships. She points to the importance of what she has been taught along the way about how we work, from places and teachers including Interaction Institute of Social Change, Change Elemental, and Norma Wong.[6]

"When relationships aren't strong," Aisha sums up, "it makes it difficult to achieve results." She explains how teams with weak relationships "have to create work-arounds to make up for the lack of relationships," often compensating for this lack by constructing systems, operations, and process-flows that have superfluous steps. Their processes become cumbersome and counterproductive. Aisha sees strong relationships as the key to "reducing bulkiness in the process."

Taking time to nourish relationships creates the conditions to support teams in going farther and faster than they might have imagined, and to arrive with offerings that reflect their individual and collective best. When groups prioritize relationships outside of the transactional, they enable an explosion of system-wide creativity, because everyone involved feels free to express the full richness of ideas they hold. The practice of prioritizing relationships melts the ways in which business as usual upholds the social construct of an other, restoring a group's ability to operate in ways that see one another as full, complex peers who deserve mutual care and respect. This works to deconsolidate rights to design.

Prioritizing relationships also creates conditions for a group's resilience and resourcefulness in the long run. Breakout actors share that in times of great challenge or opportunity, the quality of a group's response depends on the quality of its relationships. In our entangled, relational realities, innumerable variables present themselves. Challenging turns of events defy our ability to imagine them in advance, let alone predict what will play out. We need a bedrock of authentic, trusting relationships to *together* navigate the infinitely complex living world in which we work.

. . .

INCOURAGE COMMUNITY FOUNDATION

KATHERINE TYLER Scott first traveled to Wisconsin Rapids in 2005 and met with the staff of the Incourage Community Foundation and the chamber of commerce to help plan the launch of a new local leadership program: the Adaptive Leadership Institute. This program grew out of the Incourage team's decision to fundamentally question the business-as-usual role of community foundations in order to support their own community during a time of hardship. The local paper company, which had been the center of the regional economy for nearly a century, had downsized operations and been acquired by an overseas company. Within five years of its initial wave of downsizing, nearly 40 percent of total employment in the region had been lost, disrupting the economic life of the community. Through many conversations with residents and through the Incourage team's own soul-searching process, the organization decided to focus on a sustained approach to support residents in strengthening their capacities for adaptive leadership—and taking initiative to create opportunities in times of profound change. Their approach emphasized the community's many rich assets that continued to exist despite the downsizing of its largest employer. Ultimately, their goal was to support the community in seeing and charting a new path forward.

When Katherine arrived for the planning session with her colleagues Irma Tyler-Wood and Joanna Murray from Ki ThoughtBridge, which specializes in transformative leadership development, she asked the Incourage staff what their families, neighborhoods, and community groups were experiencing. "The loss of the company really triggered and exposed a vulnerability, sadness, and depression among the residents," Katherine observes. Not only that, the adverse impact of this change led many town residents, who were suffering under the strain of the loss, to "turn on each other rather than deal with the real problem," she reflects.

Katherine and her colleagues worked with Incourage to develop a program that would equip community leaders with resources and tools to overcome the dramatic economic changes. The most important element of the program was its inception. The institute started with an activity that explored the town's history—from past centuries to more recent decades—by weaving individual participants' personal stories and values together with the larger community narrative.

Katherine describes what it was like that first day, as approximately twenty of Wisconsin Rapids' most respected municipal officials, teachers, business owners, and other local leaders were asked to do something that none of them had expected to do at a leadership training: share their individual and family histories. "We actually started with helping them to understand the significance of their history, from the present time all the way back to when the town was founded. As they told their individual stories, they began to see how these stories fit together into the larger community story."

The participants' initial discomfort with the activity soon transformed into an outpouring of stories, both in the full group and in small conversations, and through speech, writing, and drawing. Together they created a collective timeline for the town—one that soon covered three whole walls of the large event space in which they were gathered.

Joe Terry, former director of public works for the City of Wisconsin Rapids, was one of the participants in that first cohort of the Adaptive Leadership Institute. We asked him about this exercise more than a decade later, and he still vividly remembers that initial day: "What it did was, it demonstrated that some perspectives are sometimes worlds apart. Some people, when we're looking at a particular time frame, they weren't in the country, much less the area. So their timeline and their history was very, very different. But it was through that storytelling that you started to get to know some people." Joe pauses, then adds thoughtfully, "There was truth being told, and so you trust people because they're truthful."

Joe and Katherine recall the transformation they observed that day and how the energy of the room shifted palpably. Shared histories wallpapered the room; people laughed together or listened to one another with deep attention; some silently soaked in what others had written on the wall. "As this huge timeline... unfolded," Katherine says, "people began to see, one, that there is a sense of community stability, solidity, and core values that have held true for generations, but there has also been adaptation and change." She pauses to emphasize this point. "They begin to see there is some efficacy in their ability to do something now. They can do something now about the situation." Connecting residents—who each came with different backgrounds and life stories—to a shared sense of history and resilience thus opened the door to having a conversation about a collective path forward for their town.

Katherine and Joe also speak to the way that bringing shared histories into the room called people into their higher selves, reminding them that everyone has their own family stories, struggles, and journeys to this moment. "People began to hear each other," Katherine comments. "It wasn't only that people now saw one another more fully; they also began to perceive the deep intertwining of their stories— their interconnectedness with one another. As their stories came out, they also saw the larger story: that longer view of the community, beyond their own individual existence."

This collective remembering process created space for what Katherine recalls as a strong and shared reverence for place. What became clear to Katherine was "people's love not just for families but for this place." She continues,

> And I think that emotion really did infuse the group and helped them to loosen up a bit and not feel so defensive. Because it is sort of magical when you drive through the roads of Wisconsin and see the beautiful leaves turning, and those fields of red cranberries and the sun is shining and the blue sky, and the lakes. This is beautiful, this is heaven. And beneath that is a lot of stuff that they have to work on. But the beauty of it was really something that people shared and the love of that place was something that brought them together.

By the end of that first meeting, a new current of energy ran through the room: one of hopefulness, care for one another, trust, and even a sense of possibility that many had not felt for months. Rooted in a new awareness of what had come before, the group was now ready to begin the work ahead.

In the coming months and years, Incourage continued to integrate Adaptive Leadership training into more traditional skill-building workshops, with more and more people in the community participating.

Building on the spirit of the Adaptive Leadership Institute, the Incourage team decided to try something boldly different in their community, inspired by the burgeoning ideas and leadership they were witnessing among fellow community members. The idea was to invite residents to come together to imagine and build a shared community space in the heart of the city's largely shuttered downtown, which would serve as a hub for revitalizing their local economy. Residents themselves would determine what revitalizing their local economy meant, and what this space could be and do in that spirit. The idea was met with strong interest and enthusiasm. The Incourage team identified a potential space downtown on the riverfront: the Tribune Building, the former headquarters of a local newspaper that had been a source of community information for years.

From the outset, the Tribune Building design process shared the same ethos of the Adaptive Leadership Institute— that of "holding the community and each other in trust," as Katherine describes it. "This was an underlying principle of the Tribune process," explains Incourage's former CEO Kelly Ryan. She emphasizes how important this principle came to be to residents—and to how Incourage approached each decision in the Tribune Building process. "From buying the building and immediately informing the downtown neighbors that we would be seeking community participation in determining end use, by going door to door with flyers stating details about the transaction with great transparency," notes Kelly, they sought to embody holding the community and one another in trust.[1] This principle is a core value for

Incourage, which the organization strives to integrate in all it does—including in sharing openly and inviting community input on how to direct both its grant dollars and investments.

The community design process was launched with a series of monthly community design meetings, which hundreds of residents attended. At each meeting, residents worked in small groups, sitting at shared tables and rolling up their sleeves to work on everything from defining the big-picture goals of the space to adjusting budgetary line items to fit within projected funding amounts. Incourage coordinated volunteers who stepped up to serve as "table hosts" and help to plan each meeting and facilitate the small groups. Many of the table hosts were graduates of the Adaptive Leadership Institute.

Joe served as a table host throughout this process. While the participants were focused on imagining the future of the Tribune Building and of economic possibilities for their city and region, Joe reflects on how residents often looked back at their community history for inspiration and ideas, as well as for guidance on what should never again be repeated. History arose as a guide on everything from imagining what a revitalized economy could look and feel like to specific ideas for art that would make the building's walls both beautiful and meaningful, as a reflection of this unique place that everyone in the room called home. By reckoning with shared history, in a spirit of holding one another in trust, Joe reflects, "We created the *foundation*... and it's going to last for potentially generations. And whenever portions of it, or the entire thing, ends up being built, it's going to be solid."

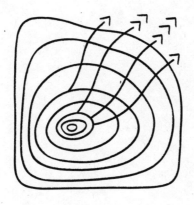

CHAPTER 6

RECKON WITH HISTORY

LOOKING BACK ON their experiences in Wisconsin Rapids, both Joe Terry and Katherine Tyler Scott recall the importance of grounding the community leadership and planning processes by acknowledging history—both shared history and distinct histories among individuals in the room.

In business as usual, history is often viewed as irrelevant to current work and as something to be retold only by expert historians. For breakout actors, history is inextricably connected to the present; it is a group's living teacher, and all group members have histories to share and teach one another.

Katherine speaks about "how important it is to look back and reflect"—both for individuals personally and for teams, organizations, and whole communities. For Katherine, exploring history together in a shared space is about creating "an opportunity for everyone to tell our stories... to understand the larger context in which you live and work. Because that context is always affecting what you do and how you respond."

Critically, she adds, reflecting on history enables us to be aware of contexts that we are inheriting, often unconsciously, and it also reminds us that we can choose what to carry forward or to change. "You always have a choice about what you want to do with your understanding of the larger context," emphasizes Katherine. Looking back at history together helps groups discern a wider range of possibilities for how they can move forward, both personally and in community.

> **Reckoning with history** is the practice of creating intentional time, space, and processes to unpack and address the past in ways relevant to the work at hand. This practice is about groups welcoming in history to guide their work—with great care, trust, and respect for one another's viewpoints and experiences. Through this practice, groups address the past in order to acknowledge and learn from it and then to channel this learning into building reparative, breakout futures.

Shifting how we understand history

This practice concerns what we call capital-H History—histories of broader communities, countries, and peoples over generations—as well as lowercase-h history, like the history of one's family or of one's team or organization. This practice is about a commitment to listen to and understand the histories that affect team members in various and often inequitable ways.

When groups are conscious of how the past influences their work, they are better positioned to identify and create breakout opportunities. Whether learning from a group's recent events and choices, understanding individual group member's life experiences as they relate to the group's current work, or comprehending the intergenerational history of a group's field and communities, reckoning with history provides an opportunity to gain new insights into what is possible. When groups don't take the time to reflect on the past, they risk making the same mistakes or perpetuating unintended harm. Katherine sums this up with a particularly memorable quote from her colleague Bob Lynn: "Historical amnesia is always debilitating and occasionally fatal."

While the influences of histories are an undeniable part of any current context, it can be hard to decipher these influences and how they play out on one's own. But when a group—rich with meaningful forms of difference among its members—comes together to bring forth elements of the past that feel relevant to the present work, myriad historical forces come into focus. The group can then choose how they want to respond in the present, rather than unconsciously continuing harmful legacies.

As co-learner Steven Bingler sums it up, "Knowing our history and owning our history are two different things." This practice, Steven says, is "a pathway to both." Breakout actors recognize that reckoning with history is about making sense of the past and its present implications together to determine what a group will do in response.

Co-learners Aisha Shillingford and Kataraina Davis reflect that this practice is not only about looking back to learn from mistakes or acknowledge grave harms; it is also about looking back for wisdom. "We carry so many people with us," points out Kataraina, "and we take responsibility for our forebears and what they did for us. So really we look back to them to give thanks, and then move forward accordingly." In this way, reckoning with history can also involve elevating triumphs, resilience, and beauty.

"Looking back to move forward is a very important Māori concept," Kataraina shares. She explains that the Māori phrase for going forward includes words that mean to move backward. Both from her cultural roots and from her professional experience leading initiatives in social design, Kataraina understands that "in order to move forward, you have to look backward." Many Indigenous Peoples' languages, traditional teachings, and lifeways echo this sentiment. Aisha shares a similar symbol and concept from the Akan people of Ghana: Sankofa, which means look back to go forward.

What does reckoning with history look like?

Breakout actors follow this practice in a variety of ways, in settings ranging from strategic planning meetings to seasonal celebrations to somber circles. Across the infinitely varied histories that groups surface and address together, there are common elements of how this practice looks. These include:

- Prioritizing repair,
- Proactively creating time and space for history, and
- Embracing team history.

Prioritizing repair

Breakout actors recognize that repair is sorely needed because the loveless economy is rooted in practices that have and continue to create significant harm. "In this country in particular," reflects co-learner Edgar Villanueva, "we have not had a process of truth and reconciliation. So many folks don't understand our history or don't know our history because they're not told the truth." In the US, workplaces exist within a national context in which, as Edgar explains, "we have never officially apologized for slavery. We've never apologized for every broken treaty with Native American tribes. We have tried to not only put parts of our dark history under the rug, we've tried to erase it."

Breakout actors point to repair as a guiding value—and North Star—of reckoning with history. Co-learner Jessica Norwood of RUNWAY speaks to repair as being both an aim and a skill. "Whatever thing we imagine going forward," she asserts, "the reality is that it must do the repair work. What it has to focus on is the healing—of the relationship, of the money, of the people, the healing post-COVID, the traumas. Every part of all of this is actually the business of repair."

Breakout actors prioritize unpacking the impact of capital-H Histories that tend not to be acknowledged in business as usual—including histories of racialized oppression, white supremacy, patriarchy, genocide, land theft, and colonization. In sharing how they do so, numerous breakout actors point to the work of economic theorist Nwamaka Agbo and her framework of restorative economics.[1] This framework emphasizes that efforts to build new and alternative approaches risk replicating the same disparities in wealth and well-being that currently exist if they do not address how specific communities have been harmed disproportionately, within both historical and present contexts. Restorative economics points to ways that groups can build alternatives that are reparative and redistributive.

Breakout actors shine a light on the living legacies and present-day impacts of history, including how it may affect a group's projects, day-to-day work, and the structure of their organizations. They also bear witness to the ways that histories have shaped team members' lives, those of their families, and how they show up in the workplace. Together they find ways to take steps toward repair and healing.

Co-learning community member Tatewin Means, executive director of Thunder Valley Community Development Corporation in South Dakota, emphasizes that reckoning with underrecognized history is necessary for everyone.

Looking back at the histories of the Lakota people, and challenging the ways that these stories may be told—or not told—in business as usual, is central to everything that the Thunder Valley team does in its work with fellow community members in Oglala territory of the Oceti Sakowin. Their groundbreaking work in affordable housing, regenerative food systems, and education is all rooted in their history as Lakota people. By reckoning with history, they can co-create visions of what they want to carry forward into their shared future.

Tatewin notes that none of this is possible without lifting up and acknowledging history that the loveless economy has made invisible or distorted. "That's how you have healing, is if you have that reckoning," says Tatewin. "And that's all levels, right? I think that's a really important part of healing as a nation, healing collectively from colonization, because we *all* have to do that. That's not just something Indigenous Peoples have to do. Or just Black people have to heal from slavery. *Everybody* does, and that includes white people, and I think that's important not to forget."

Regardless of our identities, our histories influence what we carry with us into the workplace, what we assume about one another, and how we react. We can choose, one step at a time, to chart pathways toward healing. It is in this intentional choosing that we have extraordinary opportunities for repair. For teams and organizations, this requires deep work as a group and also at the individual level—what Katherine calls the inner work.[2] Many breakout actors speak to the fact that group members' commitment to do such inner work is a vital ingredient to reckoning with history. Co-learner Antionette D. Carroll expands on the concept: "Reckoning with history isn't just a professional thing; it is something that's personal. If we do not allow our personal selves to show up, we're never going to spend the time and the due diligence needed to really deepen our understanding of, and relationship to, history."

> **Tip: Bring in outside facilitation.** If the focus of a group reflection session is likely to refer to traumatic or otherwise emotionally intense histories that involve your team members, their families, or communities, we recommend bringing in facilitators and support persons with expertise in guiding teams toward healing insights and outcomes, without inflicting emotional harm. Antionette points out a time when the Creative Reaction Lab facilitated a process to identify interventions for preventing gun violence. Many of the people participating—including members of the Creative Reaction Lab team—were themselves victims of gun violence and had lost loved ones. Antionette cautions that in such contexts, doing the brave work of reckoning with history can be immensely painful; it even risks retraumatizing participants. She shares that, in the instance above, one measure her team took was bringing on site a neutral therapist to serve as support for both the co-creators and facilitators.
>
> Another example comes from the work of Heart Research Alliance, in which the facilitators and participants explicitly reminded one another that exploring learnings from past negative experiences did not mean that participants needed to go into detail about traumatic moments, such as receiving a diagnosis or a frightening trip to the emergency room, unless they wanted to. The practice of reckoning with history requires treading with care and reverence as we welcome history as a teacher. This includes doing one's best to put in place the support structures that may be needed for reckoning. Working with the right facilitators can also provide teams an opportunity to grow their own internal capacity to reckon with history in ways that embody strong support and care.

In describing her vision for a future centered on repair, co-learner Jessica shares that she imagines, "We all have this skill that then expands out into the way that the whole economy, the whole world starts to operate. Then when there's injury here, I know how to do repair here, and when I've been hurt, you know how to do repair for me, and so forth. That we are in right relationship means that you take the responsibility—the accountability—to do the work of repair, over and over and over again. And that you recognize the interdependency, recognize your link, your Ubuntu, the highly relational pieces of all of us together." Jessica continues,

> I always had this imagined vision that if every person that was born was taught that your only job in the world was repair. The only thing that we actually say is "Welcome to the planet. I'm so glad to meet you, little person. We only have one requirement here, and that's your job here. You can go off and do lots of other amazing things, but the core job that you have to do is repair. Your job is to do repair work." And I imagine if every single human being knew that their job, their only requirement in order to be hanging here at this moment in time, is just to do repair work.

Similar to Jessica's future vision, breakout actors place repair at the center of their practice. Reckoning with history is not simply about acknowledging the past but unlearning the narratives of harm that enabled that history in the first place, and then consciously moving toward healing.

Proactively creating time and space for history

In business-as-usual workplaces, history is rarely given time in the agenda. Breakout actors recognize that in order to move beyond the loveless economy's historical amnesia, groups have to be intentional about devoting the time and care needed for history to become a teacher in illuminating ways forward. Co-learner Eugene Eric Kim of Faster Than 20 speaks to this point: "The way you address history is you make time to address it. That's the number one thing." He has seen with clients over the years that, regardless of how much a group wants to improve its work—and escape from a cycle of missteps and missed opportunities in which it may be stuck—a team will be unable to do so unless and until it makes time to "deeply understand existing conditions," as Eugene describes it.

Breakout actors come together, in groups with diverse experiences and perspectives, to build an understanding of the past and how it influences the work at hand. They know that co-creative sense-making of history is what unlocks its greatest teachings and guidance.

"When I'm bringing a big group together to co-create, it's often quite helpful—even essential—to do a participatory history exercise early on in the process," shares co-learning community member Brooking Gatewood of The Emergence Collective, which designs and facilitates collaborative social change projects for "those who dare to dream toward a more just and healthful world."[3] Brooking reflects that with any of their clients—whether a large hospital department, small business firm, or multimember nonprofit network—"inviting people into developing a shared experience of history" can transform a group.

"Key to this practice is recognizing that we revisit mistakes and past pain for the purpose of learning and growing—and for repair, not shaming or dwelling," adds Brooking. "This courageous learning orientation is in no small way the difference between us evolving as a species and cycling around in the same oppression-themed grooves."

Reckoning with history is not a one-off activity. Instead, it is an active stance and a commitment to return to being with and learning from the past as often as necessary.

One important juncture at which breakout actors reckon with history is when groups are preparing to begin a new project. As a first step, they research and discuss the historical context that may affect their upcoming work. Co-learner Isabella Jean, in her work listening to and learning from people around the world who have been part of humanitarian aid and development projects, has found that projects tend to be ineffective if they do not engage everyone involved, including those the project should benefit, in understanding relevant capital-H Histories and assessing related lower-case-h histories including "past struggles, efforts, failures, and successes" relevant to the context in which the project is being developed.

"This is why we always begin our community planning work by collecting, summarizing, and honoring all of the planning work that came before us," shares Steven, emphasizing a similar sentiment. "We gather together all of the previous plans, summarize their findings, and acknowledge the people who gave their time to the process."

Tip: Set a cadence for reflection. Whatever pace and format make sense for your group, plan in advance the times you'll look back to ensure that reckoning with history happens and that everyone comes prepared to do so. Breakout actors build in regular processes that assess what has happened and what everyone can learn from it. They recognize that without scheduling these activities in advance, they tend not to happen. The Concordia team holds an "after action review" at the end of every community meeting and after every significant event. Concordia regularly does this reflection step with clients and community members as well as internally. Other breakout actors hold a team-wide retreat once a year to assess what unfolded that year and what can be learned. Others hold a reflection process at the start of each new initiative or of each quarter.

Embracing team history

Co-learning community member Kalsoom Lakhani points out that in the relentlessness of business as usual, it can often feel as if "so many things just kind of happen, and there's no strategy at all. You're just doing what's ahead of you." Through her work with Invest2Innovate (i2i) and i2i Ventures, Kalsoom and her team have built a different kind of support ecosystem for early stage companies, rooted in inclusion. i2i includes a wider array of entrepreneurs than business as usual would typically fund, and it broadens the communities of people served by such investment, through its portfolio enterprises' groundbreaking offerings in education, technology, healthcare services, and clean energy. Working with investors in the US and entrepreneurs internationally, i2i's work in Pakistan is supporting enterprises of which 60 percent are led by women.

While Kalsoom's team and community of entrepreneurs, investors, and accelerator partners are focused on a future of evermore inclusive business opportunities, Kalsoom is emphatic that they focus on the past as well—of the sector in which they operate and of their own team. It is essential to pause and reflect regularly, she notes. When teams take the time to reflect on their own histories, Kalsoom points out, they unlock learnings that allow them to operate in more effective ways and to continually innovate and evolve.

When teams don't do this, adds co-learner Jessamyn Shams-Lau, they pay a price. "Without reckoning with history," says Jessamyn, "you are more likely doomed to repeat mistakes and contribute to a slower timeline for change than might otherwise be possible." Breakout actors prioritize making time to address their own team's history as a vital source of guidance.

Antionette emphasizes that when groups come together to reflect on and discuss their team's history, it is vital to acknowledge both the intentions of a project or person's actions and to make explicit the impact of past choices. Intentions and actual impact, Antionette points out, might be quite distinct. When groups reflect on both, they can honor best intentions while identifying impacts—including unintended ones that may have caused harm—and reckon together with what needs to change.

Breakout actors view challenges and missteps of their team's past as sources of invaluable insight—essential to enriching and strengthening a group's shared work moving forward. They emphasize that missteps are inevitable; everyone makes mistakes. When groups reflect on them together, they can create an opportunity for learning and growth.

Breakout actors point out that the process of reckoning with a group's own history is not only about making time to address what has caused harm; it is also about identifying what is worthy of celebration. These successes and joys point to what the group might want to do more of, to build upon, and explore further.

> **Tip: Reckon with the history of your field or industry.** Breakout actors share that some of the most energizing participatory history sessions happen when people get the chance to learn about and reckon with the history of the field in which they are operating. For example, Antionette and her team at Creative Reaction Lab frequently start design processes by engaging groups to assess the history of their fields and how business

as usual within it has operated over the decades. This step tends to spark a vibrant discussion on how and why the field— whether it's the field of design, elementary education, high tech, or museums—should be different, and together people come to clarity around ways they'd like to depart intentionally from the status quo. Many breakout actors affirm this aspect of reckoning with history. Co-learner Connor McManus, a former member of the Concordia team, sums it up: "Sometimes when we learn a discipline, we adopt a lot of assumptions and attitudes along the way. Tracking back and questioning those can bring new insight into what to preserve and what to update."

Reckoning with history in action

The rich history of Buffalo, New York, and its surrounding region—including the legacy of Black-led cooperatives and progressive economic projects across the city—is a key source of inspiration for the work of PUSH Buffalo and partner Cooperation Buffalo, which supports residents to start and sustain cooperatively owned, community-led businesses. "As a city, we were once the sixth largest economy in the United States at the turn of the century," explains co-learner Rahwa Ghirmatzion, executive director of PUSH Buffalo. "We had premier architects, authors, writers, musicians. We had one of the first Black musicians' unions in the country. Buffalo played a major role in the founding of the NAACP; we have the underground railroad; we have all of these things."

Despite the city's rich history and the transformative potential of cooperative businesses, Rahwa and her colleagues at PUSH and Cooperation Buffalo found that in their work to mobilize residents around cooperative business opportunities, they encountered noticeable distrust. The present-day stereotype of cooperatives is associated with white-dominant cultures and institutions that many Buffalonians didn't identify with. "Buffalo has an incredibly rich history of co-ops in Black communities specifically and other communities of color," shares Rahwa. "Some of that history we're lucky enough to have in archives here. But when most people think of co-ops these days, they think of granola or a housing co-op—something that feels like a very white project." This stereotype stems from mainstream historical narratives about the US economy that omit the rich history of cooperatives, especially their roots in Black communities and Black-led movements for economic justice and self-determination.[4]

In response, the teams of PUSH Buffalo and Cooperation Buffalo have embraced popular education about Buffalo's economic history as a core priority. In doing so, they have created a new opportunity for community members to see themselves in this history and feel a stake in building on that legacy. They engage as teachers, people in the community who lived that history and who experienced Black co-ops and co-ops of color in the 1960s and '70s. They create opportunities for residents to come together and hear the stories and accounts from these older residents about Black-led organizing for economic justice in Buffalo, as well as to learn about current opportunities offered.

In response to growing interest from residents, PUSH and Cooperation Buffalo launched a new initiative called Cooperative Academy, which trains cohorts of thirty cooperative entrepreneurs over a three-month program. "This is a big leap for us and Buffalo," reflects co-learner Andrew Delmonte, executive director of Cooperation Buffalo, pointing to the growing number of cooperative enterprises that Buffalonians are starting up as a result of Cooperative Academy. Andrew is as passionate about being a Buffalonian as they are about the potential of cooperative ways of working and living. Andrew shares that as a queer nonbinary child of an artist father and a working mother, it really wasn't until they found cooperative living that they felt able to build family and community in the way their "heart has always been calling out for." Their house sits in the same neighborhood where their great-grandparents, Sicilian immigrants, lived decades ago. "The west side of Buffalo," Andrew explains, "has been the home of my family for generations, and has held the stories of a diverse range of refugees, immigrants, Black folks, and Latinx Buffalonians over the years."

For residents of many identities and lineages, bringing to light Buffalo's own rich history in cooperative businesses and economic self-determination has been a vital aspect of the increasing interest and action by residents in forming cooperative enterprises that support their families and benefit their community. They know they are building on a proud tradition when they do so.

"This country needs to heal its soul in so many ways," reflects Rahwa. She points out that much of this need for healing stems directly from harms perpetuated by the current economic structure, as well as from the way the loveless economy tends to hide histories that could inspire us to work differently. Rahwa has always questioned injustice—and the assumption that this is simply the way things are and have to be. She and her family came to Buffalo when she was eight years old, when her family emigrated from Eritrea amid civil war. "The experience of that trauma and challenges that resulted from that circumstance also made me resilient," shares Rahwa. "As a child, I was always questioning and challenging 'Why?'" She carries this spirit still. "I listen to the deep convictions of my belly and often make decisions based on instincts, rather than thinking about the political or a respectable decision," she says. "I think about the people, fairness, justice, and find the courage to do what feels right."

Grounding in personal and community history is a way that Rahwa helps her whole team connect to deeply held values and convictions. In PUSH Buffalo's decision-making processes, the team uses a Seven-Generations Principle, which they credit to teachings from Indigenous colleagues and which honors the history of Indigenous Peoples in their region. Two of the questions related to this principle are: Will the decision we are making today create a sustainable world for seven generations forward? and Will it reverberate to heal our ancestors seven generations back? In this way, PUSH Buffalo seeks to honor history in all major decisions, in ways that can help steer plans for the future toward outcomes of healing and repair.

How does reckoning with history unlock breakout innovation?

Antionette emphasizes that when groups not only *reflect* on history but also swiftly move into *taking action* in thoughtful, reparative ways, they can build trust among everyone involved, many of whom may have had negative experiences with similar processes in the past. The trust that this builds, Antionette explains, is critical to a group's ability to achieve breakout innovation:

> Think about the times when you came into a space and you trusted people. And about the times you came into spaces and you didn't trust someone. What was the difference in

those experiences? And take into account that same reality for other folks, when they come into a space, you have to take the time to build that trust. And if you don't, the outcomes are not going to be as effective because I'm only going to give you a sliver of me if I don't trust you. But if I actually trust you, I'm willing to give you more than I even thought that I can give, because I trust that you'll be able to grab me and hold me if I fall.

Reckoning with history is often fraught and rarely without grief. It requires group members to grow in how they address accountability and practice a stance of repair. But when groups step into the practice with bravery and care, making time for reflection and taking action accordingly, the trust that they build together can be transformative.

A foundation of shared trust is critical to deconsolidating rights to design, bringing everyone around the table. Reckoning with history helps build a shared understanding of how rights to design may have been previously consolidated—whether in one's country, field, or own team—and enables groups to identify ways to adopt power-with, versus power-over, approaches in the present.

Reckoning with history unlocks breakout innovation by building the community necessary to intentionally elect pathways forward that break from the status quo. If we understand from where we have come, and how this impacts the present, we can *choose* ways of work that align with our values.

As bell hooks wrote, "As a nation, we need to gather our collective courage and face that our society's lovelessness is a wound. As we allow ourselves to acknowledge the pain of this wound when it pierces our flesh and we feel in the depths of our soul a profound anguish of spirit, we come face to face with the possibility of conversion, of having a change of heart."[5]

. . .

TENSQUARED

IN A TOY factory in the Brazilian state of São Paulo, the average temperature of the production room hung at a suffocating 100°F (38°C). Workers struggled through the extreme conditions; managers were frustrated by the heat's drain on productivity. Standard top-down problem-solving approaches consistently failed to produce a lasting solution. However, something changed when factory managers decided to participate in an innovative program called TenSquared, which helps teams of workers and managers find new solutions to seemingly intractable challenges in the workplace. They accomplish this by—you guessed it—deconsolidating rights to design within those teams.

TenSquared was created and implemented by two partner organizations, Rapid Results Institute (RRI) and Social Accountability International (SAI).[1] RRI brings its 100-Day Challenge methodology to the program, and SAI offers its expertise in workers' labor rights in supply chains. As explained by Stephanie Wilson of SAI, TenSquared "begins by facilitating the development of worker-manager teams. All workers must be peer-selected. We then work with these teams to identify the root causes of their health and safety challenges. Following this, we work with the teams to identify and create ambitious yet measurable goals."[2]

Over the course of one hundred days, a team of five workers and five managers at the Brazilian factory drew on the insights and knowledge of those traditionally in charge, as well as those who labored within the processes they were redesigning. They co-created and implemented a plan to build twelve ventilation hoods within the factory, using recycled materials, which caused the average temperature of the workspace to drop by 25°F and resulted in a much healthier working environment. In addition, the team's novel construction method saved the factory about $12,000 in the cost of ventilation hoods.

This is just one example of the results that TenSquared's approach makes possible.[3] At the heart of its co-creation process is a space for workers and managers to share diverse perspectives, expertise, lived experiences, and ideas on issues of shared importance. The program is rooted in the recognition that dissolving perceived separations to bring together workers and managers as peers allows for truly transformative, lasting solutions to emerge. Perhaps most notably, TenSquared's approach has led to improved communication channels and increased trust between workers and managers, making future workplace challenges much more manageable to confront and resolve.[4] As shared by a TenSquared worker participant, "Before, my colleagues had some hesitations about talking to their supervisors. Now, after TenSquared, our approach is different and we can address any problem."[5]

Breaking down silos to make this exchange possible requires recognizing and addressing cultural barriers and power dynamics. Because differences in rank, class, education, and lived experience among workers and managers are so significant in the contexts where TenSquared operates, program facilitators are often met with resistance by factory workers of all levels when they first propose the idea of cross-rank, cross-class innovation teams. TenSquared's program is intentionally designed to support participants in moving through initial resistance or discomfort so that workers can feel safe to bring their opinions to the table, and so that all participants can roll up their sleeves to imagine and implement breakthrough solutions together.

The first step guides the team through workshop sessions in breakout groups—the five laborers together, and the five managers together. These initial parallel processes are essential to ensure that all participants are able to speak up, share their ideas, and focus on analyzing the problem without fear of retaliation or judgment. During these concurrent sessions, both groups are asked to capture and express their ideas through several activities, including presenting, storytelling, visualizing, drawing, and role-playing. "The range of ways to share input serves to put everyone on a more level playing field," explains Stephanie. "If you bring everyone together off the bat and just ask people to verbally present their analysis of the problem, then our experience is that the laborers stay silent."[6]

Only after these initial steps are the participants willing to share their ideas and begin to find new approaches together. During the one-hundred-day process, laborers and managers join together as one team to identify a single specific goal related to occupational health and safety—invariably also linked to factory productivity and quality—and then work to achieve it. Since its founding, TenSquared has assisted more than 38,000 workers in over forty companies across fifteen industries in Brazil, China, and Turkey. Ninety-three percent of all TenSquared teams achieve their ambitious goal within one hundred days, many surpassing their original targets. TenSquared's co-creative program has led to a four-fold improvement in evacuation time efficiency at a factory in China, a 50 percent reduction in limb trauma accidents at a factory in Turkey, and a 90 percent reduction in burn-exposure areas at a chemical plant in Brazil. Other results include improved worker productivity, less absenteeism, millions of dollars in savings, and better reporting of factory problems that need immediate attention.[7]

Beyond these impressive measurable results, however, are the relationships of mutual trust that can emerge when the separations between workers and managers begin to dissolve. This is noted by Emma Taya Darch in a video on TenSquared's website:

> What we see at launch is a lot of nervousness at the beginning—some division and tension between the workers and managers. And by the end of it, you can't tell... who's a worker and a manager. It's completely transformative, and it's palpable in the room. You see the workers explaining things to the managers. You see the managers suddenly understanding the perspective of the workers—and similarly the workers understanding the perspective and concerns and priorities of the managers. So, it really helps them to understand where they have common ground, where there is potential... to collaborate and to bring in new ideas and new perspectives on challenges that perhaps they weren't able to see from the other side in the past.[8]

In many cases, these shifts in relationships between participating workers and managers, which bridge previously perceived differences, have led to more open channels of communication, especially when it comes to reporting problems. This type of co-creative process can begin to shift underlying dynamics of power and trust in the long term, as workers begin to trust that sharing their ideas will make a difference, and managers begin to understand and believe in the importance of worker input and leadership. In many of the factories that have engaged TenSquared's program, employees at all levels have continued to work together to take initiative and innovate together when challenges arise. There is genuine curiosity about the different takes their colleagues might have on an issue, and workers and managers alike begin to embrace the value of a range of lived experiences and points of view as foundational to the factory's success.

CHAPTER 7

SEEK DIFFERENCE

T HERE'S A COMMON response that many people have to this practice: "I get it! It's about diversity!" And while that's correct, this practice is about something more than the way diversity is often sought in business as usual. The practice of seeking difference is *not* about superficial efforts that aim to check a box or do a one-time step to expand the demographics of a group's members. It is instead a commitment to continually seek out relevant forms of diversity and create team cultures that effectively engage differences. It is a stance of genuine curiosity and eagerness to hear and act upon the pulsing brilliance that exists when the richness of diversities is tapped into.

Co-learner Jane Hwang, president and CEO of from Social Accountability International (SAI), shares how her team deepened their understanding of truly meaningful diversity, learning what kinds of differences are essential for a group's ability to come up with breakout ideas and pathways. Prior to generating the idea for TenSquared, the SAI team conducted research on how to spark breakthrough change, looking at examples across industries and studying change management. What quickly began to stand out, shares Jane, was that "so much of it involved bringing people that are typically working in silos, or in different hierarchies, *together.*" This realization was key to the TenSquared program. Its results have been— and continue to be—resounding evidence of the power of connecting people separated by the workings of business as usual.

Like Jane and her team, breakout actors recognize that something magical happens when they come together as peers and respected collaborators across the false lines of separation in the loveless economy. Limited viewpoints become far more expansive. Good ideas become visionary. Collective thinking and offerings become more robust. Groups rich in different experiences and perspectives—and that, as Dr. Wood says, "honor the autonomous power of everyone's story"—are the life force of a beloved economy.

> **Seeking difference** is the practice of refusing to accept business-as-usual assumptions about who should be at the table. This practice is about continually broadening the circle and range of perspectives present by being intentional about who is invited in and how that invitation happens. It is about everyone involved assessing who else should be present and committing to a process where vital differences commingle in a way that everyone feels supported, respected, and safe to share their perspectives.

Shifting how we understand difference

In recent years, overwhelming evidence has shown that when teams and enterprises prioritize diversity, it is not only the right choice but also the smart one.[1] There is growing acknowledgment that diversity on teams is key to success.[2] And while this shift toward valuing differences among group members is occurring even in business as usual, we have found that breakout actors do something distinct in their practice of seeking difference.

Breakout actors view difference not as a key metric to achieve but as a great teacher that sparks curiosity, respect, and care. They welcome being challenged by one another's unique perspectives and divergent viewpoints because they recognize that everyone holds pieces of what needs to emerge. They know that the best outcomes can only come into view through a variety of vantage points, life experiences, and ideas.

Seeking difference includes bringing together the forms of difference that are most commonly thought of: racial and ethnic identities, age, ability status, gender and sexuality, learning type, neurodiversity, and geographic diversity. In addition, many breakout actors also emphasize arenas such as rank and department within an enterprise, people's work experiences and personal histories, as well as important forms of difference in worldview, politics, and even level of support for the task at hand. Breakout actors recognize that the most vital forms of difference among group members will be unique to each endeavor.

Breakout actors recognize that engaging across differences requires inner growth as well. Words they commonly share in describing this inner work include *courage*, *flexibility*, *humility*, and *openness*—both to having one's perspective challenged and to engage in brave conversations. They accept that this practice almost always necessitates, as described by facilitator and author KA McKercher, that "people... be able to hold the tension,"[3] to feel the discomfort of disagreement and to lean into it, instead of shutting it down or trying to make it go away. When curiosity and openness are chosen, rather than rigidity and fear, there is a far greater chance for the diverse perspectives each of us hold to inform bolder thinking and innovation.

What does seeking difference look like?
....

Naturally, a practice about forms of difference tends to look many different ways. Yet there are clear commonalities in how breakout actors seek difference. These include:

• Inviting multiple perspectives on diversity,
• Creating conditions that support safety and bravery, and
• Using varied channels for contribution.

Inviting multiple perspectives on diversity

In business-as-usual workplaces, aims and objectives for increasing diversity are often decided by a few people in traditional leadership roles or by a consultant or specific team responsible for the task. While such approaches can be effective, breakout actors recognize that everyone in a community of stakeholders holds unique insights on who else might be needed around the proverbial table to steer the shared work toward the wisest outcomes. Breakout actors recognize that seeking difference works best when decision-making power is shared even in the process of how a group defines and acts on including the diversity needed. In other words, diversity is necessary to build diversity. This may sound like a chicken-or-egg situation, but breakout actors find ways to make this happen.

Co-learner Aisha Shillingford recommends that group members regularly ask themselves and one another the guiding question: Who is impacted by this work or has a perspective on this work that isn't present at this table? The Concordia team poses a similar question to the initial small group they convene at the outset of each of their projects, to generate what they call "the plan for the plan"—a proposed approach, in broad strokes, for how the project's process might happen. This small group includes people who reflect diverse perspectives and experiences that the Concordia team believes will be vital for the particular project. The group is asked to determine criteria for who else needs to be invited and in what way.

Whether it's a question regularly asked at meetings or a special type of group convened at the start of every project, seeking the opinions of many different people to identify the forms of diversity needed results in far more robust and inclusive groups.

Breakout actor Innovation Engineering, which supports companies to find the next big idea by sparking innovation from within their own teams, insists on sourcing ideas from people across all ranks and departments within a company. "Every time we work on a specific problem together," explains Innovation Engineering CEO and co-learning community member Maggie Nichols, "we ensure that there's going to be a diverse set of stakeholders internally. We call it the 'diagonal slice.'" She explains that this diagonal slice consists of "people across the organization from all sorts of different roles—and up and down, as well."

Collaborative innovation specialist Russ Gaskin, of the group CoCreative, emphasizes the importance of intentionally seeking a type of difference many people dismiss: divergence in people's level of belief in and support for the endeavor or organization. In other words, skeptics. Russ and his team have found that intentionally involving skeptics can be a key element in achieving success, especially when the endeavor is controversial, contentious, or complex. CoCreative specializes in helping "people who don't know each other and often don't even like each other to solve tough problems together," as their team describes. Russ points out that a key to their successful track record is embracing skepticism and resistance. "Ninety percent of the people involved need to be 100 percent committed to the goal, and ten percent need to be the resident skeptics," he advises. Skeptics not only raise critical questions, Russ notes, they also can end up serving as a bridge to bring along fellow skeptics, both within and outside the participant group, as they come to believe in the process and what they are building.

Co-learner Katherine Tyler Scott shares Russ's appreciation of tough questions from skeptics. "There is no healthy system that does not have some resistance," Katherine reflects. "You need to have someone sometimes pushing up against you so you can clarify, 'Well, what am I doing? And why am I doing it? How important is this? And am I doing this for the right reason at the right time?'" This is directly linked to the concept of feedback loops that we discussed in Chapter 2: the essential role of correcting feedback, along with reinforcing feedback, for the health of a system. When teams rich in different forms of wisdom do the inner work to meet tough questions with grace, and then work together to refine the answers, their shared efforts and the results they achieve are far stronger.

Breakout actors emphasize that diversity of many forms is something that groups need in all arenas and levels of their work. As members of a group continually update and refine the forms of difference they are seeking and welcoming in to guide their shared work, this practice is about a commitment to make the group itself reflect this diversity, beyond stakeholders who may be invited to join for a particular initiative. Specifically, many members of the co-learning community point to the importance of leaders, and others with positional power, being individuals who reflect these forms of difference.

> **Tip: Be careful not to tokenize.** Breakout actors point out that
> there should be clearly communicated reasons for each form
> of diversity or differing perspective that is sought out. "Be
> clear about why someone is in the group," suggests co-learner
> Bryana DiFonzo. Doing so "is key to creating an environment
> in which people know and trust that their participation or that
> of others is not 'checking a box' and is instead about valuing
> specific insights and vantage points they bring."

Creating conditions that support safety and bravery

In addition to including a wide range of diversity, a practice
of seeking difference must also actively create systems and
a group culture that enable everyone to share their insights.
As co-learner Edgar Villanueva puts it, "[H]aving a seat at
the table is not the same as feeling free to speak in your own
voice, to offer your own divergent ideas, to bring your full self
to bear on the work."[4] If people are at the table but do not feel
comfortable speaking their minds, then rights to design are
not actually being deconsolidated. Intentionality and care are
essential to break out of the homogeneity reinforced through
loveless ways of work and to unlock the collective brilliance
of truly diverse groups.

Breakout actors often start by breaking down the barriers
that keep people from joining the table in the first place. For
instance, when Incourage Community Foundation launched
a community planning process to redesign the Tribune Building, a historic building in Wisconsin Rapids' largely shuttered
downtown, they sought to understand what it would take
to make these community design meetings truly inclusive.
"After talking to residents," explains co-learner Kelly Ryan,
former Incourage CEO, "it was clear that providing food
and childcare was going to be key." Incourage decided to
include free hot food for everyone and on-site childcare at

the meetings; they also partnered with local cab companies to provide free vouchers for transportation. This type of action can be critical to creating a shared work environment that honors not only what people have to say but also what it takes for them to show up and participate.

Another way that breakout actors activate the richness of insight within our differences is by recognizing that people may require varying on-ramps to the work and by proactively creating these strategies together. Recalling her experience as a patient during the Heart Research Alliance, participating alongside doctors and medical researchers, co-learner Debbe McCall notes that it took focused effort and intention to support people like herself who came in with less technical training to feel comfortable enough to share. "It's not fair to throw a researcher, a clinician, and a patient together into the deep end... most people will give up." In the case of Heart Research Alliance, the participants designed an approach that ensured everyone—including patients participating for the first time in this kind of environment—would feel safe and able to share their ideas. They created a phased approach that included information-sharing and increasing levels of engagement with opportunities for skill-building at each step. "It can be done," Debbe says unequivocally. "I was sitting in a group with some PhDs, some pharma folks, some epidemiologists, and then there was me, the patient, and everyone was confident in sharing the different focus they each were bringing." The Heart Research Alliance members also co-created ground rules and working principles that supported everyone involved to voice their questions, ideas, and concerns.

Tip: Actively value everyone's time and insight. As co-learner Antionette D. Carroll points out, it is not enough to invite people to join in—especially if the people participating in the shared work are not paid employees of the enterprise. Break-out actors find ways to demonstrate through actions, not lip service, how much they value everyone's time. For instance, financially compensating people can make a tremendous dif-ference in conveying the degree to which their contributions are valued. Other ways include providing delicious food or other offerings that go beyond the usual fare of business as usual. Concordia, for example, ensures that their meetings with residents include abundant food and great music, gener-ally from favorite local vendors and live musicians. There is no formula. Regardless of how it is expressed, the key is valuing people as true experts of their own experiences and respect-fully thanking them for their contribution.

To enable everyone to, as Edgar describes it, feel free to speak in their own voice and show up fully in the work, seeking difference is not only about bringing additional peo-ple and perspectives into a group. It's also about fostering respect for difference in a team. A practice of seeking differ-ence is most successful when it is woven throughout entire systems—from the culture and practices of a workplace to the ways each step of a project is approached and run. This may mean that institutional changes are necessary to allow the richness of varying perspectives, knowledge, and ideas to be expressed.

Using varied channels for contribution

The presence of difference alone does not automatically translate into breakout innovation. Equally important are the multiple ways people are invited to learn, express ideas, and roll up their sleeves together.[5] Breakout actors underline that we miss countless opportunities if our diverse groups fail to operate in ways that actually engage their range of differences.

People learn, communicate, and contribute in many varied ways. If a group uses only a limited set of approaches to sharing information and inviting contributions, it's likely that many people will feel what they have to contribute doesn't fit into the available channels.

Antionette emphasizes that groups must shift away from having only one mode of collaborating, running meetings, or brainstorming and instead recognize the need for many. "As we all learn differently, we talk a lot about approaches or interventions," she says, emphasizing the plurals, "understanding that we need a variety of approaches to actually get to an intended outcome."

The TenSquared program is designed to leverage a multitude of different channels and approaches, including work in pairs and small groups, drawing or diagramming ideas, time for individual reflection before sharing in a group, and more. For instance, the TenSquared facilitators note how essential it is to have factory laborers and managers initially work separately in small groups before they come together as a full innovation team; this step builds participants' confidence and clarity about ideas they want to bring to the full group.

> **Tip: Make use of smaller groups.** If the only tool in your collaboration toolkit is hours of large-group meetings, then it's likely that many insights will go unshared and critical questions unasked. Instead, consider balancing full-group time with time in small subgroups. Breakout actors point out that it is often easier for people to express thoughts and questions in smaller groups than with a full team. Smaller groups also allow more time for each person to contribute in depth, which can help streamline a broader process. For instance, each subgroup can take the time it needs and then synthesize and refine its members' findings, which are then shared with the

larger group. In this way, the full group can be informed by the insights of many, avoiding the risk of hearing only from the few who might speak up in a large group.

Seeking difference in action

Antionette and the team at Creative Reaction Lab are passionate about the importance of bringing diverse lived experiences around the table. As Antionette points out, far too often in business as usual, groups fail to ask themselves the question "What is the actual topic that we are looking to address, and are the relevant living experts at the table?" Including those with lived experience related to the issue at hand is critical if the work is to meet its highest potential. In business-as-usual workplaces, lived experience tends to be dismissed as less important than technical training or professional expertise. And even when groups do invite people with relevant lived experience into a planning process, Antionette has observed that too often the ways groups do so result in no one showing up.

"They always say, 'Well, we invited them!'" shares Antionette, "And then I ask, 'Well, are they *paid*?' And they say, 'Well, no, but how would I pay them?' And I'm like, 'Just like you wrote in the budget you're paid; you write in the budget they're paid!'" Antionette laughs and throws up her hands, then adds with gravity, "For Creative Reaction Lab, in every budget that we write, there is a living expert stipend."

In addition to compensating lived experience as a valued form of knowledge, Antionette explains that a fundamental shift is needed for lived experiences to truly shape innovation processes. Rather than seeing people with relevant lived experience as "beneficiaries" who are passive recipients of an "expert solution" developed in isolation by people with "letters behind their names," Antionette and her team view them as experts whose insight is central to the problem-solving process. She advises those problem-solving or seeking innovation to acknowledge the multiplicity of solutions only visible when they bring different perspectives and forms of knowledge into the process. "In our organization, we don't say *solution* because it has this silver bullet mentality," explains Antionette. "We talk a lot about how we need a variety of approaches to actually get to an intended outcome."

By inviting people with many forms of expertise, and enabling everyone to shine in their capacity as experts through a multiplicity of approaches, Creative Reaction Lab is redefining what it takes to arrive at truly inclusive innovations.

How does seeking difference unlock breakout innovation?

"We use an equation to help people innovate," reveals Maggie. "It goes like this: in order to create meaningful, unique ideas, you need stimulus, raised to the power of diversity, divided by fear. This math says it all. The notion of seeking difference isn't just a little bit better than working on your own or with a homogenous group. It's not twice as better. It's exponential."

Why does seeking difference generate this exponential uptick in insight and innovation? By inviting in a fuller range of perspectives and ensuring the wisdom therein is heard and incorporated, we deconsolidate rights to design and reconnect to a far broader informational field. When we come together with intention and care in groups rich with differences among us, our shared work is vaulted beyond what's possible within the limited silos of the loveless economy and toward beloved alternatives.

· · ·

STANDING ROCK

PAULA ANTOINE, program coordinator at the Rose-bud Sioux Tribe's Sicangu Oyate Land Office, became involved in the Standing Rock movement when the concept of a spiritual camp to oppose the Dakota Access Pipeline was still a radical idea. In 2016, she was approached by several members of the Cannonball community of the Lakota Sioux Standing Rock Reservation, the site most directly affected by the building of the Dakota Access Pipeline, a massive oil pipeline designed to transport approximately 500,000 barrels of crude oil per day.[1] Paula and fellow members of the neighboring Rosebud Sioux Tribe had organized a spiritual camp on the Rosebud reservation just two years earlier. This temporary camp let people come together to protect sacred land and waters from "development" projects that threatened them, through strategies rooted in prayer and spiritual practices. Their well-planned spiritual camp, Sicangu Wicoti Iyuska, had successfully boosted efforts to shut down a proposed pipeline slated to run through their lands and aquifer.

Paula was clear that it was not going to be a cut-and-paste situation. "There were technical differences between the projects that the communities were up against," she points out. While these differences in the project and the permitting processes were important to consider from a strategic angle in designing the advocacy and legal campaigns, Paula affirms that the overall situation "was basically the same—we were out to protect a large water source." In Paula's community, the spiritual camp had been focused on protecting the Ogallala Aquifer. The nascent effort at Standing Rock was "to protect the Missouri River, and the people and the drinking water of everyone from that point downstream—the millions of people below that mark."

Paula helped community members of Cannonball to launch a social media strategy, which they then maintained. Several months later, in July 2016, when the initial permit for the pipeline was approved, members of the Standing Rock community put out a call over social media and other channels asking people to come support them by joining a spiritual camp at Standing Rock called Oceti Sakowin.

Paula was one of four people designated by her Rosebud Sioux Tribe to go and assist the Standing Rock Sioux Tribe. "What we were going to do was take our spiritual camp and put it in the area to support them spiritually," says Paula. "The Standing Rock Sioux Tribe gave us a location to camp in—and we abided by their wishes because we were guests."

Soon after, many people began arriving in response to the call for solidarity in numbers that grew—and grew and grew. The organizing strategies of Standing Rock youth and tribal members of all ages were sparking an unprecedented response, resonating with a wide variety of people across the United States and beyond. "During the time that we stayed there, we offered spiritual support and tried to accommodate the overflow, because at some points in time, there were, during the peak amounts at the Oceti Sakowin camp, I'd bet twenty-five thousand people in the area." At one point, the members of Standing Rock were running the equivalent of the twelfth-largest city in North Dakota.

Standing Rock achieved something unprecedented in the United States. Though there are many communities across the country and globally who organize to challenge large extractive projects—such as mining, oil, and gas—that threaten their homes and ecosystems, these efforts usually struggle to gain traction. Standing Rock, on the other hand, generated a response so powerful that it made headlines nationally and the world over—for months on end. The life-affirming effects of the movement reached far beyond challenging the permit processes of the Dakota Access Pipeline.

"As time went on, I don't think that North Dakota was prepared to receive that amount of people in opposition to one thing," Paula reflects. "And it ended up not just being one thing; Standing Rock became like the starting point for a movement on protecting water and defending the land and defending Unci Maka, Mother Earth."

A hallmark of the Standing Rock organizers' approach to this breakout work was the way in which they honored—and leveraged—various forms of expertise, both among tribal members and the thousands of allies present. Everyone was treated as having valuable insights and skills to offer.

Given the sheer number of people camping and arriving every day, navigating the logistical complexities alone required many forms of know-how. "There had to be organizational structure within that camp," explains Paula, "just as any traditional camp would have—like security. There was a high amount of donations, so distribution [was important], and being able to make sure that people within the camp received donations that they needed. And there were people that needed help with putting tents up, and just having living arrangements while they decided to stay there." In addition, "We also had to deal with media issues, and," she adds, laughing, "infiltrator issues!"

These logistical demands of the camp were managed almost flawlessly, and daily life at the camp was not only highly functional but also a life-changingly beautiful experience for thousands of people, tribal members and allies alike. At the same time, Standing Rock organizers and allies were leading a complex, multistate legal and advocacy campaign to challenge the pipeline's permit. How was all this possible?

Paula emphasized that a key factor was how the organizers of Standing Rock regularly sourced from the professional expertise and formal training of tribal members and their allies, while also recognizing that if they overprioritized such types of knowledge, it would have undermined the movement's potential. Although crucial to their success, legal and technical information did not take precedence over the insights of tribal elders or the guidance that emerged from spiritual practices. All these sources of information were held in equally high regard.

In their breakout work organizing the far-reaching campaign and prayer camp of Standing Rock, the organizers spoke to the invaluable insights that elders brought to their work. "One of the major responses when there was an issue or when an idea or guidance was needed is 'We need an elder,'" says Paula. During the peak of Standing Rock's prayer camp in the winter of 2016, when the movement's organizing strategies were achieving unprecedented success in capturing media coverage and huge numbers of new allies nationally and around the world, Paula points out that it was very often the input from the elders that provided the key "wisdom and knowledge... that we needed to keep us going."

Throughout the campaign, the organizers made sure they sourced multiple ways of knowing, treating different forms of knowledge as equal. Individuals with top-notch technical expertise—from social media strategies to clean energy technologies to legal advocacy—showed up from all over the world to offer their knowledge and skills in defense of water and life. And they were welcomed to do so in a way that also honored prayer and age-old tradition. At Standing Rock, new tech and old ways felt mutually reinforcing, even synergistic.

This embrace of multiple ways of knowing also reinforced the movement's approach to sharing decision-making power and leadership. "There was never just one leader," Paula shares. "Because the groups that also emerged in there were based around the camps. The medic and healing people, the media groups, the security, there were women's councils and men's councils, also the International Indigenous Youth Council." She also notes, "Nothing was ever decided by one person. They brought the issue up and then everybody that was involved had a chance to express their opinion, suggestion, or comment on any decision that was being made."

Paula explains that this way of operating—through shared leadership in service of self-governance across a large group of people—was not unique to the Standing Rock movement; it reflects a cornerstone of Lakota lifeways. "I think that throughout the entirety of the camp—and this is the same way with our tribe in general—at different points in people's lives, they step up and they assume a role; they assume the leadership role in an event or gathering," Paula reflects. "To me, it was so consensus-based that the leadership came from so many different people. We had young people that stepped up and took the leadership role in so many different ways."

One of the mentors to the Lakota and Dakota youth organizers of Standing Rock in the International Indigenous
Youth Council, Eryn Wise, shared with us how powerful it
was for their movement to connect with and source guidance
and strength from the living world all around them.

"As a guest from the Jicarilla Apache Nation and Laguna
Pueblo, it was imperative that I take time to listen to everyone's voice, and that was wise because we definitely were
informed by the animals," Eryn shares. They spoke to the
birds and other wildlife that came to the banks of the Cannonball River in the early months of the campaign. These
animals stopped coming when the river was drained in prepa-
ration for drilling and construction of the pipeline. There
was also a nearby buffalo ranch. The buffalo, Eryn explains,
"are sacred to many Indigenous Nations but in particular,
and most importantly during this historical moment, to the
stewards of these more-than-human kin. Tatanka Oyate, as
they are known to the Lakota, are the buffalo nation. A lot
of times, people would go out and pray with the buffalo, and
they would route our prayers to the ancestors for us."

On the day of one of the first major raids of Standing Rock
by the police to try to break up the resistance to the pipeline,
"the buffalo," Eryn explains, "showed up." As a wall of police
in riot gear pressed in, a herd of buffalo came over the hill and
thundered into camp. "It scared the shit out of the police,"
Eryn chuckles, "it was a phenomenal, cacophonous explosion
of sound and movement. It was hilarious to see everyone who
shouldn't have been there jump and to see those that should
lean into the moment. They were letting us know we weren't
alone that day." Shifting back to a more serious tone, they
continue, "We definitely consult a lot with those that cannot
speak for themselves, and that's part of what our ceremonies
are for—for us to be able to enter the spirit world, where the

spirits can speak for themselves, although the physical beings may not be able to, and teach us how to take our cues from them too."

The organizers and thousands of participants who answered the call at Standing Rock to help protect water and life were able to contribute as whole people in whatever multifaceted ways each had to offer on a given day—whether that offering was in the form of relevant words of wisdom from one's own spiritual tradition, a skill honed in graduate school, or an intuition felt upon standing at the edge of the Missouri River.

What stands out most to Paula about Standing Rock is "how the entire world kind of came together from that one prayer, you know, because that's what it was all about—is Mni Wiconi." In Lakota, *Mni Wiconi* means water is life. "That's one of the prayers—Mni Wiconi," Paula emphasizes, "because water is our first medicine. It's how we're all born. It's how we're all created. Every living creature on the planet needs water." Rooted in this undeniable truth of the interdependence of water and life—amplified and mobilized through multiple ways of knowing—Standing Rock became one of the most powerful movements for Indigenous sovereignty, self-determination, and environmental justice in recent history.

CHAPTER 8

SOURCE FROM MULTIPLE WAYS OF KNOWING

P AULA ANTOINE reflects on how for many well-intended allies at Standing Rock, it was a jarring experience to find their technical knowledge was not treated as the only valid source of information for the task at hand. "I've seen people in the camp who have come thinking that they had the best idea in the world," says Paula. "And they went to Cambridge, or they went to Stanford, or they went to Harvard, and they studied with whoever for so many years, and then they walk into the camp and they demand that their idea be heard, and that action be taken on their idea, and it was going to save this poor culture that has no idea about this new technology." Paula's tone shifts from softly sarcastic to deeply respectful. "And I have seen some of the people humbled."

She continues, "I have seen them turn around and have so much respect after they've experienced a ceremony. Or after they've experienced the nature and the surroundings, and being treated as a human being and a relative." Paula thinks for a moment. "I've seen them cry—because they were so overwhelmed with what they didn't know was going to happen to them there. And it was not a bad thing."

In the status quo of the loveless economy, it can be jarring for some people to reawaken and realize that technical expertise or academic learning, for example, are not the only ways of knowing that have value. Though such a transition in perspective can be uncomfortable for some at first, our research shows that it is often joyful and restorative for people to see themselves as part of a broader web of knowledge.

> **Sourcing from multiple ways of knowing** is the practice of considering, valuing, and attuning to multiple types of knowledge, ranging from technical training to lived experience to spirituality to what we sense from the living world around us. This practice actively examines and unravels biases that keep groups from appreciating certain ways of knowing, and it breaks down power dynamics that prevent people from expressing intrinsic knowledge. A practice of sourcing from multiple ways of knowing reawakens inherent capacities to access and understand information from sources other than those prioritized in business as usual. This practice honors and leverages technical expertise and formal training, while simultaneously welcoming a host of other rich sources of guidance.

Shifting how we understand knowing

In business as usual, forms of knowledge that are taken most seriously tend to be rooted in technical training from formal learning institutions. In this context, other forms of knowing, such as wisdom gleaned from lived experience, intuition, physical sensation, and spiritual practice, are often dismissed or actively silenced. However, a shift in this balance has begun to occur, which represents an increasing recognition of the value of long-dismissed types of knowledge.[1]

For example, it is becoming more common for companies to encourage sparking innovative ideas through activities like holding a group brainstorming session outdoors or including a guided meditation at staff meetings.[2]

Breakout actors go even deeper when it comes to incorporating varied ways of knowing into their work. Not only are they turning to knowledge from sources outside of business as usual, they are also strengthening their own capacity to access inner knowing. They recognize that transforming the ways in which they work is about more than just upgrading existing methods and tools; it is also about attuning awareness.

When the understanding of knowing fundamentally shifts, so does the axis of knowledge that is trusted and given power. "For most of my adult life I thought there was one way of knowing, reading, listening, developing a cognitive expertise," shares co-learner Aisha Shillingford. "In recent years, I embraced embodiment, art-making, and breath work, all of which have provided access to a way of knowing that has reconnected me to my ancestors, myself, and visions of the future that previously were impossible to access." Aisha's experience is echoed by many co-learners and even by entire teams and communities who find that welcoming in a wider array of knowing unlocks breakout innovation and also brings meaningful new insights into their own lives.

What does sourcing from multiple ways of knowing look like?

Members of the co-learning community use different words and phrases to describe the unique blend of ways of knowing they draw upon. There is no formulaic set of sources, terminology, or methods for tapping into them. However, among these varied approaches to broadening knowledge, common elements include:

- Proactively welcoming multiple ways of knowing, and
- Building team capacity for greater awareness.

Proactively welcoming multiple ways of knowing

Breakout actors source from multiple ways of knowing by acknowledging explicitly that many people carry varying levels of bias against, and discomfort with, ways of knowing traditionally dismissed in business as usual. The status quo severely limits opportunities to incorporate multiple ways of knowing into work, let alone to experience the benefits of doing so. To counteract this reticence and dearth of experience, breakout actors provide frequent encouragement and validation to legitimize sharing a recommendation based on, for example, something observed in decades of work on a factory floor, despite never studying industrial engineering; the story a grandmother passed down that explained why and how often the coastline floods from hurricanes; an intuition perceived during a walk through the woods; or even something realized in a dream. They recognize that if we do not explicitly encourage sharing from these ways of knowing, key information and wisdom will too often be left unspoken.

Co-learner Bobbie Hill of Concordia shares that when she and her team facilitated a Louisiana state initiative on climate-crisis preparedness, residents of multiple coastal regions contributed to plans for preserving the heart and soul of their communities in the face of rising sea levels and receding coastlines. "It wasn't enough that we included valuing lived experience as one of our initiative's guidelines, which we recapped at the start of every community design meeting," remembers Bobbie. "We found that the table hosts had to explicitly invite folks to share what they knew from their experience, or their family's stories over the years. Otherwise people just assumed that what they had to contribute wasn't welcome or going to make any difference, alongside the data shared by the climate scientists." By intentionally creating a group culture that valued these forms of knowledge alongside the technical reports, more residents felt comfortable sharing their insights and recommendations and encouraged one another to contribute. What they brought to the meetings was critical to revealing opportunities and innovative strategies for adapting coastal infrastructure that might have otherwise been overlooked.

Breakout actors actively think about the many facets of their lives that may provide relevant insights to the work at hand. They notice what is habitually ignored or actively suppressed and deliberately shift where they look for value. Co-learner Tatewin Means of Thunder Valley Community Development Corporation speaks to the strength demonstrated "when community members come together. What you're able to accomplish doesn't have to come from the tribal government, doesn't have to come from the federal government or some outside source, or relying on white people and their 'expertise.' We have the inherent knowledge and wisdom to find a path forward, trusting in ourselves." Thunder Valley has developed strategies across all its program areas to support staff and community members in contributing ideas from their experiences and lifeways to complement, for instance, quantitative results of an evaluation survey or written report.

To help level the playing field, breakout actors tend to dissolve boundaries between formal (academic, trained) and informal (lived) expertise to create inclusive and accessible spaces where all can participate. "I believe the fundamental way of knowing is practice," comments co-learner Ed

Whitfield. "Worldwide, people engaged in agriculture, and other aspects of life in community, have ways of knowing and are connected with ways of producing that have to do with keeping them alive—which are different from the kind of knowledge that the academy elevates." He speaks to the importance of incorporating these crucial forms of productive, practical knowledge into how teams and groups learn. Ed also notes that the knowledge produced through practice is not only about people "knowing how to do their jobs," but also that they are "creating theory in the course of it." Like Ed, breakout actors encourage fellow group members to realize that their knowledge from life and practice can provide sophisticated analysis and valuable recommendations.

> **Tip: Affirm everyone's authority on their own lived experience.** When someone shares information from their lived experience, it is important they are seen as the authority. It can take enormous bravery to share a personal journey in a workplace setting. It is natural that colleagues will have varied experiences, and therefore people in a group may disagree on the conclusion a peer has arrived at. However, it is important to stay focused on expressing a divergent perspective on the conclusion in a way that honors the experience the person has shared. Breakout innovation can best be achieved when sharing lived experience is truly received as a gift for the benefit of a collective effort.

Breakout actors offer a note of caution when welcoming many ways of knowing: it is important that groups do not overcorrect from business as usual and thus create other imbalances. Sometimes when groups deliberately source from multiple ways of knowing for the first time, they inadvertently create new hierarchies of knowledge. For instance, they may conclude that an insight gained through meditation is of greater value than insights gained through technical expertise or quantitative assessment. While sourcing from multiple ways of knowing may mean giving more time and space to forms of knowledge that have been invalidated by business as usual, this practice does not mean prioritizing these above formal education or technical information. Co-learner Brooking Gatewood shares how she's seen teams "working so hard to not overly worship the written word"[3] that they end up tipping into "an absolute lack of documentation, which can then create new problems, such as a lack of transparent information-sharing, or creating unwanted power dynamics or access issues." The trick with this practice—as well as all the practices—is balance.

Building team capacity for greater awareness

Innovation scholar Otto Scharmer of the MIT Sloan School of Management has led groundbreaking work on how intuitive ways of knowing relate to innovation. Several members of the co-learning community frequently speak about Scharmer's work and a framework he developed called Theory U—a methodology for "learning from the future as it emerges."[4] Theory U was inspired by Scharmer and his colleagues observing patterns in how groups and individuals were able to generate breakthrough ideas and solutions, even in the face of extreme complexity. A striking commonality was that they reported having some form of relationship with a deep source of knowing—something that enabled them to actually shift their consciousness, to become aware of new possibilities.[5]

Each in their own ways, breakout actors encourage their colleagues, teams, and groups to tap into sources of knowing that help shift and expand thinking. Tatewin describes Thunder Valley Community Development Corporation's practice of regularly sourcing guidance from Lakota spirituality and lifeways: "I think it's important because it takes you out of any predetermined box or parameters—those limits that we think are there to the work. So when you remove those, and you're looking at the world from a different viewpoint, from a different perspective, you really start to see the possibilities, and not the barriers."

Breakout actors turn to many different sources to spark more expansive thinking and awareness. Key among these are:

Emotion. Simply affirming that emotions are a valuable source of knowing can go a long way, especially since business as usual encourages a separation from emotions in favor of "rationality." Co-learner Katherine Tyler Scott's decades of work in a whole-person approach to leadership development strongly affirms this. Business as usual aims to convince us that our emotions are not as important as our cognitive ability, which, she believes, "is another thing that keeps us stuck." Emotional capacity, she emphasizes, is "what makes you a human being—and your innate, intuitive sensing of truth is the wisdom that makes the universe go 'round.'"

Embodied knowledge. Even in business as usual, there is growing recognition that movement and intentional embodiment practices designed to bring awareness to physical sensations can help with problem-solving, dealing with challenges, and responding honestly and creatively to the world.[6] Plenty of physical movement practices and mind-body connection techniques can heighten somatic awareness.[7] Breakout actors might invite group members to move their bodies in whatever way is accessible to them, or turn a break into an impromptu dance party. They also emphasize that care and ample movement, coupled with dedicated attention to signals from the body and determination to interpret them, can open up new awareness and knowing.

Art. From visual arts to music to poetry and more, many breakout actors incorporate art into their work of imagining and building together. Several emphasize the ways in which engaging in art-based approaches helps level the playing field; the business-as-usual knowledge hierarchies seem to fall away when group members have the opportunity to, for instance, draw their idea for a next step. Art can also help group members tap into a sense of play, which unleashes creative ideas and insights that might not arise in the business-as-usual mindset of "working." According to co-learner Jessica Norwood, "It's about integrating a lot more art and creativity and play and pleasure and joy into what we're doing."

Spiritual insight. For many people, spiritual practice is a personal and powerful source of insight. Whatever their chosen practice, breakout actors have found value in attuning to information whose origins lie beyond the mind—from a source some would call divine. They find it can offer not only profound insight but also strength and motivation to keep going when the work is difficult. Paula notes, for her Lakota people and for many people around the world, spirituality is a source of inspiration in multiple ways and deeply intertwined with embodied knowledge as well: "Our culture and our prayers—they *are* song and dance." She explains that spirituality and physical movement are not disconnected concepts in her culture. At Standing Rock, "Our prayers played a major part in everything we did. It's like in order to survive, you need to breathe air. It's part of the beating heart. You need that drumbeat to live."

Connecting with the living world. Breakout actors recognize that interacting with nonhuman living beings as well as surrounding ecosystems awakens healthy connections. For instance, co-learner Debbe McCall of the Heart Research

Alliance notes that "a cat's purr reduces pain and regulates heart rhythm." A host of recent scientific studies have found that connecting to natural ecosystems—even in ways as simple as walking through a grove of trees—activates the brain in ways that enhance problem-solving and insight.[8] Simply stepping outside can ensure that ideas are linked and aligned to the particular places where the work is most relevant. KA McKercher points out, "Connecting to place is an integral part of respecting cultural protocols, honoring and designing for where we are working, and ensuring that our solutions don't neglect our natural environment."[9] In their work, KA encourages this connection by providing teams with time for walks through a natural landscape or time together around a fire under the stars.

Breakout actors integrate a combination of emotional, embodied, spiritual, lived, and technical knowledge in their work.

> **Tip: Practice self-care to tap into multiple ways of knowing.**
> One of the most loveless aspects of business as usual is the expectation of efficiency and overwork to get the job done. This way of work takes a tremendous toll on physical, mental, and emotional well-being, as discussed earlier in this book. It also affects the ability to be wise.[10] In a state of overwhelm, it is harder to tap into the wisdom within and around us. Breakout actors find self-care is an essential part of being responsible to their collaborators and work. When members of a group tend to their minds, bodies, and spirits, they are more adept at tapping into complex and varied sources of knowledge and can build upon one another's insights effectively. This leads to information emerging that's beyond what could have been accessed individually. When we care for our body and spirit, we can most powerfully exercise our rights to design.

Sourcing from multiple ways of knowing in action

In order for the Heart Research Alliance to successfully build a patient-powered research network, facilitators Brooking Gatewood and Rebecca Petzel put great care into ensuring the culture of the design process was built around the needs of those who had the most at stake as well as the expertise gained from lived experience: people managing and living with atrial fibrillation (AFib) and other heart conditions. This happened in several ways.

Patients were treated as the primary experts in the room from day one. Additionally, patients with heart conditions were the majority of participants in the research design process. This was critical to shifting the balance of power away from doctors and researchers, who have the default authority in business as usual, allowing patients to drive the conversations. Centering patients' voices required more than just numbers; facilitators worked together with participants—including patients, doctors, and researchers—to set expectations based on the realities of patients' lives. Attendance was expected to fluctuate based on participants' health, and medical jargon was broken down into accessible terms. The culture and ground rules that participants co-created enabled conversations that rarely occur at the hospital or in medical research settings.

"Patients have lots of great ideas; we just aren't used to framing it the way a researcher can," shares Debbe. "It's two different languages. There's research and there's living with it. It's like there's a medical language and patient language." The culture and ground rules, along with support from the facilitators, made it possible to source insights from both these languages. "Every time that the researchers and clinicians got too far ahead, the facilitators slowed them down. They made sure the patients were comfortable, they made sure we understood, they made sure we caught up. And if we got off on a tangent, like ranting... which we do sometimes... they would pull us back to the center and go, 'Okay, so here's actually the question.'"

Debbe reflects on how Heart Research Alliance's success in identifying research questions with groundbreaking implications for patient quality of life would not have been possible without sourcing from patients' unique ways of knowing: "Like most patients, I know my disease very well, and most patients who are very involved in their disease and treatment are experts at a different level, of course, than a clinician or researcher will be, but we bring a wealth of information to the table when you are talking about any disease process. Because we live with it 24/7. It's only recently that we've been respected, and by that, I mean treated as experts on our disease."

Through co-creating a group culture that values all forms of knowledge in the room, with specific ground rules and practices for bridging the "languages" that participants spoke, Heart Research Alliance not only shed light on critically important and innovative research questions but also expanded the knowledge of everyone involved.

How does sourcing from multiple ways of knowing unlock breakout innovation?

Within business as usual, vast amounts of key insights are often prevented from ever making it to the table. Within the loveless economy, who delivers information, how they deliver it, and where it comes from are shaped by business-as-usual biases, which ultimately determine which insights are actually heard and acted upon. As a result, groups again and again operate with a shortsighted view of what is, what has been, and what could be.

"I think playing out business and finance in the head has made it possible for the negative impacts of our economy to become abstractions," offers co-learner Bruce Campbell of Blue Dot Advocates law firm, "just more data that sits in a spreadsheet and is considered dispassionately along with other data, like revenue and profits. Somehow business needs to become personal, in the sense that people experience what they are doing with their whole selves. If they do this, then it will make it harder to continue harmful practices."

By tapping into greater awareness and insight from a varied array of sources of knowing, listening deeply to themselves as whole beings, as well as sensing into realms beyond, breakout actors not only generate ideas that are innovative, they become aware of the wider expanse of vital possibilities. Even in the face of daunting challenges, when deconsolidating rights to design by sourcing from multiple ways of knowing, breakout pathways can reveal themselves.

. . .

CREATIVE REACTION LAB

C REATIVE REACTION LAB's clients range across sectors—museums, tech companies, government agencies, and more—and locations, from their hometown of St. Louis, Missouri, across the United States and internationally. But they all tend to share a similar motivation for reaching out. "In the face of increasing recognition of multiculturalism across their institutions and communities, in some cases realizing that internally they have been upholding white supremacy tenets, they want to design a more inclusive and equitable lens to how they work," explains Creative Reaction Lab founder, president, and CEO Antionette D. Carroll. "And that's why they call in our team."

The Creative Reaction Lab team designs and facilitates customized learning experiences using Equity-Centered Community Design, an internationally acclaimed method they pioneered. This creative problem-solving method integrates key practices such as building a team of diverse co-creators; reflecting, acknowledging, and challenging one's power biases, privileges, values, and assumptions; integrating analysis of history into the process; and designing in healing elements. Throughout the process, those with lived experience play a lead role as designers of solutions that will be effective and meaningful. The experience and results of Creative Reaction Lab's approach to design have been embraced with such enthusiasm that thousands of people have joined the growing network of "Redesigners for Justice," inspired by this approach and committed to reflecting it in their everyday lives and work.[1]

In every Equity-Centered Community Design process, the multigenerational age range of Creative Reaction Lab's team is not the only kind of diversity in the room, as they center racial and ethnic equity in their work. Antionette and her colleagues always support the co-creators in advance of the kickoff with effective outreach to include an array of stakeholders with vital perspectives on the issues being tackled.

Antionette and her team begin the first gathering with a reflective activity quite unlike kickoff meetings in business as usual. Explains Antionette, "We always start with language-setting." This includes addressing a concept that the Creative Reaction Lab team refers to as the case for equity. "Usually, the way we look at the case for equity depends on the topic at hand. For instance, let's say, philanthropy. If we are working with a grant-making foundation that wants to identify and make changes in how it operates as an institution, what is the reason for us to design equity into the philanthropic industry?" she asks. "And what's the history of inequitable processes and design within the field?"

In exploring this question, co-creators are invited to look at "both sides of the coin," emphasizes Antionette. "This means both the problems in that space and also learning about groups that are leading existing efforts to address these problems." Creative Reaction Lab takes a nuanced, highly intentional approach to that second side of the coin. "The question is, How do we fit into that work—acknowledging the history of what has already been done—and how do we build upon that, rather than erasing it?"

Language-setting also means participants are asked to identify the most important concepts for their shared work—the interventions they will be designing—and co-create their own precise terms and definitions. Antionette shares a recent example of this, when a team of youth impacted by the criminal justice system, training to become Redesigners for Justice, were tackling an issue related to food justice and access in their communities. "The community design apprentices took terms like 'food desert' and determined a more accurate term, based on their experience, is 'food apartheid,' and then they co-created their own definition." While clients or participants might initially dismiss this language-setting step as peripheral to the core work, the Creative Reaction Lab team is clear about its central importance. Antionette sums it up: "If we can't co-create language and clarity together, through people bringing in their diverse perspectives and living expertise, then how are we going to co-create interventions?"

The Creative Reaction Lab team then introduces the group to the next activities: personal reflections, followed by an exercise in pairs to expand on what was unearthed and then an exercise as a full group. In describing this step, Antionette gives a bemused grin. What happens next "almost every single time" is that her team receives pushback. Some people in the room are deeply uncomfortable with being asked to spend time on something that seems unrelated to efficiently achieving the task at hand. The problem they are supposed to be addressing in this workshop is urgent. People have taken time away from pressing responsibilities. They want to get to the final product as fast as possible. Antionette and her team calmly respond, "This is our framework; this is our process. This is not typical human-centered design or design thinking, because, for us, it is not enough to think about how you're going to develop interventions without also analyzing how you are showing up in a space."

The group is then skillfully guided through reflections that touch on an individual's own experiences with power, the often unspoken dynamics related to power within the participants' own teams, and how these dynamics relate to the group's ability to work with fellow stakeholders to truly address the issue at hand, which everyone in the room cares deeply about.

The resistance and worried impatience that hung in the air quickly dissipate. In its place, something emerges that is hard to name, but words that come to mind are *awe*, *reverence*, and *focus*. In the small groups around the room, people bear witness to a colleague sharing something never spoken aloud; others suddenly see an entirely new approach for change at the root of the issue; many grapple with a realization about how they show up in their work every day.

Everyone is deeply *in* what they are doing, speaking, listening, reimagining and redesigning. No one is looking at the clock. People in the meeting room are no longer experiencing time in the same way they were at the start of the meeting. Even if for only this fleeting part of their day, they have moved into a different quality of presence with one another, revealing new universes of awareness and possibility.

As Antionette describes how her team moves through the inevitable early resistance, she smiles. "Almost every single time—actually, I may say every time they originally opposed this part of the process—after the engagement, the organizers will come up to us and say, 'That was fantastic! That was amazing; we were able to reflect on ourselves.' And sometimes we're looking at them, like, 'Did you forget you didn't want us to do that?!'"

Antionette points out that the key to their widely embraced approach is in creating time for reflection paired with action. "The problem with a lot of equity, diversity and inclusion work is that, while it sparks important reflection on our biases and how we show up, the process then stays there—in reflection, in the theoretical, in the individual, and *not* to systemic action." Similarly, she notes, the problem with a lot of design work is that it doesn't do reflection and instead jumps straight into action. "We are trying to bring these realms that are already synergistic *together*. Reflection throughout the process, and getting to that space of action: let's test some things, let's learn. We have to have a futuristic approach and a creator's mindset to actually produce something from our reflection."

"When we reflect not only on the makeup of the room, but also on our personal and community histories," shares Antionette, "we can look at this process as a form of our healing as well. For me personally, as I get more involved in more initiatives in St. Louis, reckoning with community history has been a part of my healing."

Through their own experiences and those of their clients and program participants, the Creative Reaction Lab team has seen that the time spent in this kind of profound reflection can spark healing—and strategic insight—that continues to guide action for years to come. They frequently hear from clients, even long after their initial work together, that the teams and organizations regularly look back on those grounding conversations and the values and aims that were so powerfully clarified by everyone involved. It turns out that the initial hours and days they spent in language-setting, building trust, and reckoning with histories become an invaluable north star to which the group returns to find their way, time and again.

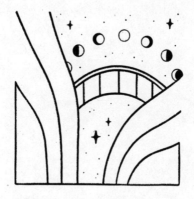

CHAPTER 9

TRUST THERE IS TIME

NTENTIONALLY counteracting the culture of urgency while creating space to relate to time in a more expansive way are cornerstones of Creative Reaction Lab's efficacy. Trusting there is time—to build relationships and shared language, to confront the exclusive histories within their field, and to account for power differences in the room—is a central practice of breakout actors to ensure that their efforts will result in meaningful outcomes.

We hesitated to use the word *trust* in this practice. On the one hand, we heard the word used in a positive light innumerable times by breakout actors, to mean having faith in the importance of taking the time to get things right. On the other hand, being asked to trust can be triggering, especially when one has had experiences of the loveless economy *not* being oriented toward one's protection and care.

Additionally, we recognize that combining trust with an insistence that there is indeed enough time can make the invitation feel unfeasible—even offensive. How can the research indicate to trust there is time, when so many of us are struggling to stay afloat financially, working multiple jobs, racing the clock to meet deadlines that have real-world consequences—all the while reading news of the latest climate crisis report about time slipping inexorably away? Time is the resource that no one seems to have enough of. And in the current economy, the ability to keep up with this frenetic pace is tied to the very ability to survive.

Perhaps because of this context, the practice of trusting there is time was the last practice to come into view through our research process. We were several years into the research before we noticed that, across dozens of interviews with breakout actors, a strong pattern emerged: the co-learners all treated time as an abundant and elastic resource. The ways they make this true—even amid the time-starved context of the loveless economy—include intentionally shifting the quality of one's attention, revising team priorities to ensure they are aligned with the team's values, and challenging business-as-usual narratives related to urgency and the nature of time.

Breakout actors trust there is time for building strong foundations for their work—such as nurturing authentic, caring relationships with team members—and that doing so supports, rather than detracts from, getting the job done. They trust that finding ways—however small—to approach time as something spacious and abundant dramatically improves the quality of their work.

Trusting there is time means believing there is always time available to prioritize engagement and care in how we work. This practice invites us to question the assumed urgency that is so pervasive in business as usual and to be critical of the frazzled state in which so many of us frequently operate. This practice applies the paradox of going slow to go fast. It means strategically investing time at the front end of a process—and at points all along the way—to nourish the solid foundations necessary for lasting transformation. Breakout actors approach this practice as a foundation for the other six practices in that it facilitates the time needed for each of them. When time is taken to build strong foundations—such as authentic relationships, insights gathered from many perspectives, or clear structures of co-ownership for shared work—it can be surprising how quickly processes reach and surpass even the most audacious hopes.

Shifting how we understand time

In the current context of generalized urgency and economic duress, a practice of trusting there is time is not easy. As co-learner Dawn Neuman, CFO at Incourage Community Foundation, points out, "It is hard to see how to get off the hamster wheel when you don't remember how you got caught up in it in the first place, and when it is all you can really remember!" More than any other practice, this is one that cannot be done alone. Breakout actors demonstrate ways in which whole teams, enterprises, and communities can practice trusting there is enough time and, in doing so together, make it true.

This practice requires a shift in mindset as well as a change in how time is invested. Breakout actors cultivate an active relationship with time that is far more complex than allocating the number of hours in a workday.

Co-learner Enoch Elwell reflects on what he has learned through the shared efforts of working with first-time entrepreneurs and business owners in the CO.STARTERS community to resist the intensive urgency and instant growth demands of startups in business as usual. CO.STARTERS is a network that supports grassroots leaders working to start their own enterprises; it equips individuals and groups with top-notch tools and resources of all kinds to fuel vibrant entrepreneurial ecosystems. Since founding CO.STARTERS, Enoch has consistently brought to his work equal doses of business savvy and soulfulness. "Rather than looking at time as something that happens to us, which we are a victim of, time is something that we can choose to engage with. When we are fully present, time stands still," reflects Enoch. "Those transformational moments transcend time!"

Enoch points out that shifting the relationship to time in this way is not easy, and it requires continual inner work and intentionally "practicing openness, gratitude, and emotional and physiological awareness." Breakout actors confirm that this type of personal growth takes time and effort but is profoundly worth it. Trusting there is time lays the groundwork for groups to achieve truly meaningful change sooner, and more easefully, than they otherwise might have.

The shift away from urgency and toward trusting that there is sufficient time to nurture what matters most allows groups to work together in a way that gives rise to the kind of profound outcomes breakout innovation yields.

What does trusting there is time look like?

Breakout actors readily admit that this practice is often the most challenging because of the intense culture of urgency in the loveless economy. Nonetheless, they find that even small steps can help shift their team's relationship to time toward abundance. Several ways that breakout actors trust there is time are:

- Honoring people's time constraints and real urgency,
- Pointing out that varied approaches to time exist, and
- Prioritizing the fundamentals.

Honoring people's time constraints and real urgency

A key way breakout actors foster a feeling of safety for their teams and communities with regard to this practice is by demonstrating respect for people's time and for their existing constraints and commitments. Co-learner Bobbie Hill shares, "Establish a clear timeline and communicate it in every way possible to those that will participate." Doing so is essential for people to "feel their time is valuable and contributing to the work. They need to see this reflected in documentation of the work and watch the project advancing to meaningful and viable solutions."

Many breakout actors echo this point—emphasizing the importance of not only clearly sharing a timeline at the start of a project but also every time things change. When teams work in ways that deconsolidate rights to design, the resulting higher level of attunement to what is trying to emerge can mean that timelines and plans frequently shift as groups respond to new information, opportunities, and course corrections. In the current economic system, when those with positional power change deadlines, everyone else scrambles, regardless of the cost. Breakout actors, instead, expect things to shift and approach any changes by demonstrating care and seeking consent and discussion with anyone impacted.

Breakout actors note that sometimes it's not about changing a deadline but changing the approach to meeting a deadline. "There are a lot of ways to use time well in pursuit of a given deadline," reflects co-learner Connor McManus of his experience working with breakout actor Concordia. "That doesn't necessarily mean working flat out at a computer. You have to make room to unlock creativity and take breaks, and optimize your headspace."

Co-learner Jessamyn Shams-Lau adds a further dimension to navigating the balance between honoring true urgency and refusing the constant rush. "It's false urgency, or unexamined urgency—that is what we have to move away from, not urgency as a whole," she clarifies. "I often find that I'm torn between the philosophical instinct that taking time leads to better outcomes, whilst also incredibly impatient to act, knowing so many people need change yesterday." Jessamyn emphasizes that it is vital to operate with respect for the fact that "so many have endured generations of trauma and injustice, yet are still infuriatingly told 'Go slow.'"

In navigating the tensions Jessamyn speaks to, several breakout actors reference the work of author Dr. Tema Okun, who has examined and written extensively about the topic of white supremacy culture, including how its dominance influences the relationship to time. Dr. Okun notes that many people are struggling "to hold the volatile and tender contradiction of an underlying urgency about our immediate need for justice which is with us always with the day to day sense of urgency that too often defines our organizational and community cultures." Dr. Okun writes: "White supremacy culture is not urgent about racial justice; white supremacy culture is urgent in the name of short-term power and profit. And white supremacy culture likes to engender a culture of urgency in those of us who are working to dismantle it because it knows that living with a constant sense that everything is urgent is a recipe for the abuse of power and burnout."[1]

Breakout actors appreciate this analysis and note that this practice—like all seven—is about achieving a balance that fits one's group. It means rejecting unquestioned urgency; at the same time, it is not a license for endless navel-gazing. Trusting there is time is about cultivating a quality of awareness that allows the spaciousness to choose the pace that best serves the work at hand.

Tip: Create a culture of asking for help. In business as usual, time constraints are often navigated by struggling alone. A key way to help teams and groups shift away from survival mode and into a relationship with time that best serves their work is to intentionally build a culture of support and "nimble time constraints," as co-learner Antionette D. Carroll describes it. If a deadline is fast approaching and seems far harder to meet than anticipated, relevant collaborators can assess together: What's most important here? Is this deadline indeed fixed, or is there wiggle room? If it can't move, what else can shift to make it feel more possible? By doing so, what may have felt impossible individually usually becomes easier to sort out together. When information, ideas, and responsibility for outcomes are shared, a situation tends to rapidly reveal itself as one that contains many possible paths that support well-being and identified priorities.

Pointing out that varied approaches to time exist

Many people in the United States may never have questioned the way their workplaces approach time. It has been deeply ingrained in business as usual that the way to be a good, professional worker is to be laser-focused on moving from point A to point B to get to the outcome as quickly as possible. After all, time is money, right?

In this paradigm, time is strictly linear and a commodity: there is only a certain amount of time in the scarce marketplace, and it is spent in one way or another. This conception of time is rooted in shifts during the industrial revolution when the ownership of time became a currency.[2] "As employers consolidated control over their workforces," writes economist Dr. Juliet B. Schor, "the day was increasingly split into two kinds of time: 'owners' time,' the time of *work*; and 'their own time, a time (in theory) for *leisure*.'"[3] This approach to time is directly linked to the stressors so many people experience in the current loveless economy. It is also, as many breakout actors note, a construct of white supremacy culture. Several people in the co-learning community reference Dr. Okun's identification of a sense of urgency as one of the characteristics of white supremacy culture.[4] They emphasize the importance of explicitly discussing the nature and origins of business as usual's approach to time as a first step in the practice of trusting there is time. Doing so supports group members in realizing there are other approaches that exist, which one can choose. Doing so builds a shared awareness that the predominant approach to time in the loveless economy is simply one way of doing things, linked to one particular worldview—and an approach directly linked to maximizing extraction and accumulation at all costs.

Equally important is pointing out that other ways of viewing and experiencing time exist. Many Indigenous cultures, for instance, have a long-term and cyclical view of time. As co-learner Kataraina Davis says, "Māori think long term. We're not here for the quick fix." Another approach to time is common among communities of individuals with chronic health conditions: time is viewed through a lens of quality rather than quantity. "As patients like to say," shares co-learner Debbe McCall, "'Clinicians look at quantity of time; we're looking at quality of time.' How good do we live? How happy are we? How well are we coping with things? Not just 'Are we living longer with our disease?' Because anyone who's cared for elderly parents or a child with a terminal disease knows you are on limited time. So, let's make the best of it we can."

"It's not just about believing that there is enough time," reflects co-learner Brooking Gatewood, "but choosing to act this way—as its own radical and transformative act in a world addicted to running on scarcity." In the current context of the unquestioned, urgent pursuit of deadlines, it can seem improbable that this way of operating is a choice and that this relationship with time is one option of many. Yet when entire teams choose to operate with a newfound sense of choice in their approach, breakout actors find that their work tends to benefit immediately and profoundly. This shift allows teams to explore approaches to time and agenda-setting that may be far more effective and values-aligned for any given task, and which helps unlock breakout possibilities that previously felt impossible.

> **Tip: Ensure leaders practice trusting there is time.** Breakout actors note that in order for teams to be able to intentionally choose how they approach time and for collective transformation to occur, this practice requires buy-in from both those in formal leadership roles and those who hold positional power. Active support is critical to a group's ability to actually trust there is time. As Dawn notes, "Without a level of trust between those involved, it would be harder for the element of allowing time to play out to actually work out okay." Support from leadership also helps ensure the job security and economic safety of the group as a whole, as they dare to depart from business-as-usual approaches to time in search of breakout ways of operating.

Prioritizing the fundamentals

A key ingredient to effectively sharing decision-making power, forging strong relationships, reckoning with history, bringing people together across differences, and learning from multiple ways of knowing is allowing the time necessary for these practices. For this reason, nourishing strong foundations often requires a significant initial investment of time—sometimes to a degree that clashes with mainstream expectations of pacing. Breakout actors explicitly question business-as-usual assumptions about what is most important in their work. They ask, What priorities do we want to set as a team, and why?

Once a strong foundation is in place, breakout results spring from this healthy soil faster and bolder than many anticipate. Summing up the importance of tending to these foundational elements, co-learner Isabella Jean reflects, "I've seen it many times: quality process leads to quality outcomes." Many breakout actors boldly trust that building solid foundations results in the time for breakout results to emerge.

> **Tip: Co-define the foundations your group will prioritize.**
> Work together to determine the foundational elements that will be your team's North Star. What does your team want to intentionally dedicate time to? When time pressure gets intense, as it invariably does, what are your team's priorities? Plan scenarios to anticipate how team members can support one another to find a sense of spaciousness and choice to stay true to these fundamentals amid the inevitable time pressures that arise.

Trusting there is time in action

Co-learner Banks Benitez is the former CEO and co-founder of Uncharted, one of the longest-operating social venture acceleration programs in the United States. Banks transitioned from his role after ten years of leading the organization as a member of its leaderful team. During his tenure, one of the major ways Uncharted created a culture of doing things differently inside their workplace was pushing back on business as usual's urgency and instead establishing approaches to time that make sense for the team and community of social ventures they support. Uncharted intentionally departs from the quick-fix approach to time so common among business accelerator programs. Their team trusts in the time it takes for a new venture to create and show positive change.

"There is a lack of support for organizations that are not overnight successes," Banks shares. "And so Uncharted tries to stand in that breach and say, 'We will bet on the things that will take time to mature, that are not overnight, that are focusing on leverage points in systems change, that aren't the easy wins right away.'" These attitudes and approaches to time have yielded powerful results both for Uncharted's own ability to fulfill its mission and for the success of the growing, diverse community of enterprises it supports.

As an accelerator dedicated to "elevating and supporting organizations that are overlooked and underrepresented," the Uncharted team works actively across all fifty states in the US to identify promising enterprises and encourage them to apply. "This year, we got 344 applications for our program—77 percent of which were from people of color, and 63 percent were women or nonbinary founders," Banks shares with pride. "Those stats significantly outperform other accelerator cohorts." Uncharted also continues to attract top-notch levels of additional investment for participants in its cohorts. Every dollar that goes to Uncharted, on average, translates into $8 of additional capital invested into the social ventures it supports. "That means that we are redistributing capital into early stage organizations and helping fund the most audacious early stage ventures that are out there," explains Banks.

After several years of bringing this ethos to their work with the social ventures Uncharted supports, the team began asking some bigger questions internally about time and what would make their work its best. Reflecting on the kind of relationship to time that many hold in the current loveless economy, Banks notes, "When working hard is a badge of honor, everything's urgent, everything's a priority. We are incentivized to essentially keep ourselves busy and to fill our time." Uncharted's team members considered a shorter workweek. "We tried to really say, 'Let's move away from the hustle culture or the brute force mentality approach.'" To help release this unexamined urgency and busyness, the Uncharted team underwent an organization-wide reflection process. "It was about challenging some of those norms in a way that says, What's the most important work? How long will that work take? And let's cut away all the things that are unimportant," explains Banks. "Doing that changes our relationship to time."

Uncharted ultimately chose to adopt a four-day workweek, but that change was not about simply reducing the number of working days in a week. Without a larger cultural shift related to time, a four-day workweek can result in employees feeling stressed and cramming everything on their to-do lists into fewer days but longer hours. Banks shares, "It's actually about pausing and recognizing that we have been socialized into needing to be busy, needing to be productive."

To support a shift in their team's culture, Uncharted has encouraged team members to create their own schedules based on the rhythms and ways of working that will help them move forward on the things that truly matter. "We trust our team to be available in a small window of time every day, and they can then structure the rest of their day how they please," shares Banks. "We placed ownership at each person's level and said, 'If you were in full control of your week, how would you do it? And could you get your work done if you were to be the author, the sole author of your week?'"

When Uncharted staff members thought deeply about these questions, many experienced a newfound sense of abundance. Banks recalls people on the Uncharted team realizing that there is plenty of time to get work done. "There's powerful agency in restructuring your week in a way that reclaims your time—and your control over your calendar, as opposed to your calendar controlling you." Uncharted has inspired similar questioning processes and shifts in many other groups, not only funding partners and social ventures it serves but enterprises across the country, thanks to national news coverage of its inspiring approach to trusting there is time.

How trusting there is time unlocks breakout innovation

Breakout actors emphasize that when they trust there is time to work in ways that deconsolidate rights to design, then "when the outputs come out, they tend to be stronger," as Antionette puts it. "There tends to be more confidence in it. They tend to be sustained more because we've had a shift to co-power; we've had co-ownership and co-investment."

In the process of trusting there is time, breakout actors often end up defying the assumption that collaborative processes take longer or that investing time up front slows the overall project. On the contrary, they frequently demonstrate how well-run collaborative efforts reach impact faster. Ten-Squared does so in only one hundred days, even for problems that proved intractable for years when tackled with more traditional top-down approaches. The Unified New Orleans Plan that resulted from Concordia's broadly participatory process was not only the first plan to gain citywide approval and unlock desperately needed federal funds for recovery from

Hurricane Katrina, but it was created in only five months—more rapidly than either of its top-down predecessors. "It was in many ways a magical experience," recalls co-learner Steven Bingler of Concordia, "where time was suspended as the power of purpose and human relationships took over."

However, in speaking to the importance of this practice and why it works, what breakout actors emphasize most strongly has nothing to do with speed: when groups practice trusting there is enough time, group members *change the quality of their awareness*, including the quality of their presence with one another. This practice brings teams into a space in which they are able to tap into a completely different realm of imagination and insight—both individually, and as a group—than that which they can access when they are frantically keeping pace or anxiously watching the clock. Writer and philosopher Dr. Bayo Akomolafe sums this up beautifully: "[S]lowing down is not a function of speed; it's a function of awareness... [I]t's a function of presence."[5]

It is hard to see breakout possibilities when in the throes of surviving the relentless pace of the loveless economy. When groups find ways to create spaces together that help them feel outside the grip of this fevered pace, they are more able to drop into a grounded place in which they can hear the whisperings of what wants to emerge. "So slowing down seems to be a hacking of the machine," continues Dr. Akomolafe. "It... allows us to penetrate into different kinds of realities, other worlds if you will."[6]

Many breakout actors speak to this dynamic. "I think of the studies—and personal experience," reflects co-learner Bryana DiFonzo of PUSH Buffalo, "about how things like financial scarcity negatively affects people's character and ability to think, and I've had the same experience with time scarcity. When you can feel that spaciousness, it shakes you out of unhelpful, limited ways of thinking and being, and helps you see more clearly what fundamental things you should be doing. It's similar to 'work smarter, not harder.'"

Many breakout actors find that when they practice trusting there is time at work, change is sparked in their lives beyond their workplaces—creating new possibilities for how time can open up in their own lives, families, and communities. They point out that this can in turn reinforce our capacity—in both how we work and be—to stay present, clear, and attuned to care for one another and our highest aims.

. . .

CONCORDIA

"**A**LL RIGHT, folks, what do we think?" asked Bobbie Hill, as she unveiled three potential floor plans for what the old Tribune Building could one day look like. Bobbie posed this question to the over two hundred residents of Wisconsin Rapids who had shown up that evening for a community design meeting on the future Tribune Building. They were reimagining the space to best serve their local economic revitalization. This was the eighth of ten design meetings held monthly over the course of a year, facilitated by Bobbie and the Concordia team. Concordia, a New Orleans–based community-centered planning, design, and architecture firm, had been suggested to Kelly Ryan, then CEO of the Incourage Community Foundation, by a key ally. Observing the crowded room, buzzing with excitement, Kelly understood the wisdom of the recommendation.

Over the course of that year, meeting turnout had grown dramatically. While only about fifty people had turned out for the first meeting, word had quickly spread about the unusually creative—and fun!—nature of the meeting. The second meeting began with an unexpected scramble to find dozens of additional chairs and folding tables to seat the two hundred community members in attendance. Concordia's team was used to turnout growing from one meeting to the next, as word gets out about their far from business-as-usual design processes. Because of this, Concordia kicks off every meeting in a way that ensures everyone present can participate fully, even if they weren't there for past meetings.

As with every project they are invited to facilitate and design, the Concordia team was disciplined about *not* bringing any preconceptions or plans about what the design of the Tribune Building should be. Instead, they use an iterative brainstorming and refinement process with residents to uncover together a vision and detailed plan for how the new space could best serve the community. They also intentionally start all of their projects with an engagement process to assess what activities and methods will best support stakeholders to effectively and joyfully participate in the design process itself.

Now, eight meetings in, the Concordia team had welcomed everyone with their usual warmth, heart, and humor; the Incourage team then briefly grounded everyone in the broader context. After the opening, Concordia gave everyone in the room an overview of the big-picture goals of the process, how tonight's meeting fit in, and what had happened at the previous design meeting. As part of their recap, they explained what they had done to integrate residents' ideas from previous meetings into the initial floor plans to be shared that night. Bobbie explained that she and her team had cataloged all the ideas that people had shared—whether these were written, drawn, or spoken. The Concordia team had analyzed these ideas for frequency and similarity, tracked the specific design features that came up, then synthesized all of this information into three different scenarios—which she would now share with the group.

Bobbie paused before turning on the projector. "These are just initial attempts to turn what y'all are saying into possible designs. But we always get a lot of parts wrong," said Bobbie emphatically. "So please know that these are just a starting place, and together we're going to be going through a process to help us figure out what we may want to throw out entirely, and what we may want to keep refining."

When the projector's beam of light revealed three renderings for a completely reimagined Tribune Building—each depicting specific uses and activities inspired by residents' ideas—you could have heard a pin drop in the packed meeting hall. It was not only the elegance and professionalism of the diagrams that captivated people or being able to see for the first time what the space could be. What was perhaps most mesmerizing for many in the room was beholding their own ideas being taken so seriously, and heard so deeply, that they were now reflected in vivid detail in these diagrams.

Ben Joosten, a high school junior at the time, was one of the people in that meeting. "I guess a lot of us weren't used to our ideas being taken seriously, and you know, having a big process like this act on people's ideas," Ben shares. "That's when I realized that this process really was different. It *really* was going to be about residents designing and deciding together."

Bobbie turned off the projector and let everyone know that each table would have a large printout of the floor plans. She invited each group to start with just thinking about the basic floor plan, before getting to the details. Each group discussed, ranked, and described their top choice of the three floor plan options and/or described alternative recommendations they might have. Every small group had a "table sheet" to work from with clear graphics and sections to help group members organize their ideas. In less than two minutes, the room transformed from a spellbound crowd into a noisy sea of animated conversations with drawing and note-taking happening at every table.

Later that evening, Bobbie introduced the second and final activity of the meeting with a smile; it was time to dive into some "fun details." In their small groups, residents chose design elements, such as an aquarium or a fireplace, to furnish their floor plan. As in the first activity, each small group had a table sheet with graphics to guide them: the Concordia team had listed all the design elements that Wisconsin Rapids residents had suggested at the previous meeting, along with pricing for each element (which Concordia team members had researched). Each group also received a hypothetical budget to spend on their design element choices.

"It became clearer to folks which elements were important enough to the community that they were willing to spend their money on it," shares Bobbie. "For example, though it would be expensive to install and maintain, residents highly prioritized having a fireplace in the building. Many residents wanted a water feature, but overall residents felt that they weren't willing to spend the money that it would require to install and maintain." With all the information and constraints on the table, residents were invited into a process of self-determining how best to use available resources to meet their own and their community's needs. By the end of the evening, everyone in the room had grappled with tough choices and learned about their neighbors' priorities for the future space. Many groups had even brainstormed brilliant new ideas, with some revising their earlier thinking and finding ways to satisfy both constraints and aspirations.

While the reconstruction of the Tribune Building has not yet happened due to a series of frustrating hurdles and funding delays, many participants share that they still look back fondly at the community design process as an experience that awakened their sense of agency in shaping the future of their city. The process also made an impact on the Concordia team: the experience of getting to know so many residents and working together toward such a visionary plan inspired the team to bring in new tools and techniques. A decade after the design meetings took place, Bobbie and her Concordia colleagues identify the Tribune project as a turning point in sharpening their work. Bobbie elaborates, "At that time, our vision for what it takes to prototype, and what it means to have a meeting that is respectful, and all the little things that are important, had all been iterated and in place for quite some time already. But the tools we use—graphics, computer programs and software, and methods for integrating many points of feedback on a prototype—all those kinds of things really took a huge leap through what we did with the Tribune project."

Concordia's former team member Connor McManus agrees: "The Tribune project was kind of a new iteration in terms of the tools that we were using. The past two years of COVID have been a new transformation, because we have had to completely shift the tool set to an online setting and rethink... how we're trying to bring the same intent with just a completely different set of tools to do these engagement meetings."

Regardless of tools and technicalities, every process Bobbie has participated in over the years has prompted the same awareness in team members and residents alike: upon sharing an initial idea and then refining it through prototyping, "We'll probably realize," says Bobbie, "that our idea needs some tweaking. And then what we've just done there is quickly move ourselves from big pie-in-the-sky ideas to refining them down to what will actually work—and work best." Whether in small groups or rooms packed with two hundred people, Concordia and many breakout actors have learned that inviting participants to join in the shaping and reshaping of ideas—before all the details have been worked out—is key to unlocking innovation that transforms rather than reinforces the status quo.

CHAPTER 10

PROTOTYPE EARLY AND OFTEN

L EARNING ABOUT Concordia's approach to resident-led design sparked a realization that profoundly influenced our research. While many business-as-usual organizations are increasingly using elements of collaborative design when engaging with clients, community members, and other stakeholders, quite often this engagement still means sharing predetermined scenarios already passed through multiple rounds of tweaking and technical review behind the scenes, before getting feedback from external stakeholders. Too often it is unclear how stakeholder input informed the presented scenarios, if at all, and often it is too late in the process to incorporate substantial feedback. What made Concordia's approach stand out was their commitment, rigor, and creative practice of inviting participants into a process often hidden from public view: the development and refinement of the options—or prototypes—being considered in the first place.

A prototype is a draft, model, mock-up, or a verbal description of a proposed idea, which can be presented for others' consideration. Prototyping is testing out that idea with other people and gathering their feedback, and then refining or transforming the idea into a next version based on what was learned together. It is an iterative process: a draft or model reflecting initial thinking—the best first guess, so to speak—is refined step by step, until the weaknesses and opportunities identified by those sharing feedback have been addressed.

Concordia and other breakout actors demonstrate an approach to prototyping that enables refinement of ideas in response to what stakeholders consider most important for viability and success; this way of prototyping is also at the heart of what sparks breakout innovation.

> **Prototyping early and often** is the practice of sharing and testing ideas at each step of a process. Prototyping early means that from the very beginning of working together, assumptions are tested and space is allowed to course-correct and refine before ideas are finalized or launched. Prototyping early and often means that along the way, there is transparency about the ways in which feedback and ideas from colleagues, collaborators, and other stakeholders has been assessed and integrated.

Shifting how we understand prototyping

This practice may sound familiar to many; the concept central to prototyping has firmly taken hold within the world of startups, tech, and design in recent years. A focus on prototyping is the cornerstone of the hugely influential lean startup methodology from entrepreneur and author Eric Ries's bestselling book, *The Lean Startup*.[1] The lean startup approach advocates testing ideas early with clients and end-users in "minimal viable product" form—the simplest, least costly format in which to test an idea effectively. Iterations are made based on crucial early feedback long before massive investment in a new product launch. The lean approach is enormously effective and cost-saving. It's also common sense: a tested product yields better results than one that goes from idea to fully built and launched without being shared with potential users. If one's assumptions are off the mark, sunk costs can be so large that they tank the whole enterprise.

As co-learner Enoch Elwell says, a key concept of prototyping is "the notion of starting small. It's about creating as quickly as possible the smallest effort iteration that is useful for testing, but not polished and perfected." And as co-learner Maggie Nichols puts it, "It's about failing early to win in the long run."

Breakout actors embrace this lean approach, and they take the practice of prototyping to a new level. Their approach is set apart by a spirit of accountability and peership: everyone involved in the process not only tests out the ideas and shares feedback, they also share in determining next steps. Breakout actors also practice prototyping internally in their teams, organizations, and workplaces. Following this ethos supports groups in being courageous, embracing uncertainty, and sharing accountability and a sense of ownership for what they are creating together.

Whether with their team or with circles of stakeholders connected to a breakout actor's work, the prototypes they use can be simple; even a hand-drawn sketch or thoughtful conversation will do. But breakout actors always put utmost effort into the ways they assess these prototypes and collectively determine a wise way forward. They continually and intentionally create space for this vital learning—a space in which everyone feels free to share ideas, however incomplete or imperfect, that may contain a crucial starting point. They also feel free to question, welcome in voices uniquely able to foresee where an idea could falter, and brainstorm what else might be possible. With this brave process and deep relational care, breakout actors are able to realize together the next best step and move in leaps and bounds from prototyping to building powerfully grounded breakout realities.

What does prototyping early and often look like?

Breakout actors use a wide variety of prototypes—from a phone conversation with a client to invite their ideas on a new potential offering to a top-notch graphically designed rendering. However, there are clear commonalities in how they prototype. These include:

- Testing basic assumptions before beginning,
- Working together to synthesize learnings and decide next steps, and
- Replacing perfectionism with a culture of learning.

Testing basic assumptions before beginning

Prototyping in the loveless economy is often driven by an underlying inquiry into which version of a potential solution will be most successful. Do people like version A or version B? While prototyping in this way is informative, breakout actors engage prototyping long before they arrive at specific options for an outcome. They ask one another questions such as "These are the goals that we think should guide our project. Are these indeed the right goals, or do you feel they should be different?" Or "We think the main problem that we need to address together is this. Do you agree that this is the priority problem?"

Co-learner Katherine Tyler Scott discusses the importance of assessing whether the right questions are being asked when entering any planning and design process: "It's not the answer; it's often the questions you have to ask to get the answer" that determines whether the work starts off in a good way. The Concordia team often tests their "plan for the plan" by first gathering feedback on the design for the overall planning process *before* they take steps to design a physical space itself. Participants of the patient-powered research initiative Heart Research Alliance emphasize that its success stemmed from its focus on gauging patients' priorities about what research questions should be studied. This enabled researchers to identify the best questions and refine them *before* initiating research.

"Assume you are wrong," shares co-learner John Ikerd with a smile. "Too often, we are so sure we are right that we are unwilling to admit that we made a mistake until it is too late to correct it. Assuming we are wrong helps to offset whatever biases we may be bringing in." Regular prototyping with this spirit of humility and openness can be a way to stay attuned to what is emerging and evolving, rather than staying locked in our own beliefs.

> **Tip: Gather feedback through individual and group reflection.**
> Breakout actors note that different information is available when engaging people individually for their feedback (such as giving them the opportunity to review the prototype on their own and write up or verbally share their thoughts on what works and what could improve) and people in groups (such as sharing trends in feedback and collectively discussing). Both kinds of feedback are invaluable. Individual feedback preserves independence of thought, which is key to revealing patterns and trends in what collaborators want. Group reflection enables ideas and insights to build on what individuals share. Breakout actors find that alternating between individual

and group assessment throughout a prototyping process can be highly effective. This could be as simple as inviting people to spend five minutes reflecting in silence and individually noting any key reactions before starting a group conversation.

Working together to synthesize learnings and decide next steps

One of the biggest differences between prototyping in business as usual and the way breakout actors follow this practice is the way ideas and feedback from a prototyping session are incorporated. Do a handful of facilitators or leaders make sense of everyone's feedback and decide the next iteration? Or are the people providing that feedback also involved in deciding what to do next? Breakout actors lean toward the latter, and they skillfully work together, even in huge groups—as was the case in Wisconsin Rapids with the Tribune Building design process. Their groups become experts at synthesizing information into key insights and proposed options, as well as effective decision-making with those involved in prototyping to determine needed changes and next steps. They engage everyone involved to roll up their sleeves and work creatively to integrate many ideas into the next iteration, while also carefully tracking how the prototype evolves, so that the changes incorporated can be communicated to those who offered input.

To enable broad participation in determining what to do with input, the Concordia team uses several methods. One simple way is asking participants to share their reasoning; whether community members are proposing a new idea for the next iteration of a plan or suggesting an existing idea be removed, the Concordia team always invites participants to share why. When participants have the opportunity to articulate their reasoning and also hear from others, groups can have transparent, open discussions about what input should be incorporated into a plan, what should not make it in, and why.

Another method Concordia employs is transparently sharing any constraints in the design process. For instance, Concordia shares cost implications for specific ideas community members have suggested, along with the overall project budget, so that community members can grapple with any trade-offs needed to fit within financial constraints. They have found that when groups operate with this kind of shared awareness of the full scope of the challenge at hand, participants' ideas become even more imaginative, precise, and useful.

Over the years, co-learner Bobbie Hill has observed that transparent and collaborative prototyping enables a change in participants' mindsets from me to we. "Those kinds of shifts," shares Bobbie, "don't just happen overnight. You can't do that without having people own these recommendations and idea creation. They have to be part of the process. It becomes not just 'my idea,' but 'we're really listening to each other.'"

Tip: Differentiate between what you heard and what you're proposing. When we first started our own practice of prototyping early and often, we would present an initial idea, gather a ton of feedback, get excited about realizations inspired by that feedback, and then return to a few next iterations to decide on together. When we unveiled our next-stage prototype to the group, they met us with puzzled looks. What happened to X thing they liked in the first prototype? What did other people think about Y? Why did we do Z? We realized we needed to change how we were presenting the group with each prototype—and once we did so, it improved our prototyping sessions by leaps and bounds. The simple change was shaped by learning alongside breakout actors. Whenever we

shared new iterations, we divided the information into two cat-
egories: what we heard and what we proposed. In presenting
what we heard, we summarized the feedback quantitatively
and qualitatively. This allowed everyone to understand how
their reaction fit into the larger response to the prototype, and
it also let them learn from others' feedback. Then we outlined
what we were proposing based on the collective insights generated, and participants could react to that information as a
separate prototype, sharing what they liked and what alternatives they might recommend.

Replacing perfectionism with a culture of learning

For many breakout actors, the heart of this practice requires
releasing perfectionism and committing ourselves instead
to shared reflection and learning as we go. Co-learner
Antionette D. Carroll elaborates, "When we think about this
idea of being perfect or this idea of 'I've officially accom-
plished everything and nothing needs to shift or change,' it's
many times perpetuating a lot of the systems that have been
based on exclusion and inequity."

Breakout actors share that unlearning perfectionism takes
time and vulnerability, especially in the business-as-usual
culture that values speed and optimizing profit at all costs.
When teams step out of perfectionism and into a culture
of learning, they reawaken a sense of self-determination—
a sense that it is possible to continually iterate to create worlds
boldly distinct from the status quo. Failing and then prototyping out of failure creates a team environment conducive
to taking risks, learning, and co-creating the best possible
solutions—ones that address and undo pervasive inequities.

This practice is effective when the way mistakes and failure are perceived changes. As KA McKercher articulates it,
the practice includes "building resilience for the reality that
while some ideas won't work and will need to be repurposed

or discarded, that need not negatively impact the self-esteem of the person who suggested the idea." Indeed, they point out, "Failed ideas make great compost."[2]

Breakout actors support their teams and groups in making this shift by unpacking attitudes about perfection and failure. These discussions can be revelatory for many people; they realize that business as usual, in which we wait to share an idea until it feels sufficiently polished and bulletproof, often comes from an attitude of perfectionism that is deeply embedded in constructs of white supremacy. A sense of obligation to exhibit perfection is one of the attributes identified as part of white supremacy culture[3] by Dr. Tema Okun. Many breakout actors also note how the origins of the loveless economy continue to influence workplace norms and expectations, including what is considered to be perfect. Achieving business-as-usual success can mean feeling as though one has to get it all right all of the time, or perhaps work harder and appear more polished than one's peers in order to be treated with the same respect. Indeed, the demand for perfectionism in business as usual is so pervasive that it's difficult to disentangle the idea of what it means to be professional, or a good worker, from always being correct and speaking only when fully prepared and able to share comprehensively. All of these experiences affect how teams work together.

Breakout actors point out that this obsession with perfection is not an innately human trait; in fact, as Dr. Okun and many breakout actors note, it is a deviation from how many groups have approached things for millennia. Realizing this helps to spark a sense of choice. Perfectionism can be unlearned together, while also creating a culture in which learning, or failing forward, is valued—and even celebrated.

Letting go of perfectionism is key to being able to catch problems early on via prototyping, well before implementation. Breakout actors note it's important to prime all collaborators to adopt a prototyping mindset from the very beginning of a project. Breakout actors remind group members that the purpose of presenting an early prototype is to intentionally surface problems when it is still easy to make significant course corrections or even go back to the drawing board. Prototypes often need not be fully fleshed-out renderings. They can instead be imperfect offerings perfectly suited for sparking insight and guidance from collaborators on a good next step.

This practice, like all the practices, is about balance. In that same spirit of anti-perfectionism, teams need to create boundaries around how many prototyping iterations they will do. Since there's no such thing as perfect, at some point a judgment call does need to be made as to when the design will be called "good enough" for implementation. Then feedback loops can move into the realm of evaluation rather than prototyping.

When teams fully embrace this ethos, prototyping early and often shows up in everything they do. At Thunder Valley Community Development Corporation, for example, prototyping is deeply ingrained in the team's ways of working and being. "Everything we do at Thunder Valley," shares co-learner Tatewin Means, "even down to the constructing of a community, is about prototyping." Her colleague, deputy director and co-learner Lynn Cuny, reflects on an example of their team prototyping internally:

> Everything that we do is adaptive. An example that comes to mind is our directors' meetings. We have all of our initiative directors meet once a month. Before, some of the organizational leadership staff would be there to hear the ways that the directors were working through things, and peer-mentoring each other. Now we've moved away from

leadership being there, and instead we're just giving directors a chance to be there and find new ways to coexist, to do some of the same events, and meet different objectives for each initiative together. It's just really giving them the chance to liberate, to come together and have that peer mentorship. This is something that was tested, and it seems to be working well.

In a way, observes Tatewin, you could think of every single initiative of Thunder Valley CDC as a prototype. "And why is it a prototype? It's a prototype for us because we refine it continually. That's why we emphasize so much evaluation— so that iterative processes happen naturally and organically, where we're reviewing, we're evaluating ourselves, and we're making improvements," she explains. The Thunder Valley CDC team is clear that this way of operating is not only smart, it's also liberatory. "This is us living our own sovereignty, our own liberation," shares Tatewin. "It can be different for different communities. But this is a way you can exercise your self-determination, right?"

> **Tip: Practice prototyping internally to build a culture of learning.** Within teams, prototyping can be used to test out a new approach to staff meetings, a new annual process for developing next year's budget, or even an out-of-the-box idea for a team retreat. Breakout actors note that when teams adopt a spirit of trying something despite knowing the results will be imperfect, they are better able to learn and improve together. As they continually innovate, they deepen the ways work can break free from what isn't working in the status quo.

Prototyping early and often in action

Breakout actor Institute for Native Pacific Education and Culture (INPEACE) embraced an ethos of prototyping to successfully launch the Kaulele Project, an Indigenous pop-up science center. For the Native Hawaiian staff leading INPEACE's work with children, youth, and families in predominantly Native Hawaiian communities of Oʻahu, Kauaʻi, Molokaʻi, and Hawaiʻi islands, prototyping is nothing new. "Of course, we ask our community members of all ages—from the youngest keiki [child] to our elder kupuna [grandparent]— what would make our work most valuable to them and what ideas and advice they have for our team," shares co-learner Maile Keliʻipio-Acoba, CEO of INPEACE.

After years of successful work in education through its innovative early childhood programs that engage both children and caregivers, as well as its many well-loved programs in middle schools and post-secondary programs, INPEACE realized there was an important gap in educational outcomes. Testing data from schools showed that students in the communities INPEACE serves were struggling in STEM (science, technology, engineering, and mathematics). The INPEACE team wanted to address this need—and to do so in a way that was uniquely Hawaiian.

"For thousands of years," shares Maile, "Native Hawaiian seafarers have successfully utilized systematic observation of their environment to traverse vast expanses of open ocean and thrive on the most remote islands on Earth." The INPEACE team wanted to bring to life STEM concepts in ways that would not only support students to thrive at school and in future work opportunities, but also instill in them a profound sense of pride for the scientific knowledge systems that Native Hawaiians and Pacific Islanders perfected over millennia. The idea of the Kaulele Project was born to serve as a bridge between the values and concepts of 'ike kupuna (traditional knowledge) and STEM concepts and technology.

Initially, the staff dreamed grand visions of a world-class museum. But once they rolled up their sleeves to start turning this vision into reality, through iterative prototyping, their vision for success started to shift—from a traditional museum to something quite different, and unique to the priorities of INPEACE's community. "We began by generating a series of ideas for specific exhibits—such as one about constellations in the night sky, or an experiential exhibit on the creation of kapa cloth from the fibers of the wauke plant," explains Maile. "And we took these ideas to students in schools and asked which exhibits they would most like to see." From all the input from students as well as an advisory group of community members, many points of clarity emerged. One major finding from the community feedback was that, rather than trying to fundraise for a building and permanent museum, the right next step was to launch the Kaulele Project as a pop-up museum with traveling exhibits that could go to schools and community centers across the state. Additionally, "It became clear to us," shares Maile, "that as part of exhibit design, we needed to ensure that it was grounded in mo'olelo—the traditional Hawaiian stories that serve as the conduit to pass down ancestral knowledge."

This approach not only was much easier and quicker to fund than it would have been to finance the building of an entire museum, but it also turned out to be incredibly resilient when the COVID-19 pandemic hit. Even when large gatherings were prohibited and museums were closed, community members were still able to engage with the exhibits, one ohana (family) at a time. Despite the pandemic shutdowns, INPEACE was able to prototype many different exhibits and determine which to invest in further. The initial exhibits were built in creative ways by the INPEACE team themselves, supported by family members and friends. After rounds of prototyping, INPEACE was ready to fund a collaboration with an experienced museum design firm to develop its exhibit on kapa cloth into a top-notch museum experience.

Since its launch, the exhibit has traveled to multiple locations and communities in Hawai'i and is already sparking new interests in STEM, alongside excitement for the rich traditions and knowledge held by generations of Native Hawaiians. INPEACE also received the largest grant in their organizational history from a funder who was impressed by the value of INPEACE's work to its communities.[4]

"Prototyping at each step made us confident that what we were building was of real value to our students and their families," shares Maile. The INPEACE team has its sights set on a future in which the Kaulele Project encompasses multiple exhibits traveling and rotating throughout the state and potentially nationwide, with its pop-up approach enabling Kaulele to reach even the most remote locations. In the process, INPEACE team members have been learning and honing a powerful approach for bridging Indigenous knowledge with current STEM concepts. "This is a process that we want to be able to develop in order to assist other Indigenous communities to do the same with their own mo'olelo," says Maile. By taking one step at a time, guided by the youth and families at the center of everything the organization does, the INPEACE team members are confident—like their ancestors who voyaged across the vast Pacific Ocean—that they will reach their destination.

How prototyping early and often unlocks breakout innovation

This practice is effective for several reasons. First, it taps into the collective intelligence of a diverse group to refine and improve ideas. "Nothing that makes sense on paper ever shakes out exactly that way once it's loose in a world full of real people and events," points out co-learner Bryana DiFonzo of PUSH Buffalo. "So many actions, decisions, policies, et cetera, end up having negative unintended consequences that could have been mitigated if they had done more prototyping." Speaking to the central role prototyping has played in enabling PUSH's success in expanding access to affordable green housing, along with nourishing a vibrant sense of community and civic responsibility in the city of Buffalo, Bryana reflects, "So much of our work revolves around this, and seeing the value in the learning process." Prototyping early and often dramatically enhances the learning and course-correcting a group is able to do.

Second, this practice serves as a powerful method by which to gather both correcting and reinforcing feedback. It opens the channels wide to all kinds of input. In doing so, prototyping early and often enables shared work to be informed by robust, balancing sources of information that guide it toward greater positive impact and wisdom. Rather than passively waiting for feedback to arrive, this practice is about ensuring it is invited in, at every step.

Third, the effectiveness stems from, as co-learner Brooking Gatewood says, "that sense of collective investment and buy-in and relationship-building" that is built through prototyping and "serves to strengthen the work." When prototyping is practiced in ways that deconsolidate rights to design, it does far more than sharpen ideas and prevent missteps. In contrast to loveless ways of work, where a few wield power to decide which ideas are accepted and which get scrapped, "having a lot of people involved and directly influencing solutions and decisions," explains Bobbie, "builds in public ownership and accountability." In other words, a feeling of trust and ownership of what is decided can encourage more robust support of the project's success.

Prototyping allows collaborators to engage in all steps of imagining and building together—from identifying the problem to implementing the solution—even in the more technical aspects of a process, such as drafting floor plans. Even if not everyone shares the same technical expertise, prototyping allows everyone to contribute—sharing their preferences, ideas, and lived experiences—just as meaningfully as the technical experts do.

Prototyping early and often requires humility and bravery in sharing half-baked ideas, hard work to turn input into draft possibilities, and inquiry at each step on how to improve. With this approach, the practice can make the difference between an innovation effort that generates business-as-usual results and one that leaps from brainstorming to breakout innovation.

· · ·

INNOVATION ENGINEERING

EVERY TIME the Innovation Engineering team launches its program with a new client, whether a large company or a small nonprofit, what participants share initially tends to have more to do with fear than imagination. People are afraid to speak up and share their half-baked, out-of-the-box ideas. They are nervous about even taking time away from their to-do lists to participate in seemingly unrelated exercises to spark imagination. They are worried they'll suggest something that their boss doesn't approve of. The list goes on.

"I'm hard pressed to find anybody who would look at themselves and go, 'I'm living in fear and that's why I'm not imaginative.' But the exhibits are all over the place," shares Maggie Nichols, president and CEO of Eureka! Ranch and Innovation Engineering, an innovation firm and program for businesses.

Over three decades of work with dozens of corporate and nonprofit clients across the United States, including big-name brands, Maggie and the Innovation Engineering team have noticed—and documented in thousands of participant surveys—the growing presence of fear in their clients' workplaces. "The exhibits of fear can be things like 'I'm too busy.' They are 'I couldn't possibly; I'm exhausted; I just can't go there with you.'" On the surface, these statements may seem to have nothing to do with fear, but don't be fooled; they're just a cover. Fear stops imagination and innovation in their tracks. "Fear steals all the oxygen that imagination needs to even get going. Fear makes you create an agenda for yourself that takes every minute of the day. There's no moment to step back. It feels wasteful to be imaginative. It feels frivolous. It feels like I could wander and come up empty, and that feels defeating."

Innovation Engineering is "a complete innovation operating system" for teams and enterprises, and it's also a field of study. The Innovation Engineering team is proud of the fact that all the practices they teach and tools they offer are informed by decades of research and data collection that their team has done through their work with clients.

Maggie and her team are clear what makes their approach stand out. In contrast to the business-as-usual approach to innovation—in which a handful of experts, consultants, or designers conceive a company's next big idea or breakthrough pivot—Innovation Engineering turns inward to awaken the profound capacity for imagination among every single member of a company. Their approach is also deeply rooted in transforming leadership approaches by coaching founders and leaders to shift away from a top-down approach and toward one that supports leaderful teams to thrive. Innovation Engineering is big on supporting companies in implementing systems that help entire teams to develop and share bold ideas; they also assist people on those teams in stepping into leadership roles for prototypes of ideas they're particularly passionate about, helping them move toward strategic implementation.

This approach is *very* different from the Eureka! Ranch that Doug Hall founded in 1986, as a think tank to help large companies solve big challenges. Maggie first got involved as a business student in the 1990s when the company was based on a more business-as-usual approach to innovation. "When I joined the company," recalls Maggie, "we were in the heyday of a different company every week—whether it was Nike, American Express, Walt Disney—all those." Their approach at that time, as Maggie sums up, was "So you've got a big challenge? You come to us, and we'll give you the big idea. You have to come to the clever place to do creative things—and play with Nerf guns and all the fanfare."

However, several years into Maggie's time with the company, Doug and the team began to ask some big questions about what truly meaningful forms of innovation could look like. Around 2000, Maggie and Doug were discussing the future. She remembers their most recent clients were working on innovations for "caskets, cookies, and credit cards." As they thought about what all their efforts were adding up to, Maggie says, "You had a moment to step back and kind of go like, 'Really? That's the legacy we're leaving for this world? The next low-fat Fig Newton and the next low APR?" They realized that if Eureka! Ranch continued operating in the same way, then, as Maggie puts it, "the world doesn't get better." Simultaneously, they saw tremendous potential for change by way of equipping teams to find inspiration and to create their own ideas. "So that's when the notion of innovation engineering began," explains Maggie.

They launched Innovation Engineering and reoriented their efforts to focus on fundamentally changing how innovation works, in a way that systematically deconsolidated rights to design. The mission statement is "To change the world by enabling innovation by everyone, everywhere, every day." Their approach centers on two concepts: stimulus and diversity. This includes intentionally stimulating people to help them think differently; the stimuli can be randomly generated words, findings from participants' "homework" researching questions or possibilities that they have been curious about, scanning news about a particular topic or trend, and beyond. Diversity among teams is the key ingredient that makes the ideas resulting from these stimuli add up to something groundbreaking—or, as Innovation Engineering terms it, "meaningfully unique."

But when Innovation Engineering embarked on this new direction—challenging and inviting everyone across teams and even whole enterprises to step up as innovators—Maggie says, "we started to really see the fear come out." Sometimes it was subtle; other times they experienced "toxic cultures and terrible things" at client companies in which people were afraid they'd be fired immediately for sharing an idea that didn't land well with higher-ups, or if they were viewed as misusing their time imagining rather than getting things done. "We used to have an assumption," shares Maggie, "that the critical ingredients for invention were stimulus, diversity, and fun. And then in that decade, we were like, 'Fun is too superficial. Fear as the denominator is actually the real deal. People are scared, and, okay, well, big ideas are scary. So how do you make people not scared?"

Maggie and her team have found that making changes in the workplace to address root causes of participants' fears around sharing unorthodox ideas—and subsequently implementing practices and systems to nurture their expression—catalyzes people to share boldly, initiate idea-testing with enthusiasm, and take steps to realize those ideas. Maggie is passionate about encouraging enterprises of all stripes and sizes to overcome fear and build workplace environments that embolden everyone on the team to fully express their imaginations and rights to design. She also facilitates development of new skills and robust systems that will stay with people and their companies for the long haul. "If you build a system for imagining," says Maggie, explaining Innovation Engineering's focus on systems, "you can bake it into how you work, and into life. You can make it a bigger part of what you do."

These elements, plus encouraging enterprises to shift how leadership occurs across their teams, have added up to remarkable results for Innovation Engineering. While there is an array of impressive statistics demonstrating the value of the company's packages for clients, there is one so outstanding that the team actually stopped mentioning it publicly because people didn't believe it. "When our team looked at our most recent training class where students had well-documented projects, we found the average projected value of the innovations from their projects was about 250 times what they had spent on the course, with even the lowest value in the set exceeding three times what they had spent on the course," Maggie explains.

Where is this financial value coming from? Sometimes it comes from big ideas for new products or services that team members developed through their participation in the Innovation Engineering program; this attracts new funding, clients, and investment. But most often the breakthroughs people had (which they value so strongly!) were to do with changes in *how they work* among their team and enterprise. When people are invited and have the opportunity to innovate ways to make their enterprise more successful, it turns out they most often identify processes that they believe could be far better. "Eighty percent of the time, people are working on process improvements," shares Maggie. "This shows how lots of our ways of work are... broken."

The high financial return that clients experience from participating in Innovation Engineering's programs is all the more striking because, when it comes to innovation training courses in business as usual, Maggie notes, "the expectation is that the majority of students never even apply the new skills they learn." In contrast, Innovation Engineering's approach enables each participant to determine what they most want to innovate in their current work—and to have the agency to immediately apply and enact the new ideas they and their colleagues generate. This means that the value surpasses even the impressive quantitative data that the Innovation Engineering team has documented. "Participants reflect that it's also about getting confidence to overcome their fear," emphasizes Maggie, "and this is key to what makes the training and experience so valuable on a balance sheet, but also in the culture and mindset it creates."

When people take initiative to innovate the processes by which they and their teams function, the results have far-reaching benefits. "It's not another widget that comes off the line. System improvement and process stuff is the kind of thing that shifts, that stays," says Maggie, based on the data Innovation Engineering has collected over time. And the lasting benefits are not only monetary. The Innovation Engineering facilitators regularly receive post-training feedback about the personal transformations participants experience; they find more ease, joy, and meaning in their work and often in their lives outside work too. One participant shared that the changes in his workplace had such a positive impact on his life that it inspired him and his spouse to become parents, something they had deeply desired but that had felt untenable previously, amid the demands of their work. Being parents in the way they wanted to now felt entirely possible, even joyful. Maggie treasures the feedback that so many people over the years have shared; she calls them love letters.

It turns out that through their own "meaningfully unique" approach, Innovation Engineering enables workplaces to transform into environments of free-flowing imagination, action, and leadership—and in so doing, they not only make work feel less scary; they make it feel more beloved.

CHAPTER 11

THEY MAY TRY TO STOP YOU

IN THE PURSUIT of the seven practices, some breakout actors experience resistance. While, as we discussed in Chapter 7, Seek Difference, the presence of resistance can be a part of a healthy human system, we use the term differently in this chapter. Here, we discuss two particular forms of resistance that breakout actors encounter, which they report can feel surprising and can sometimes even thwart a group's efforts. Given the frequency and degree of this resistance, we would be remiss not to provide a deeper exploration of what you might come up against while implementing the seven practices, how it most commonly takes shape, and why it might be happening.

We noted in our research that resistance to breakout actors' efforts most often happens when a breakout initiative, company, or organization is on the verge of transformational change and when they are receiving positive public recognition. In fact, some breakout actors have come to view such resistance as a signpost signaling their innovations are successfully breaking out of the status quo.

External backlash and internalized doubt

The resistance faced by the breakout actors in our co-learning community most commonly came in two forms: external backlash and internalized doubt.

In our research, approximately 20 percent of breakout actors experienced notable external backlash.[1] It took many forms: a quick shutdown of an initiative that was considered incredibly successful by those involved, a sudden firing with no stated cause, a retraction of funds, or even elaborate sabotage. This happens often when groups least expect it. The backlash can be directed at entire initiatives, as well as individuals within projects.

In an example that we've been asked to share anonymously, the staff of a grant-making family foundation was collaborating with the foundation's grantees to reimagine how the foundation worked. They addressed everything from how the staff conducted meetings with potential grantees to a new community-driven process, which would identify future groups to fund. A couple of years into this transformation, all collaborative efforts came to an abrupt halt. They were shut down by the board of trustees, who were all family members of the founder. Despite the family members' prior and consistent support for what the staff and grantees were building together, they suddenly notified the team that every staff position would cease to exist within a few weeks and that the family would be taking over operations, including the selection of future grantees. This reversal of support occurred as the staff's new collaboratively created practices were being heralded in their field as raising the bar for effective philanthropy. In a matter of weeks, everything the staff and dozens of grantee groups had worked together to build was dismantled.

Throughout all of the cases in our research, those who initiated such backlash were accustomed to having control over the welfare of and decisions for a larger collective. They were used to a consolidation of rights to design. For the grant-making foundation, the family was used to having complete power over how the foundation's money benefited others. Rather than engaging the stakeholders most affected or involving them in decision-making, these individuals were instead accustomed to deciding things on behalf of those stakeholders.

Backlash from those who currently enjoy consolidated rights to design, however, only makes up one type of resistance that breakout efforts meet. In our research, a subtler type of resistance came in the form of internalized doubt arising in the people involved in the enterprises and who do not necessarily benefit from the status quo remaining as it is.

Breakout actors shared that sometimes resistance bubbles up from their closest collaborators—or even from themselves. Co-learner Maggie Nichols and the team at Innovation Engineering have substantial data on this phenomenon. "With every single team we've worked with since 1990, at the start we invite them to do a pre-assessment. It's all about their perception of their ability to innovate," explains Maggie. Team members answer a series of questions on topics such as how they perceive the need and urgency for innovation at their company, the degree to which creative ideas are welcomed, and whether they feel they have the resources and support to succeed in their own work. From Innovation Engineering's years of data, they've learned that individuals within teams are often hesitant to voice or act on their ideas. This is particularly true of workplaces where workers believe that nothing other than *what is* will be given any credence or attention. They've found this work culture to be pervasive.

In our research, we've also seen other forms of internalized doubt that limit what groups do, even when there isn't necessarily a work culture that people perceive as discouraging new ideas. For instance, some people report feeling nervous the first time they are invited to join together as peers with people they perceive as different from them in terms of class, race, gender, professional background, or ability. Others—when faced with the prospect of sharing decision-making power, for example—worry that everything will fall apart if they release control. Some people share feelings of confusion: will they still have a place in the work once change happens?

We also personally brushed up against people's trepidations. When we broached the topic of expanding who is involved in decision-making, people not only often vented about the negative experiences they'd had with, for instance, consensus processes gone awry, but they also sometimes looked at us confused, offering, "What about the tragedy of the commons?" or "... the dangers of mob mentality?" Sometimes they asked us—half-jokingly or quite seriously—whether we were communists.

The hesitations people express are varied, but we believe they reveal common currents throughout the loveless economy that are central to what keeps us perpetuating it. We believe the majority of us are unsure whether there will be anything on the other side to catch us if we break out of the status quo. Breakout actors note that those resisting may often feel trepidation sparked by a fear that what was about to happen would ultimately not work.

We've all been trained to perpetuate the lovelessness, even as we suffer varied impacts from it. The constructed separations and otherizations of business as usual reinforce that a few must act upon the many, that it would be dangerous for all of us to decide and create for ourselves. This belief is so pervasive in business as usual, that many of us reinforce these constructs every day without thinking about them as anything but ordinary.

Designing *for*
....

As an outgrowth of the consolidation of rights to design, in business as usual it is considered normal for individuals and groups to decide and implement on behalf of stakeholders.

Loveless ways of work are often about speaking for, creating for, marketing toward, or managing on behalf of—all of which in practice uphold a conceptual notion that there is a homogeneous other, a subject apart from the person doing the action whose (unchosen) role is to receive it. Such dynamics are not just embedded within the work of profit-seeking multinational corporations. Nonprofits, government agencies, and volunteer groups also replicate separations in these ways, stunting innovation. While it may seem obvious that an action such as extracting both creates and benefits from separations between the actor and the subject, we may lose sight of the fact that many other actions do so, too, including in fields dedicated to "helping."

Indeed, socially minded organizations or businesses that set out to have a positive impact are not immune to consolidating rights to design. We have been struck by how often efforts—across nonprofits, social enterprise businesses, international development projects, and philanthropic institutions—work in ways that implicitly infantilize, dehumanize, ignore, and even fear those they are trying to benefit.[2] Within business as usual, it is easy for a complex mosaic of individual people to be othered by the homogenizing category of "beneficiary."

Designing programs, policies, products, and services *for* stakeholders who are not in the room, or who might be consulted but do not have decision-making authority or the ability to share in the benefits from their insights, actively reinforces the separations that keep us locked in business as usual. However well intentioned, such efforts reinforce the consolidation of rights to design.

These ways of work have deep roots. For several hundred years, those who benefit from the status quo of consolidated influence have intentionally spread the false supremacist idea that some people are naturally superior to others and should be entrusted with decisions that affect everyone. Historian and author Dr. Heather Cox Richardson sheds light on ways this notion has been repeatedly promoted throughout US history, always with the goal of compelling people to believe that everything operates best when "controlled by a few wealthy, educated, well-connected, and usually white and male leaders." Dr. Richardson explains that "the argument goes that they are the only ones with the skills, the insight, and the experience to make good decisions about national policy, particularly economic policy. And it is important that wealth concentrate in their hands, since they will act as its stewards, using it wisely in lump sums, while if the workers who produce wealth get control of it, they will fritter it away."[3]

Tactics that aim to enforce this ideology have been alive in the United States since its earliest days and are continually created through white supremacy, classism, and patriarchy, among other exclusionary ideologies. In 1858, for instance, South Carolina planter and US Senator James Henry Hammond argued before the Senate that, as Dr. Richardson sums up, "the South had figured out the best government in the world. It had put a few wealthy, educated, well-connected men in power over everyone else—which he called 'mudsills'—

workers who produced the capital that supported society, but had little direction or ambition and had to be controlled by their superiors."[4] His assertion and the fact that this view was shared by many in power at the time reveal the degree to which the perspective that only a few are capable of designing society has long been embedded in the United States.

Alongside arguments that most humans are incapable of managing shared resources, there exists a pervasive ideology that those with consolidated influence in an extractive economy are morally superior or justified in this act because others—particularly those considered less fortunate—are not able to manage for themselves. For instance, in the late nineteenth century in the United States, as Gilded Age elites began to amass private fortunes of the scale previously seen only in the hands of monarchs, new ways of work developed for the purpose of "giving back" to the very communities from which they were extracting wealth.[5] This reinforced the notions of an other, who could not manage on their own and from whom it was justifiable to extract. An apparatus of enterprises like nonprofits, charities, philanthropic entities, and later socially conscious businesses developed and perpetuated such a separation by aiming to save, uplift, complete, and otherwise help such persons rather than engage in mutualistic partnership. The charitable aims of such projects may have sometimes come from authentic intentions to give back, but because these efforts were—and are still today—often based on the premise that beneficiaries are less capable than those "helping," the projects hoarded rights to design while ignoring root causes of inequity, such as community wealth extraction.

Over the years, alarmingly explicit exclusionary arguments have resurfaced, including recently. In spring 2021, *National Review* correspondent Kevin D. Williamson published a piece suggesting that "the [US] republic would be better served by having fewer—but better—voters."[6] Representatives, he offers, "are people who act in other people's interests" and know what is best for them. Similarly, US Republican lobbyists Mike Solon and Bill Greene wrote an opinion piece in the *Wall Street Journal* in summer 2021 advocating that governance by specialists—whom they literally call "somebodies"—allows the rest of us, who they refer to as "nobodies," freedom not to trouble ourselves to pay attention or participate.[7]

Through conversations with breakout actors, we learned that the conditioning of business as usual instructs people to be unsure of our collective ability to survive *without* a consolidation of rights to design in the hands of a "capable" few. Breakout actors know that, of course, subject-matter experts and technical expertise are key. There are countless scenarios in which the expertise of, say, a surgeon or electrician or lawyer is crucial in determining the best course of action. The challenge arises if everyone else is assumed to be "nobodies" rather than thoughtful peers who may also have vital insights.

Breakout actors point out that we have been conditioned to believe we live in a world of scarcity where things must be carefully managed toward one end: productivity. Many of us have learned to fear entrusting one another with our collective well-being—believing that if we share power, bad things will happen. Order will devolve into chaos. People will pursue only what's good for them in the short term and all will be lost.

Because of this, when faced with emerging breakout innovation, people sometimes feel a trepidation sparked by disbelief in humanity's collective abilities. We believe this is often the place from which resistance arises.

Many of us have been taught to believe in the idea of tyranny of the masses—that humans will naturally devolve into chaos and violence without a select few in charge who hold consolidated rights to design. Such notions go back centuries and were in part popularized by seventeenth-century philosopher Thomas Hobbes. He argued in his book *Leviathan* that human nature was a war of all against all;[8] that ungoverned, there was no guarantee that any two people would not try to kill each other for their resources. If humans aren't kept in check by strict rule, he warned, "there is no place for industry; because the fruit thereof is uncertain... And the life of man, solitary, poore, nasty, brutish, and short."[9]

A similar story was told through the concept of the tragedy of the commons, which began as a particularly sticky article in *Science*, published in 1968 by ecologist Dr. Garrett Hardin. The premise was that if left to our collective care, the commons—our collective resources, such as fisheries, the air we breathe, or a community garden we share—will naturally end in ruins, due to human nature. Dr. Hardin argued that people will act independently according to their own self-interests and counter to the common good, which leads to the inevitable depletion of the resource. Like many of those promoting consolidated control over common welfare, Dr. Hardin had an agenda. According to the Southern Poverty Law Center, for almost sixty years Dr. Hardin "used his authority as a respected, if controversial, ecologist at the University of California, Santa Barbara, to integrate nativist attitudes toward race and immigration into the American environmentalist movement. [He] based many of his arguments on racist, pseudo-scientific assertions."[10]

Dr. Hardin's claims, along with other assertions that humans lack the ability to collaboratively manage shared welfare, have largely been debunked. Among the many researchers who have disproven such arguments, Dr. Elinor Ostrom stands out. In 2009, she won a Nobel Prize in Economic Sciences for her decades of research demonstrating the efficacy of highly sophisticated practices employed by peoples and communities around the globe to manage the commons that sustain them. What "The Tragedy of the Commons" and other arguments overlook is that, as historian E.P. Thompson wrote, "commoners were not without commonsense."[11] Even Dr. Hardin publicly retracted his thesis in the early 1990s, though its ideas had already become part of the public consciousness.[12]

In the book *A Paradise Built in Hell*, historian and National Book Critic's Circle Award–winning author Rebecca Solnit illuminates evidence that further calls into question the basic premises of Hobbes and Dr. Hardin. Solnit turned to the field of disaster sociology to draw upon studies and first-hand accounts from five major disasters, spanning a century and multiple geographies, starting with the 1906 earthquake in San Francisco. Solnit's work shows humans' propensity to become the opposite of a Hobbesian mob when order evaporates. Across the board, what she found empirically demonstrates that, in such times, the predominant response among people impacted is to step up to assist one another in altruistic ways and self-organize to create neighborhood societies of cooperation and mutual aid.[13]

Again and again, research demonstrates that—despite what we may have been told about human nature—when we work in partnership to manage our collective welfare, we do not devolve into self-interested chaos; rather, we have the capacity to organize ourselves into sophisticated systems that prioritize ethical care and mutual thriving.

The imagination deficit

The loveless economy is rife with narratives that this is not possible, and that there are no viable alternatives to business as usual. Such narratives make some people feel that when it comes to the economy, nothing else is worth trying, and that if businesses and organizations were to balance power dynamics, the result would be chaos and ruin.

A near-religious fervor exists, particularly in the United States, in the belief that the current loveless economy is fundamentally immovable, and that everything else possible has already been tried. This fervor has left our collective economic imagination significantly atrophied from underuse. Not only do people struggle to believe that alternative ways of work might be possible, but it's also hard for them to even *imagine* what those other ways could be. We observed that some breakout actors, faced with the imminent prospect of breakout innovation, actually struggle to believe in their own successes, which they are experiencing firsthand. It can seem so impossible that what they are experiencing could be true.

And yet the reality is that not only can other ways of work and other economies exist, they already do.

The existence of alternative economies

Economies that prioritize partnership and interdependence have existed for millennia.[14] For instance, in Indigenous societies worldwide, "wealth is understood as having enough to share, and the practice for dealing with abundance is to give it away," explains Dr. Robin Wall Kimmerer in her 2020 essay, "The Serviceberry: An Indigenous Economy of Abundance." "In fact, status is determined not by how much one accumulates, but by how much one gives away." In such economies, the currency *is* relationship, "which is expressed as gratitude, as interdependence and the ongoing cycles of reciprocity." Rather than benefiting only a small few, such economies are designed to nurture "the community bonds which enhance mutual well-being; the economic unit is 'we' rather than 'I,' as all flourishing is mutual."[15] In the Americas, a diverse array of economies flourished for thousands of years, many organized around the principles and currency that Dr. Kimmerer speaks to, each unique to the landscape to which it is inextricably tied.[16]

Within—and in resistance to—the loveless economy, there have always been alternative economic approaches that businesses and organizations took to step out of business as usual and lean into humans' natural abilities for mutualism. For instance, in her 2014 book *Collective Courage,* political economist and City University of New York professor Dr. Jessica Gordon Nembhard explores many instances in which Black Americans have come together to build alternative economic communities around values of mutual support and opportunity. There is a rich history of African American cooperatives beginning as early as the 1780s, often formed as a response to exclusion from white-owned spaces. Many such cooperatives continue today, and as Dr. Gordon Nembhard's work offers, the past can present opportunities for self-reliance in the future.[17] There is also a vibrant movement of Indigenous-led businesses, funds, financial entities, and networks building on the work of previous generations to keep alternative ways of economic thinking and practice alive. Their work strengthens economies rooted in a diversity of Indigenous values and lifeways.

Thousands of groups have created successful alternatives to extractive economic practice and consider themselves a part of a burgeoning "next economy movement." Whether such groups call themselves regenerative businesses, part of the sharing economy, worker-owned, community-owned, decentralized autonomous organizations, double-bottom-line enterprises, B Corps, co-ops, zebras,[18] or community-wealth-building enterprises, people continue to prove that there is an abundance of viable and alluring alternatives to business as usual and that we don't have to live in a loveless economy.

If there have been and currently are alternatives to the loveless economy, why do we so rarely hear about them? Why are they not emblazoned in our minds as living examples to expand our imagination about what could be possible for our own lives?

We believe the loveless economy is perpetuated, in part, by so many of us not knowing alternatives can and do exist. If we did know, more of us might start working toward something better. Indeed, for over four hundred years, there have been intentional and systematic efforts to dismantle and continually erode economies that stand in the way of unfettered extraction. The fabric of countless societies has been purposefully weakened to gain global domination and access to resources, while obliterating the visible and alluring alternatives to a system focused on the pursuit of excessive wealth.

Although this kind of systemic destruction has roots in diverse geographies and periods of history, it was in the actions of European elites beginning around the fifteenth century that one sees the subjugating practices that would, in particular, become the roots of business as usual. At that time in Europe, a series of consequential systemic changes disrupted feudalism; these changes included the bubonic plague and mass insurrections,[19] both of which contributed to shifting labor patterns.[20] Feudalism as an economic system had allowed the elite to extract resources from the majority, so the disruptions left European aristocrats scrambling to keep wealth and rights to design consolidated.

"Europe's 1 percent found their share of the economic surplus contracting," explain authors Dr. Jason W. Moore and Dr. Raj Patel. In response, ruling classes devised new methods to recapture wealth and continue growing it. "What followed was an epochal transition: one that reinvented the surplus,"[21] by methods that included new forms of extractive banking, violent colonization and land theft, and the genocide of peoples.

The transition to this intensified extraction represented a change in the rate and global scope at which real wealth was transformed into financial wealth by any means necessary. It fueled massive financial growth through the robbery of diverse sources of wealth, which previously had been cultivated and protected for generations within the complex economies of many societies. As we've discussed, business as usual originated from the strategies used to enable this new scope of extraction. "There were concurring and, at some level, collaborating evils," explains co-learner Ed Whitfield, speaking to a set of distinct yet interlinked historical atrocities.

European settler-colonists invaded the Americas and used brutal violence to undermine whole societies and thereby gain access to the natural resources of Indigenous Nations, including land that was and is the basis of the lifeways, economies, spirituality, and identity of many Indigenous Peoples. "Colonization," wrote Dr. Kimmerer, "is the process by which an invading people seeks to replace the original lifeways with their own, erasing the evidence of prior claims to place. Its tools are many: military and political power, assimilative education, economic pressure, ecological transformation, religion—and language."[22]

While colonizing abroad, European elites pushed much of the population across Ireland, Scotland, Wales, and England into a newly conceptualized category of "worker" by forcibly acquiring and then privatizing the land and resources such populations had managed for generations.[23] This was called Enclosure. When people refused to leave their ancestral lands, they were removed by force and driven to join the growing workforces of industrializing cities.

Concurrently, through settler colonialism in the Americas, European elites built the plantation economy—a system in which enslaved persons grew cash crops like tobacco, sugar, and eventually cotton, for the enrichment of enslavers. The scale of this system in the US South and its relationship to large-scale textile factories and other industrial entities in the US North led to the creation of new forms of finance. Through shipping cotton to Europe and supporting slavery via capital investments, New York City emerged as a financial center.[24] "It is uncanny," explains American historian and Harvard University professor Dr. Tiya Miles, "but perhaps predictable, that the original wall for which Wall Street is named was built by the enslaved at a site that served as the city's first organized slave auction. The capital profits and financial wagers of Manhattan, the United States and the world still flow through this place where black and red people were traded and where the wealth of a region was built on slavery."[25]

Though very different, settler colonialism, the plantation economy, and Enclosure each contributed to the creation of an apparatus that enabled vast extraction. "These things happening concurrently increased the amount of evil done by each one," notes Ed. "In other words, the enclosure of the commons—the normalizing of individual control over what should be collective spaces—was part of what allowed for the destruction of Indigenous communities, was part of what allowed for the enslavement of communities out of Africa." These atrocities, he explains, "happened within a close period of time and all added to the incredible accumulation of capital." Critically, Ed points out, understanding their concurrence, and at times collaborative nature, is "not a question of creating some equivalency... but of understanding how these collaborating evils influence the modern world that we have today." Born from past and current exploitations, the loveless economy is rooted in domination and supremacy.

Historically, part of the domination strategy of elite power-holders was to make participation in the loveless economy the only option if one wanted to survive at all. For example, during the beginning of industrialization in Britain, the elite made it a crime to live off the land and, in some cases, enacted violently repressive legislation that ordered the death penalty for associated offenses, such as eating wild meat.[26] The poverty that Enclosure created was also criminalized, with people being sent away or to jail for not being able to take care of themselves.[27] Work in the loveless economy became the only option. Strikingly, supporters of Enclosure at the time even defined the word *impoverished* as "not inclined to work for wages."[28]

Throughout history, those who spoke up and called for alternatives to the loveless economy have faced danger. This continues today. Globally, there are hundreds of people killed every year for organizing their communities to advocate for alternatives to large-scale development projects, such as big dams and mines,[29] and worker strikes can turn deadly.[30] Colleagues in our networks have lost their lives when they challenged business as usual: making themselves targets of powerful corporations and financial entities.[31]

In the United States, there has been a long history of both state-sanctioned and extrajudicial violence against organizers. The Black co-op movement experienced "all different kinds of sabotage," explains Dr. Gordon Nembhard, such as "banks not giving Black co-ops a line of credit, railroads not taking their product and distributing it, insurance companies raising the premium so high that they had to go out of business. And then to the other side of the spectrum of white supremacist terrorism, actually lynching co-op people, burning down the co-ops, threatening people's lives." Additionally, entire nations have been punished for refusing to adhere to the economic status quo. The World Bank and nation-states with consolidated wealth (like the United States) threatened and bribed other governments: in order to receive aid, the "borrowing countries" were required to implement policy prescriptions that restructured their economies in ways that intensified extraction of resources by cutting social spending and privatizing services.[32]

Breaking out together

Breakout actors are realistic about the challenges and are constantly reckoning with the histories that affect and—at times—constrain our present. They try to practice self-compassion and also offer compassion to one another. This work is difficult. It's no wonder some of us feel trepidation in stepping out of business as usual; many communities have been stripped of access to alternatives for generations—while being aggressively compelled or threatened to maintain the status quo. And, as we've discussed, there can be professional costs to trying to make a change, such as getting fired, and those costs fall disproportionately on people of color, women, LGBTQIA2S+ persons, immigrants, and those with disabilities.

However, even the most devastating impacts have been met with powerful defiance. For example, breakout actor Thunder Valley Community Development Corporation sources inspiration from the courageous efforts, past and present, of Lakota people to keep their lifeways alive. "There was a time when Lakota as Indigenous People were almost completely wiped out," shares Beau LeBeaux of Thunder Valley CDC. "But there were always those few who kept the language alive, kept the beliefs, kept the ceremonies, kept the culture, kept all that knowledge alive, through everything we faced as a people." Thunder Valley CDC is one of many Indigenous-led businesses ensuring that such alternatives are accessible to more and more people.

It is hard to crush economies grounded in an ethos of partnership rather than separation and domination. Even amid the devastation over the past centuries of the Western economic project, ways of work that lean into our inter-dependence as an asset have flourished. Economies based on reciprocity are resilient. If, across generations, people have been able to keep these ways alive in the face of such intentional demolition, think about what's possible when more and more of us join the effort to step out of what isn't working—and hasn't worked—about business as usual?

Breakout actors radiate palpable hope, fueled by the successes they see in their work every day. After every single interview over the past seven years, we felt uplifted. The feeling was so dramatic that whenever we were having a hard day or feeling down about the world, we wished that we had an upcoming research interview that day. This hope among breakout actors comes in part from witnessing how ways of work outside of business as usual not only benefit people most affected by the lovelessness of the economy but can be more beloved for everyone, including those who appear to be benefiting most from the status quo.

"The ironic thing is, the people with the most wealth and power—the system isn't working for them either," points out co-learner Bruce Campbell of Blue Dot Advocates, speaking from years of working with corporate executives, philanthropists, and other people who supposedly are "winning" in the loveless economy. "In fact, if you're measuring an economy based on how effectively it allows us to develop happiness and well-being, I don't think it's making many capitalists happy. At least not the kind of happiness that wisdom teachers speak of," notes Bruce. His observations over the years have made him wonder: "In a context of such extreme wealth inequality, how can folks with vast accumulations of wealth really feel at peace with themselves?"

When Bruce learned about the case at the beginning of this chapter of the grant-making foundation's wealthy family members suddenly shutting down everything the staff and grantees had been building for years, he offered, "If you think of that family that fired all the staff, were they at peace with that dynamic? With themselves and their wealth? Probably not." The reason that the current loveless economy is perpetuated, asserts Bruce, is not because the people with extreme wealth are necessarily happy about their lot. Instead, he believes, it's perpetuated by the fact that "there is an overwhelming amount of cultural and societal support for the current system. There is continuous reinforcement that we are doing the right thing if we generate more wealth and hold on to power and control. These are all things we have been taught."

In order to unlearn the dogma of the loveless economy and have a chance at breaking out of it, we have to do what co-learner Katherine Tyler Scott calls the inner work. We all have inner work to do. A part of that is reflecting on any impulses of resistance that might arise in us in the face of breakout innovation, to understand if they are true intuitions or, instead, rooted in the propaganda of business as usual. When we don't do that inner work, we risk not only harming efforts that could bring about needed change, but harming ourselves by preventing positive shifts in our own lives.

"The reality is," reflects Bruce, "that all of us have unlearning and healing to do, from our experiences in the loveless economy, including those who hold the most power." The only way out of the lovelessness, believes Bruce, is through being compassionate with one another and dedicating oneself to the inner work that enables unlearning to happen, so that beloved ways of work can emerge. Many co-learners share this sentiment: that it's not about turning the tables; it's about reimagining and restructuring the tables to be welcoming for everyone.

Two years after they experienced the backlash, we spoke with the former executive director of the grant-making foundation. "I'll never know exactly what was going through their minds," they say of the family members, "but you do get to know people quite well as you work with them for so many years on something very personal." They continue,

> I often heard from board members, 'I didn't ask for this wealth; I was born into it. I actually really struggle with my relationship to it. And I didn't ask for this philanthropic foundation either. I'm here because my name is on the door, and I am a steward of that name, and it was started with my family's money.' And again and again, I would get the distinct impression that it wasn't joyful work for them... There was a discomfort with having to play this

role, which they hadn't chosen or opted into themselves, but nevertheless they were expected to perform it with all of its complexities.

The compassion with which the former director is able to view the board's reaction doesn't mean that what happened was okay or that it was easy for them at the time. "The situation was incredibly painful," they share. "We'd all spent years of our lives—I personally had spent more than a decade—building what then was just vaporized."

With eyes wide open to the difficulty of transformational change, we held a special round of interviews specifically to ask breakout actors if changing how they worked was worth it. They unanimously agreed it was. "I think it really comes down to what are the most meaningful things we can do in life as people in our existence?" shares co-learner Enoch Elwell of CO.STARTERS. He reflects,

> What is it that we all long for as people? At the end of the day, it's to be loved and to have significance. We're all just trying to answer that fundamental question: are we loved and do we have significance? By changing how we worked, we came together around something more meaningful, more rich, deeper... and this is where we get the closest to some of the things that matter deepest for us as humans.

Many breakout actors echoed this same sentiment. They shared that it was the power of the relationships they formed, or the ways existing relationships shifted, that offered some of the most meaning and benefit. Breakout actors also reflected that what they experienced together mattered and would last, even in the cases where there was backlash. "I mean, who cares if the project happens or it doesn't, right?" concludes Enoch. "We found each other through it. We found other people who know us more deeply... we shared a common love and grew in love for each other. I know that's not a word to use in regular business. But when we love each other more deeply, we are more known to each other. We have more significance."

We asked the former executive director of the grant-making foundation about the aftermath of what had happened. Several staff members were immediately hired by grantee organizations when the grantees found out. "Our grantees snapped up our staff!" they say, laughing, and then add, "It was very gratifying to see that happen—and an affirmation for how our staff built their relationships." Reflecting on their experience, the former director shares that initially they felt overwhelmed with despair and frustration—that years of work, learning, and dedication could be seemingly undone so fast by the influence of consolidated wealth. But then they received an email from a colleague in the foundation's network. "The way this person framed it for us," they say, "helped me to see things in a slightly positive light in that time—and increasingly positive as I've gotten more distance from the situation." They still vividly recall what the message said:

> The values and the practices that you built in that organization are not held in the organization. They're not held in the folders of documents that were razed. They're not held on the website that now doesn't exist. They are held in the people that you worked with. And that means they will go with the people to whatever organizations or communities or work they move on to next. And so it's not lost. None of it is lost. It's just spread out now.

Hearing this, we were moved to tears. It resonated deeply with what we've witnessed across breakout actors and in our own lives. When you unleash economic imagination by working together as peers, possibilities and different ways of being emerge that one can't forget. From our own experiences, we cannot *unknow* the possibilities we've learned through breakout innovation. We can't go back to business as usual. We, just like our fellow co-learners, have been forever changed and no one can take that away.

· · ·

PUSH BUFFALO

RAHWA GHIRMATZION, the executive director of PUSH Buffalo, is used to skepticism. Recalling common forms of pushback she has fielded over the years from developers, city officials, and even consultants the PUSH Buffalo team hired to support their efforts, she says, "They would just say that it's impossible. We're dreaming too big. It's too much." But Rahwa and team are not easily deterred. Over the past decade and a half since the organization's founding, the PUSH Buffalo team has consistently remained rooted in their knowledge of what *is* possible when people work together. In response to skepticism, says Rahwa, "We'd say, 'Listen, we've got all the power we need to make this real and show people that it *can* be real.'"

People United for Sustainable Housing Buffalo, or PUSH Buffalo, is a community organization based in Buffalo, New York, that has been mobilizing residents to create strong neighborhoods with quality affordable housing and greater local hiring opportunities, and to advance racial, economic, and environmental justice in the city since 2005.

Rahwa describes the organization as "a container that was created of and by everyday people—working class folks who really felt like they could make a difference in their community and imagined. It was an exercise in imagination saying, 'This is how things currently are, and this is what we think it should be.'" PUSH founders and current team members embody that spirit of imagination because, as Rahwa puts it, "We think we have the solutions for something better for our own community. And we don't think that help is coming from the outside. So we are going to figure out how to do it on our own."

Over the past seventeen years, PUSH has won incredible victories for working people in Buffalo, from fighting for greater rights for tenants to developing sustainable affordable housing. Rahwa shares the impetus for the founders of PUSH Buffalo, Aaron Bartley and Eric Walker, in starting one of PUSH's current major initiatives—their effort to create a Green Development Zone in the heart of the city. "It started out with asking ourselves, 'What is the biggest problem we are trying to solve here?'" In assessing this question with team and community members, the answer was not simple. "The immediate thing that you could see in our neighborhood then was racial inequality and economic inequality, and that they were tightly linked together," explains Rahwa. These issues were also linked to environmental injustice, notes Rahwa, and all of them contributed to creating poverty for many people in the community. For PUSH and residents, they determined that the key problem to solve was "How do we address the root causes of poverty in our neighborhood?"

In answering this question, the PUSH team recognized that in the United States, land ownership and housing ownership are key pathways to generating wealth. The community and PUSH team began boldly imagining what it could look like to address the problem across their neighborhood. They knew they could build solutions that went far beyond the usual siloed approaches, to instead holistically address its root causes in ways that would enrich people's lives in the neighborhood as a whole. Through imagining with residents, PUSH team members, and partners, they came up with a vision they called the Green Development Zone.

Bringing the Green Development Zone to life meant co-creating a comprehensive plan for the neighborhood with hundreds of local residents, plus finding and mobilizing resources. With the whole-hearted support of residents across the racially and economically diverse neighborhood, PUSH has already transformed thirty-five square blocks—which they see as merely a start to what's possible for the Green Development Zone. "We have already built over one hundred units of housing," shares Rahwa with excitement, "and each one gets greener and greener and greener. We are in the midst of planning forty-nine units of housing with 30 percent supportive housing[1] built without any fossil fuel infrastructure in Buffalo."

This strategy of combining affordability, equity, and green building practices is core to PUSH Buffalo's model, explains Andrew Delmonte, executive director of Cooperation Buffalo, a partner organization to PUSH Buffalo. "Not only are we doing community development radically differently than the business-as-usual approach, we are proving to others it can be done, and doing it for those most in need first."

And it's not just housing that is being built—it's a multi-faceted, creative mix of homes and businesses and common spaces. "The last unit that we just did was a nine-unit project that has nine apartments; a community laundromat called the WASH Project, which is a benefit corporation; and an art center for immigrants and refugees in order for the youth to keep their language and traditions," explains Rahwa. "It's also for older new Americans to be able to acculturate to America and use it as a meeting place and social gathering place."

Far more than physical housing, the Green Development Zone is constructing the physical infrastructure residents need, strengthening social fabric, and also restoring the land and local ecosystem. Rahwa describes the impact of that change:

> We are bringing back tree canopy. We are bringing back gardens. We are bringing back butterflies and bees. We are also reducing the heat island effect and reducing people's stress levels because now there's more lush greenery everywhere we go. But we're also creating family-sustaining jobs for those operations and maintenance and installation. We are building renewable energy projects—both on our sites but also offsite—and providing, again, good paying jobs. We are training people in sustainable trades, green construction, green infrastructure, solar technicians, installers, operators, and maintenance folks. Next up, we're going to be working on wind. There's going to be an offshore wind project where we have to train 250 Buffalonians and negotiate their labor contracts with the unions.

Referring back to the original problem that residents identified, Rahwa smiles and asks, "So I think this is starting to meet the goal, right? These are the immediate needs." However, Rahwa emphasizes, the most important solution and approach of all is PUSH Buffalo's dedication to nourishing social cohesion, connection, and care across their community. What is most vital, shares Rahwa, "is our elders, our youth, and everybody in between coming together to plan with us, to co-conspire with us, to lead with us and say, 'These are the things that we need,' because you know what, they are the eyes and ears on the ground."

Bryana DiFonzo, director of new economy at PUSH Buffalo, adds to Rahwa's point: "Being in community means being in continual conversation with people who disagree with you, and making sure that your conversation moves things forward without leaving anyone behind." Bryana strives to bring this awareness and ethos into every area of her life, from her workplace to her neighborhood to her family and chosen family units. She emphasizes that this means paying close attention to both the present and the future simultaneously. "What are the needs right now? Do people need to eat or have a place to live? Are we reckoning with the environmental injustices that are in our community and in our bodies right now? How are we pulling toward the future and how can we make sure that the things that we need to help the planet are also helping people as well? We can't do only one or the other."

This simultaneous care for the present and future needs of the community is an ethos that the whole team of PUSH Buffalo brings to their work, including in their Community Hiring Hall program, which trains those left out of the job market to be some of the first in line for work in emerging sectors by equipping them for jobs in solar panel installation, green infrastructure, environmental remediation, and more.

When the PUSH team imagines the future they are working for, they imagine one with enough time. In this future, bolstered by an economy that supports, cares for, and enlivens all its residents as whole people, everyone has time to be with their families, be in their gardens, be active in community and civic life, and just be.

The PUSH team often reflects on how to balance practicing this more whole and spacious future with meeting the demands of the complex, far-reaching work they are doing across the city. Yes, it's busy and full-on, reflects Bryana, who is also a mother and active community member. However, she finds it is nonetheless possible to practice this future here, and now. "It's about finding the time for what is important and making sure that we're really clear on what that is," she shares. "And what is important is, well, all the things that we know deep down, like living a good and in-right-relationship kind of life. And it's the care of home and of community, and of your civic engagement, and having meaningful work, and all those kinds of things." She pauses and then adds, "Right now, we have to carve out the space and hold the line for that, because it's not there by design yet."

In the meantime, PUSH is taking steps to make a future of wholeness and well-being for everyone, something that *is* by design in our economies and communities. By daring to imagine and build together, they are making this future real, one bold step at a time.

CHAPTER 12

PRACTICING BELOVED ECONOMIES

W E THOUGHT we were going to complete this book years ago. We had the beginning of a very different version of the manuscript in the fall of 2017. But every time we almost wrapped up our research, we faced unexpected challenges: loved ones fell ill, financial hardships occurred, personal health issues arose... the list goes on. This book has been a process of building several intricate, intentional mandalas in the sand only to see them swept away, again and again, by tides beyond our control. But it wasn't just that life changed our plans. It was also that each time best-laid plans shifted, something new arose from the research that suggested there was a larger, perhaps cosmic, reason for the delay. Some unexpected finding, turn of events, or opportunity for collaboration would show us, once again, that we were not yet finished.

Eventually, a gift emerged from the extended timeline: we witnessed something interesting happening in the changes unfolding with breakout actors.

We saw how co-learner Joe Terry of Wisconsin Rapids profoundly changed his approach to teamwork, collaboration, and leadership after co-designing the Tribune Building with hundreds of fellow residents. We saw enterprises, such as Concordia, shift their governance and financial structures to embody the kind of deconsolidated rights to design that have made their work so meaningful in communities across the United States. We even witnessed standards start to shift across an entire industry, in response to a breakout actor raising the bar and demonstrating what else is possible, as was the case with RUNWAY's influence on approaches to investment in new small businesses.

As we observed the scope of change surrounding breakout actors, we sought to deepen our understanding by returning to interview transcripts and discussing the topic with more than a dozen co-learners. We explored the changes breakout actors experienced over time, which was almost half a decade since we'd first connected. Over the two years that followed, we invited updates from co-learning community members, asked and refined questions related to long-term impacts, and tracked the shifts we were witnessing.

The ripple effect of breakout innovation

This examination revealed the potential of breakout innovation to spark change in widening circles—from individuals to teams to whole enterprises to industries and geographies. We call this the ripple effect of breakout innovation, which we observed in three arenas:

- *Individuals* were experiencing permanent shifts in their own personal approaches to collaborative work, in alignment with the seven practices.

- When multiple members of a team experienced working with the seven practices, entire *enterprises* often changed their strategic approach, focus, and day-to-day work processes, as well as their governance and financial structures, toward deconsolidating rights to design.

• As peer entities of breakout enterprises were inspired by the breakout actors, they, too, made changes in practice, structure, and culture toward deconsolidating rights to design. This sometimes sparked a broader shift in how their *industry* as a whole viewed best practices and what was possible for their field. Or a breakout actor inspired numerous actors across a broader *geographic area*—such as a town or county—to transform their view of what ways of work were possible in that region.

RUNWAY exemplifies the ripple effect of breakout innovation. Funders involved in RUNWAY's work—from wealthy individuals to large banking entities such as Self-Help Federal Credit Union, which serves over 95,000 members across California, Illinois, Washington, and Wisconsin—have adopted an array of new practices inspired by RUNWAY's groundbreaking approach to customized, relational friends and family capital. Many of RUNWAY's funding partners now also bring elements of RUNWAY's approach to other entities they fund. Like RUNWAY's team, they, too, now boldly ask why finance has to follow the same old standards. They now dare to break these rules and co-create new ones that enable their financing to better contribute to what makes life good.

The process of working together in breakout ways instills in those involved a permanently different sense of what is possible in how we work, in what we can imagine and build. This capacity to understand the transformations possible becomes embodied by the people involved; it becomes a part of who they are. They seem to forever thereafter have a greater audacity to imagine and enact ways of work that deconsolidate rights to design, and they align workplace systems and structures to enable such changes in practice. Our conversations with co-learning community members over the years made it clear that people then cannot help but bring this courage into every new endeavor. Experiencing breakout innovation begets more breakout innovation.

Joe is someone who has witnessed this ripple effect unfold alongside us, in real-time, over the years since we met in 2017. As an individual, he reoriented his approach to leadership and collaboration with an unwavering commitment to broadening the exercise of rights to design, through his participation in the Adaptive Leadership Institute and through his participation in the community design process that Incourage Community Foundation catalyzed for the Tribune Building. These two experiences forever changed how Joe perceives the role of leaders and what is possible when we build leaderful teams that can better manage complexity in shifting contexts to achieve transformational change.

From these experiences, he looked for ways to ensure a wide distribution of rights to design in his work every day, for over a decade, at the City of Wisconsin Rapids as director of public works and at the Village of Port Edwards as engineer-administrator. This ethos has generated lasting structural shifts. Over the course of his tenure, the public works department quit employing formulaic community comment periods and check-the-box consultations that are the norm. They instituted new processes that invite residents to be creative partners with the city on everything from road reconstruction to sanitation services to designing a new aquatic and recreation center.

Thanks to these new protocols, residents make more robust use of existing feedback processes. Joe's engagement of people in city council meetings, for example, has contributed to an increase in viewership of their live and recorded broadcasts. The meetings are now regularly viewed by three to four hundred people. "For a community this size, that's a big number," Joe notes. And within the department, new protocols encourage staff to consider one another as peers—each with essential ideas to be heard and acted upon—rather than looking only to the "higher-ups" for answers.

Although Joe recently moved on from leading the department in Wisconsin Rapids, younger leaders with whom he collaborated continue to work in ways that defy business as usual in civil works projects. As a result, city residents and municipal employees now expect and contribute more to public works processes. We believe this shift is a huge part of what contributed to the successful launch of a new community institution, the Wisconsin Rapids Recreation Complex and Aquatic Center, in 2020, which won statewide and national awards for its innovative planning process and design.[1]

The ripple effect across a community is something we have also spoken about with team members of PUSH Buffalo. Their organization facilitates visionary, resident-driven change for whole neighborhoods of their large city and inspires new approaches to urban development and infrastructure across Buffalo, New York, and beyond. From buildings to gardens to new businesses to statewide energy policy inspired by the organization's work, the effects are tangible. This is a part of PUSH Buffalo's far-reaching impact. Even more important, though, says executive director Rahwa Ghirmatzion, are the ramifications of PUSH's different ways of working together: their focus on the how rather than just the what. It is through transforming how they work that, as Rahwa sums up, "We're actually building a whole society and economy together, not just making widgets."

Strikingly, the ripple effect in people, enterprises, industries, and regions seems to persist even if the initial effort that inspired the change bumped up against individuals trying to stop them—even when those individuals did stop the initiative. In those cases, the people involved were still transformed, and these internal shifts generated something profound beyond the scope of the specific project they were working on, something that no one could stop or erase.

Nearly a decade after Incourage's community design process began, the old Tribune Building remains empty, as the community still works toward the funding necessary to actualize its planned restoration. In the meantime, though, Joe overhauled the way that his team works. We have met with many other local residents of the area who share his conviction for transformation. Community members experienced through the Tribune Building effort what it's like for rights to design to be widely distributed, and there is no going back. For example, a young teacher models engagement with his students after ways of work he learned through the process. A working mother and food enthusiast launched her own restaurant and welcomed the creative partnership of the restaurant's entire staff; this venture has led to a unique farm-to-table experience that has invigorated a local food movement. An overhauled Tribune Building—while still something residents hope to realize—wasn't the sole key to unlocking economic vitality for the area. Instead, it was the experience of profoundly different ways of working together that vitalized place-based change across the community. Many ideas initially discussed at the community convenings are already happening in the community, and residents now have increased community pride, a feeling of greater collective ownership of their locality, and a sense of belonging.

Transforming our economies

As we discussed in Chapter 3, witnessing the ripple effect among breakout actors and their communities has led us to believe that transforming how we work can play a significant role in changing our economy. As individuals and enterprises change what they value and prioritize in their work, it can affect the larger systems in which they are operating.

Co-learner John Ikerd has borne witness to the ripple effect of breakout innovation, affirming that he, too, experienced it in his own work. He has worked in academia as an economic researcher and professor and as a team member of countless initiatives across rural areas primarily in the midwestern United States, alongside farmers, agronomists, and local business owners. In these roles, John built new programs to sustain and enliven local economies. And in his decades of experience, he explains, "The only power greater than the economic and political power of the defenders of the status quo is the power of the people—meaning a consensus of the people—to demand transformational change in our economy."

Any society's economy is inextricably linked to its rules and laws, which determine how people engage within that economy—what is allowed, encouraged, and prohibited. The rules and laws are usually established by the processes of government. For this reason, we cannot ignore the critical role of legislation, which can encourage or imperil a shift toward a beloved economy. However, as John points out, we must not assume the link between government and what's possible for our economies is something we can influence only through established legislative and political channels, or only as consumers who inform supply and demand.[2]

Our findings and experiences have led us to believe that breakout innovation and its ripple effect can shift the

boundaries and rules of how our economies at large are con-
stituted. Not only does the experience of changing work
within groups and teams have a positive impact on individuals, organizations, and, as John puts it, "community life,"
their breakout results serve also as early proofs-of-concept
for what could be encouraged within industries, regions, and
even our greater economy. "People get interested in things
they believe can exist," explains co-learner Ed Whitfield,
"and there's no better way to believe something can exist than
to know that it does exist or has existed sometime in the past
with a similar group of people. That's why it is so important
to build the embryonic models of new and old forms that better serve our community's needs, so that we can share them
with people and inspire them to create meaningful structures
in their communities on a larger scale."

Because the economy is made up of all of us and our everyday choices in our places of work, when groups successfully
break out from business as usual, they affect the overall system. As breakout actors shift the consensus on how to govern
their own enterprise or group, standards of their industries
or the bounds of community life can change in response; in
turn, the economy also transforms to reflect the shifts their
decisions represent. Breakout actors can also end up advocating for systemic changes that reflect the possibilities they've
come to believe in through their practice.

Just as RUNWAY has upleveled industry standards, other
breakout actors have reimagined how they work with results
that shifted rules and bounds on a broad scale. Uncharted's approach to a four-day workweek, for example, which
is rooted in allowing staff to manage their time and define
their top priorities, has sparked a ripple effect. When the
staff experimented and prototyped ways of approaching their
time to make work and life better, they never expected this

effort to be public. But the interest in what they created, and the approach they used to get there, has been so significant that their co-founder and former CEO Banks Benitez was interviewed on a national morning news program. Similarly, PUSH Buffalo's work to implement community-owned solar power and microgrids for their city—which they were told at the outset were logistically and legally impossible—led to a broader coalition of groups embracing this approach and eventually winning policy change at the state level, making this possibility real not only for the city of Buffalo but for communities across New York State.

In the case of Blue Dot Advocates, their work has made waves in the legal field through the results of their approach to legal counsel, which is rooted in radically deconsolidating rights to design. For instance, they invited clients' team members and fellow community members to reimagine how legal frameworks can be of service to the futures their communities are working to build. In multiple instances, the Blue Dot team has set precedents, as in its work representing investors that provided financing for Organically Grown Company to become the first company in the United States owned by a "perpetual purpose trust," a groundbreaking new ownership structure designed to uphold purpose-based entrepreneurship, ownership, and succession.[3] Blue Dot has helped bring into legal reality a variety of new ownership and governance structures, investment terms and agreements, and more, which are being adopted and replicated by other enterprises and legal actors.

They and other breakout actors exemplify how, when groups of people intentionally change how they work, the resulting shifts can extend into transforming overarching norms, rules, and laws, including what's possible for structures of governance and ownership. This kind of shift is critical to shifting systems at their very roots and is the kind of change Ed Whitfield is talking about when he says, "If there hasn't been some shift in who owns what and consequently who is in a position of power to create with or not, then it's not transformational."

Everyday decisions in our workplaces accumulate and contribute toward upholding or reconstructing the economy. As breakout actors demonstrate, it is not only *what* we work on that matters, it is also *how* we work. We believe the ripple effect of breakout innovation demonstrates that transforming how we work is a vital lever for systemic economic change. "I think the creation of beloved economies and beloved communities at local levels is the key to regaining the power of the people, rather than the powerful, to govern," reflects John. By getting the designer's pen into the hands of many, beyond the grip of the few in business as usual, breakout actors expand our collective imagination for how work and, by extension, our economy could function. "Over time," concludes John, "through the experiences of groups of people, they may be able to convince society to change the economic boundaries and rules to better meet the needs of society."

The means are the ends

We have come to believe that the degree to which alternate economies are possible in the future is directly tied to the degree to which our behavior changes in the present.

In contradiction to the old saying "the ends justify the means," what our research has shown, time and again, is that the means *are* the ends. Milvian Aspuac, a colleague who leads groundbreaking economic work in Guatemala with her

Indigenous community, related this dynamic to the Indigenous concept of buen vivir, which means good living, a life that is in balance across many realms. "Buen vivir," explains Milvian, "is not a destination; it's not something you search for. Instead, it's something you build daily. It's about walking the path of buen vivir."

Striving toward a different economy is about creating a little piece of it today and focusing our attention there, so that we may begin to live and work in beloved ways right now. The exciting part is that it's not necessary to understand all the big-picture policy dynamics of a beloved economy in order to participate in creating it. You can set out on the path to different worlds without all the answers; it's arguable this is the only way that any economy is ever arrived at, including the one we have right now. As co-learner Jessica Norwood of RUNWAY offers, "The things that we want to experience in the world, we design and create for ourselves... practice the world you want so that you get the world you want."

In our experience, the more we practice, the more we are given glimpses of what alternate future economies could be. As breakout actors in the co-learning community have continued to practice their ways into such futures, together we have dreamed into the question: When we transform how we work according to practices like the seven in this book, what is the nature of the economies that come to life?

Dr. Virgil A. Wood was the first person with whom we discussed this question. A graduate of Virginia Union University, he earned a master of divinity degree from Andover Newton Theological School and a doctorate in education from Harvard University. Although he has studied extensively and worked in many communities, urban and rural, his quest to understand and create beloved economic communities is most deeply informed by his childhood and early years.

Growing up, Dr. Wood was blessed to understand what it meant to embody a beloved economic community. His small town outside Charlottesville, Virginia, was known as one of the "freedom towns" founded by Black families owning and operating farms. Here, his experience growing up on a family farm shaped much of his outlook. "I think that experience," says Dr. Wood, "taught me about abundance."

Dr. Wood describes the richness that sprang from his family's one-acre vegetable garden every summer. "There was a hot bed right there where you'd plant little seeds. They'd give you tomato seeds and watermelon seeds," he recalls. "White potatoes over here, and squash and beans and pole beans and peas. All this growing, all the onions, all that stuff. And rows of sweet potatoes, and the corn. All of that." The ground we walk on, he shared, is in a sense a beloved economy because it embodies the resources needed for human livelihood in its soil.

Dr. Wood's mother made sure that these rich harvests were always shared. "Mother would say, 'Take Ms. Gordon these dozen eggs,' and 'Make sure Aunt Jenna has her...'—that kind of thing," Dr. Wood tells us. "It was a sense of abundance. I never knew scarcity." Sharing this abundance in ways that created rich community life and a spirit of mutual care were central to the rhythm of his childhood. In his community, people could rest assured that if they fell on hard times, there would be enough of this abundance to fall back on, to catch them. This was the ground upon which the beloved economy of his childhood flourished and has remained central to Dr. Wood in his approach to life. "I think the healthiest environment is when you can deal with just enough. And I think the sense of abundance is how you appreciate what your environment allows and your privilege to both produce and consume what makes society flourish."

There is something else at the core of his approach: trust in the face of uncertain futures, with the humility that all we can do is follow the rhythm of planting, harvesting, and sharing. "It gave you a sense of not only that we are trusting nature now, that we've prepared all of this," Dr. Wood observes. "You don't know what the weather's going to be. You don't know what the harvest is going to be. You don't know what you're going to have. So you plant in faith." You invest with your faith and a practice of abundance to help that future emerge.

As we've said, our loveless economy is not inevitable, and Dr. Wood knows this from experience. He consistently affirms to us that beloved economic communities are entirely possible and that he has watched people create practices and systems that ensure everyone is cared for. "I get personhood based on the quality of the interaction with people in my setting. So as we think about beloved economic communities, I think it's going to be helpful for us to think: Can a family be a beloved economic community? Can the school be a beloved economic community? I think absolutely so." Dr. Wood reminds us how our centers of community and our workplaces can embody the best of what we wish for our systems at large. Because it's about the ways we relate, the ways we see and create abundance, "I think of a beloved community," clarifies Dr. Wood, "as atmospheric: consciousness and geography."

He also makes clear that the concept of a beloved economy has no prescriptive definition—that a beloved economy is neither about any economic ism nor a top-down system or model. He shares that a beloved economy comes from treating with care and reverence "the autonomous power of everyone's story," and from each of us being able to contribute to, and access, abundance. A beloved economy comes from prioritizing forms of ownership that provide everyone with dignified livelihoods. "There is something I want to be very precise about," states Dr. Wood, "and that is: livelihood has to be comprised of more than labor." He lets the phrase hang in the air for a moment. "I mean that the ability to have a livelihood is not dependent *only* on work for pay. If we are talking about a beloved economy, but still assuming that livelihood is *always* tied to a job with a wage, and if we are only seeing what livelihood is and can be as constrained by that, we're missing the point."

Dr. Wood shares that labor in its current manifestation is a state of exile, because the only way for those without amassed capital to survive is to work enough to secure sufficient money to cover one's basic needs. This leaves many people feeling a weight pressing down on them: they know that if they were to stop, to take time to rest, to live their days in ways that would make them feel whole and well, their very survival may be imperiled. It's no wonder, says Dr. Wood, that so many people feel that work isn't working. This is an unbeloved way to be. He emphasizes that dreaming into the idea of livelihood *beyond* business as usual—beyond exile—is where entrepreneurship is truly needed. "It's entrepreneurial in spirit," shares Dr. Wood, to innovate out of the way work is conceptualized in the current system.[4]

In talking about a beloved economy, Dr. Wood frequently points to a quote by Dr. Martin Luther King Jr. "It's like Martin said," he emphasizes, "that the economy we need is a 'good and just society... a socially conscious democracy which reconciles the truths of individualism and collectivism.'"[5] He explains that economies arise from the ways we relate to one another. When we approach those relationships with an entrepreneurial spirit that cultivates the inherent abundance of life and prioritizes care by welcoming everyone as a creative contributor, we expand the bounds of what can be imagined. This aligns profoundly with what we've observed in the ripple effects arising from the innovative work of breakout actors. There are many examples of groups using an entrepreneurial spirit to reimagine livelihood, and such innovations have a particularly profound effect in contributing to creating the kind of beloved economies Dr. Wood describes.

For instance, the universal basic income funds that RUNWAY raised and deposited in each entrepreneur's account at the start of the COVID-19 pandemic were provided for the purpose of sustaining the well-being of each person and their loved ones and were unlinked to work, achievement, or production.[6] And within weeks, their program was used as a proof-of-concept by other funds. Similarly, "community food utilities," an approach advocated by John, extends the concept of a public utility to food, allowing local communities to cooperatively ensure no one goes hungry, regardless of market fluctuations.[7] The idea has since inspired other communities to experiment with their own food utilities.

In the wake of the pandemic, Dr. Wood spoke with increased urgency about the need for more people to see an entrepreneurial spirit as a skill that can be applied to expand our collective imagination around the concept of livelihood. We see this as a need for expanded economic imagination around the values we express through work, asking ourselves: How can we prioritize livelihood in ways that make life good for all of us? We talked with Dr. Wood about unlinking how we think about a good living from the business-as-usual constraints of how pay is earned—such as moving away from productivity standards, rethinking who gets profit, and shifting how we understand achievement. If we imagine in such directions, what economies could then become possible?

With Dr. Wood's blessing, we shared his term beloved economy with other members of the co-learning community. We did so without providing his definition. We asked co-learners if they would be willing to do a creative writing exercise with this prompt: "Imagine, thirty years from now, you step out your front door and walk out into the embrace of a *beloved economy*, whatever this means to you. Describe what you're seeing, doing, hearing, smelling. What is it like to be in this beloved economic reality?"

The poetry that poured forth took our breath away. What resulted from dozens of virtual creative writing "write-shops" formed an exquisite sort of found poem, depicting a vivid patchwork of economic futures. We share some of their words in the epilogue. Without knowing any details of Dr. Wood's life or his definition of a beloved economy, many co-learners described futures that echoed his most cherished aspects of the concept and even of the community life of his youth.

Indeed, what they wrote exemplified Dr. Wood's description of beloved economies as atmospheric and defined by the ways we relate to one another. What emerges from breakout actors' transformational ways of work are beloved economies best represented by their means of getting there. In every piece of writing, we caught a glimpse of the values and priorities of the seven practices. The nature of breakout actors' *practice* is woven into the fiber of the economies they are actually imagining and building.

Reflecting the centrality of authentic relationships and the way a relational worldview plays out in their life and work, every co-learner described an economic reality in which formerly impersonal transactions become meaningful exchanges with people they know and care about. Many co-learners described an economic future in which decision-making power is widely distributed and there is opportunity and responsibility to play a role in making life good for all—with neighborhoods filled with this spirit of shared agency, responsibility, and care. Visions of beloved economies were bustling, abundant, and artful futures. History was also present and appeared across almost all the responses. These futures feature people dedicated to repairing harms created in the economic past and to actively restoring nearly lost lifeways through realities of liberation.

In terms of day-to-day life, co-learners portrayed a wide variety of vivid scenes from beloved economic futures—everything from planting seeds with future grandchildren in a home garden to living in a community surrounded by regenerated forests; from partaking in a community workshop with 3D printers and a robotics assembly system to enjoying a spacious work schedule—all while delighting in delectable offerings of local food prepared by people they were deeply connected to.

Transforming how we work generates opportunities for futures as richly diverse as everyone involved. Every scene from the creative writing exercises was unique in its details, yet each beloved economy imagined was echoed in the others.

It makes sense. If the means are the ends, then the futures we practice our way into are natural extensions of how we practice our present.

· · ·

THUNDER VALLEY COMMUNITY DEVELOPMENT CORPORATION

THUNDER VALLEY is located in Oglala territory of the Oceti Sakowin amid rolling grasslands and the nearby sacred Black Hills of South Dakota. The community is the home of Thunder Valley Community Development Corporation, an organization that began over a decade ago with one family and a mother's commitment to providing a nurturing home for children who needed a safe place to go. As young adults, some of the children raised by this community matriarch gathered around the Inipi (sweat lodge) fire with other young people to envision a different future for their community. Hungry for change in their surroundings, they realized they could bring forward the spirit of generosity, compassion, and hope they had learned from a young age and from their own journeys of healing to support the freedom and self-determination of their people. From this early conversation among young people with a dream grew the Thunder Valley

Community Development Corporation, a fifty-person organization that is leading the field of sustainable community development rooted in Indigenous spirituality, languages, and lifeways.

From the beginning, the team knew that they would have to approach things differently. "We live in a world where systems and politics and government and ways of operation were basically placed upon us, saying, 'This is the right way to do things,' when we inherently know that's not the way that *we* would do it," explains deputy director Lynn Cuny. "But our people have adapted to those systems—the government, state systems, federal systems that don't make sense for us."

Across Thunder Valley CDC's many programs and initiatives, spirituality and a reverence for Lakota lifeways are at the center of the work. In explaining why the organization was created, executive director Tatewin Means emphasizes that "it was almost like a spiritual calling. It was a connection to prayer. And so that prayer brought this vision to life." Tatewin explains that, from its inception, "all of Thunder Valley's work has continued to be guided by prayer and spirituality and listening to the guidance of our ancestors. And things happen and fall in place because of that, we believe."

Tatewin and other team members emphasize that it is this spiritual grounding that enables Thunder Valley CDC's work to embody a spirit of audacious hope. "From our foundation as an organization, the original teaching was 'Don't come from a place of fear; come from a place of hope.'" Out of those prayers and fueled by hope, Thunder Valley CDC has achieved an extraordinary amount and become an activating force for change and healing across Oglala territory. Eight initiatives address wellness and sustainable economic development at multiple levels of community life: food sovereignty, Lakota language and lifeways, regenerative community development, sustainable energy, construction projects, Lakota-serving social enterprise, and homeownership programs.

At first glance, some of Thunder Valley CDC's program areas may seem typical of community development corporations— a type of community-based nonprofit organization that is common across the United States. Community development corporations focus on revitalizing the areas in which they are located, typically low-income, underserved communities that have experienced significant disinvestment.[1] Like Thunder Valley CDC, many community development corporations offer, for example, options for affordable housing and homeownership, or a range of education and social services to community residents. However, Thunder Valley CDC has reimagined what these offerings can be and how they can feel, which makes their work anything but typical.

This spirit of reimagination rooted in tradition permeates everything that Thunder Valley CDC offers. The organization's social enterprise program, for example, "works to make our people collectively stronger by redefining and building community wealth. We do this by building a regenerative economy grounded in Lakota knowledge and values, and by making education and entrepreneurial opportunities more accessible to the Pine Ridge reservation."[2] Within this initiative, one of their top priorities is "to assist community members in learning a decolonized approach to economic development, such as sharing resources, bartering, and communal ownership."[3]

Likewise, in their homeownership initiative, Thunder Valley CDC supports community members in building wealth and homeownership "by rooting this work in our elders' teachings and Lakota value system."[4] Through a series of "financial liberation" courses, Thunder Valley CDC is "on the journey of redefining homeownership away from a colonial mindset to being a part of Lakota liberation."[5]

Tatewin beams when she describes what they have done: "The actual physical community we're building is unlike any other in our reservation or any reservation in South Dakota. To have a grassroots community be built from the ground up is truly innovative and courageous." Tatewin emphasizes it's not just the beautiful homes and shared community spaces; it's also the intangible elements of what they have built: "To be able to put together funding to get that started, and the dream for what this place will be—how beautiful that is. I think that, in and of itself, is hopeful because people see that it is possible to live a different way and to expect higher standards and different standards than what we're accustomed to."

The Thunder Valley CDC team members believe that the root of their success lies in embracing a fundamental shift in perspective—one that the Thunder Valley CDC team and community members feel is central to their liberation as Lakota people. "Our Lakota worldview is about restoring balance—balance of our identity, our language, all those pieces that make someone a Lakota. And the physical environment around us, living in balance with that." It's about being in right relationship with all these elements, affirms Tatewin. "It's not always just about you in a selfish way because of how you want to progress through society, which is a very colonialist or Westernized way to think. But to find that balance within yourself, because then you're a better relative, you're a better mother, you're a better parent, auntie, uncle."

A ripple effect builds from the point of individual balance. Tatewin observes, "So, then there's balance restored in your family or extended family and eventually your nation. That's our initial concept of liberation. How that ripple effect starts with you and then goes out from there." Tatewin emphasizes that, with right relationship, "when you have those connections, it's not just financial. It's your spirit; it's your mind; it's that relationship and being part of something bigger."

As that balance is restored in individuals, families, and others, an interconnected, powerful community begins to move ever closer to their ultimate vision of a liberated Lakota Nation.

"As we do this work and think about liberation," explains Tatewin, "we think about, 'What does it take to get there?'" For staff and community members working with Thunder Valley CDC, there is a shared recognition that "the first step has to be healing, because of all the trauma and the genocide that our people have experienced and endured, survived," states Tatewin. "We have to have healing in order to break these cycles that we have in our community. And then from that healing leads to hope."

Lynn adds,

I think you have to be able to hope to imagine the things that you want or the things that you would like to change. And so once you have, you're able to be hopeful and have hope within yourself, you'd be able to imagine the things that you would want to change or make better, which would lead to liberation. So I think it's all circular. And so we're really promoting that here at Thunder Valley with all of our staff: to really think about their own healing journeys, the things that they may need. Maybe it's a ceremony; maybe it's something that they can do on their own healing journey. And it's definitely a process, but actively working on healing in accordance to our own Lakota lifeways is really going to help bring back that balance, bring back more of our traditional societies of being a good relative, of being responsible and liberated to do the things that we need to do as people, as employees. But it goes further than that. And so we *all* have to do it. It doesn't matter what our title is here at Thunder Valley; we all have to do it. It's a healing journey that's personal to each and every one of us.

And while it's not always easy to know where to start or how to stay the course, Tatewin shares some guidance that has helped her remember how to find the way: "I was in a ceremony recently where they said, 'What is good and what is right?' As long as you are doing what is good and right, then you're walking in the way you're supposed to be."

CHAPTER 13

REORIENTING WORK TOWARD LIFE

ONE NIGHT, five years into our research, we had dinner with leadership trainer and coach Toby Herzlich, who has served as a mentor to each of us over many years. As the evening unfolded, we shared our emerging research findings, and upon describing the seven practices, Toby exclaimed, "Woah! What are the seven practices again?"

We rattled them off, counting them down on our fingers. Toby smiled and pulled a paper out of her purse. "We just finished *this*," she said, handing over a document. Toby is the founder of the nonprofit Biomimicry for Social Innovation (BSI); her "we" referred to her team there. BSI, like the growing field of biomimicry itself, looks to biology and studies the forms, processes, and dynamics of the natural world for insight into how our human-centered systems can function in ways that are sustainable and regenerative, as natural systems are.

The BSI document Toby showed us included a diagram illustrating six "Living Systems Leadership Practices." The pamphlet detailed leadership guidelines that Toby and her research colleagues had developed by distilling a foundational body of work in biomimicry called "Life's Principles."[1] This work reflects overarching patterns embodied by nearly all living organisms and ecological systems, patterns that broadly define how life survives and thrives on our shared planet—and how it has done so for nearly four billion years.

"Essentially," explained Toby, "these are operating guidelines for being an earthling. And see how close they are to the seven practices?"

We read the pamphlet and our jaws dropped; she was right.

From these two different areas of research—one that studies life systems of the natural world, and one that investigates breakout innovation among humans—core principles/practices emerged that were strikingly similar: they reflected ways of operating together that support *life*.

As we learned from Toby and her BSI colleagues, biologist Deborah Bidwell and biomimicry consultant McCall Langford, there are many examples throughout nature of living organisms having evolved behaviors and strategies similar to those we see in the practices of breakout actors. On page 343, we share some of BSI's most striking examples of dynamics among organisms in the natural world that mirror the seven practices.

Through a multiyear collaboration with BSI, we came to understand that the seven practices reflect what life does to adapt and evolve. In other words, the seven practices reflect what nonhuman living organisms and systems do to survive and thrive in the context of dynamic conditions. When BSI pointed this out, we all noted there was something intuitive about it. "It makes sense," Toby offered. "Truly innovative human practices that work well in challenging times would naturally align with how life has adapted and evolved to overcome survival challenges over millions of years."

Indeed, what the seven practices ultimately do is enable us to adapt. By deconsolidating rights to design, these practices enable groups of people to change how they work in response to signals all around us, which seem to scream that work isn't working. The practices operate by activating the inherent potential of people across an entire system to reimagine and reorient toward that which sustains life and makes it good for all. As these changes ripple across our economic system, our economy as a whole has a far greater chance of evolving toward ways of operating that nourish, rather than endanger, life itself.

Many species demonstrate the power-sharing dynamics that lie at the heart of deconsolidating rights to design; it turns out these dynamics are also at the heart of living beings' ability to be resilient, collaborative, and self-organizing. The BSI team explained that few nonhuman species are organized around top-down leadership, with one or a few in charge imposing their will upon the many. Whether in a herd, hive, pack, flock, forest, or gaggle, organisms that meet their functional needs in community have developed myriad ways to collectively distribute power, allocate resources, make decisions, and set a direction for where they will go together.

One example of this is the western honeybee, which uses a specialized dance to share power and decision-making among members of the colony to determine the optimal location for a new hive. A colony of bees can include tens of thousands of individual bees. When the colony needs a new hive, a cohort of workers known as scout bees are responsible for scoping out locations for hive development. Dozens of scouts are sent out to explore the environs—widely, independently, and simultaneously. Each scout returns to the swarm and shares information with other scouts through a complex "waggle dance" encoded with data about the distance and direction to a potential hive site, as well as the site quality. All discoveries of acceptable nest sites are shared; no scout is stifled. Other scouts read the enthusiasm, check it out for themselves, and return to dance alongside those whose advertised site they rank highest.

This process of distributed, group decision-making builds coalitions that attract additional members, as more bees investigate and dance in relation to their site preference. As some early scouts tire, they pass the baton, thus reinvigorating the dancing coalitions. This ensures that excitement for an initially promising site must be reinforced by a new set of scouts, as the scouts begin to coalesce around a dominant pick. Before long, a threshold percentage of dancers reaches a decision, and the whole swarm moves to its new home. Biologists have tracked that these intricate dance steps reliably "lead a swarm to an accurate, speedy, and unified decision."[2]

Since we humans are just as biological in our beingness as any other species, it follows that the deep patterns within the natural world that help nonhuman species thrive can also help us thrive.[3] We were stunned, in our final years of this research, to uncover the degree to which practices that widely distribute rights to design can be tools to help our economies move in wise directions and adapt, by transforming how we work. Life's ways hold lessons for us about how we can enact shifts like those of breakout actors shared in Chapter 12.

When we orient toward what makes life thrive, we do so alongside many species who have evolved adaptive practices for billions of years. Deconsolidating rights to design allows us to reconnect to correcting feedback from both the wider human community and the even larger web of all life. Janine Benyus, founder of the field of biomimicry, encourages us to quiet our human cleverness to listen and learn deeply from the wisdom of other organisms.[4]

The work with BSI as well as our observations alongside breakout actors over time have led to what feels like the most profound implication of this research: these ways of practicing work not only echo the wisdom of the broader systems of life all around us, they also reconnect us to our place within these systems.

The loveless economy continually sells the world as a place in which only humans matter, claiming that intent, choice, wisdom, and agency belong to humans alone,[5] and the rest of the living world is dead. This is a flattened, limiting view of the world—one that kills countless other possible worlds in its constant assertion of itself.[6]

"Conceiving of plants and land as objects, not subjects—as things, instead of beings—provides the moral distance that enables exploitation," writes Dr. Robin Wall Kimmerer, "[V]aluing the productive potential of the physical body but denying the personhood of the being."[7] The loveless economy ignores that agency is more than just a human property.[8] It is easier to extract from a world that doesn't talk back. Our workplaces only engage human stakeholders; it's not often that we seek wisdom from other organisms, the mountains, rivers, or the ocean. Business as usual considers oil for extracting, water for privatizing and selling, and soil for using up. It carves up the world in the name of financial wealth, which flows to a few, rather than nourishing or replenishing all involved. Upholding the loveless economy requires us to consider the rest of the world inanimate or fair game for human taking.

Business as usual disconnects us not only from one another as humans but also from the rest of life. We believe these multiple forms of disconnection cause a collective wound of separation[9]—the pain of unnatural isolation from the rest of life. As economic thinker Charles Eisenstein explains, things don't have to be this way and haven't always been. He echoes an understanding emphasized by many Indigenous Peoples and a point expressed by several people in our co-learning community: Times have existed when a strong matrix of relationships was present for all people, when we "knew every plant, we knew every animal, every bird, we knew its song, and when it sang, and what bugs it eats, and where those bugs lived, and what the soil smells like where the bugs live, and what plants grow there, and what medicine the plants are used for. We were in this web of interbeing. We were deeply known. Therefore we knew ourselves. We felt as if we were at home in the universe."[10]

Despite what business as usual claims, the world is not dead. It is not there merely for our taking. Instead, we humans are interconnected with every other being on this teeming, complex, pulsing planet. Dr. Wood often mentions the concept of Ubuntu: I am because we are. We are only because we are a *we*. As physicist Dr. Karen Barad puts it, "We are of the universe—there is no inside, no outside."[11]

Experience has convinced us that the seven practices break down barriers by helping us widely distribute rights to design. We have come to believe that, in doing so, they reconnect us to each other. We believe they also begin to reweave our connections with the entire web of life. These practices not only train us to listen more deeply to one another but also to the whole world around us.

"I think that what we are yearning for as a society is the real connections, right?" says co-learner Rahwa. "It's about that mutuality. It's about that connection. It's about being connected to the Earth, and that makes us feel good. It's a recognition that, right now, these systems do not work, so how do we—because we're all brilliant—come together to imagine and break into that reality that will make us feel more connected to ourselves, to each other, to our communities, to the Earth?"

We believe the reconnection that's possible through transforming how we work is a gift beyond any outcome we could have imagined when we began this research—something that no loveless economy would ever think to measure: *belonging*.

Belonging means being invited to the designer's table, alongside everyone else, with a pen in your hand and also in the hands of your neighbors. It means exercising our inherent agency in a distributed web of power with mutual accountability. As Rahwa describes, "The purpose of working collectively and being responsible for and to each other is what will make us whole, what will bring us to the light, what will ultimately liberate us."

All we have to do is get started. We can create pieces of a beloved economy today.

Practice means taking one step at a time and trying, again and again.

And as we reconnect and listen to the web of life through practicing interdependence, a massive network of life comes alive again to our senses. A beloved economy manifests through our recognition of life's enchantment.

This enchanted world is the one that has always been there—right under your feet, whispering to you as you sleep, tugging at your shirt sleeve, coaxing you to turn around and see, once again, your larger home and your birthright to belong among *all of this*.

WE ASKED DR. WOOD one afternoon, "What will happen if we make our way into beloved economies?"

"Let me characterize what I think will happen," he replied. "I think when we get there, the children will have fallen in love with life, and they're dancing, and they're laughing and playing. The old folks will have fallen in love again with life and they are smiling and dancing. I'm talking about the reenchantment of life now."

EPILOGUE

WE ASKED members of the co-learning community: imagine, thirty years from now, you step out your front door and walk into the embrace of a *beloved economy*... What are you seeing, doing, hearing, smelling? What is it like to be in this economy?

The replies below are woven together from the responses of a dozen members of the co-learning community.[1]

. . .

I woke up this morning.

And I moved about feeling free.

I finished my "good morning" ritual. And I thought about the possibilities of the day. What would I eat? Where would I go? Who would I see? What would I learn? I do this routine every day—inside of the beloved economy—and every day feels the same: it feels like being free.

. . .

I wake up with my creativity engaged rather than anxiety. I enter the world outside my door with the same warmth and grace that I hold inside my door with my family, because in this beloved economy, all people are my relations, and even the ecosystem is made up of extended family.

. . .

The first thing I smell are the trees and the wildflowers. The first things I hear are the birds and the buzzing bugs of summer.

. . .

The first thing I notice are multigenerational families from diverse ethnic backgrounds sharing a common space. Children are playing together; parents are talking with other parents; grandparents are watching over the toddlers as they roam around. No one is viewed as the other. People are interested in learning about one another, their interests, passions, and ways of life. Work is not the defining characteristic of anyone, although important. What is is the contribution made to making community livable for everyone.

. . .

I am invited to make a contribution to the common good, rather than competing for my piece of the pie.

. . .

I pass my neighbors on the sidewalks and in their yards, nearly all of whom I know by name and know many personally from various activities in which we are involved in the community. Now, we meet a large portion of our day-to-day needs through personal relationships with each other, rather than by working to earn money to buy virtually everything we need or want. We have a viable year-round farmers market but also can buy our fresh vegetables, milk, eggs, and meat from local farmers by going online and having their products delivered to our door on a regular basis. Even those who were previously on government food assistance programs are now assured of having all of their food needs met, with good nutritious foods, from the same farmers and by the same means as I do.

. . .

We prioritize community care; we build neighborhoods for people, not vehicles; and we take care of each other every day, not only when in crisis. Moving through the neighborhood, I pick out family and neighbors tending to the work that benefits all of us: the washing, the cleaning, the child- and elder-care, the home maintenance, the budgeting, the resource-sharing.

. . .

There is a street festival in front of my house. A young person whom I have been teaching electronic music, music theory, and regional history of the Mississippi Delta comes to my door to borrow a microphone and amplifier system to perform newly arranged Spirituals we had been talking about. They tell me that their mom and dad like the new apartment they have and are thinking about buying it as a condominium now that their worker cooperative jobs voted themselves a bonus after the workers' assembly reported another quarterly increase. Their mom is also on the town council, planning to do another public art installation in the downtown area. There always seems to be plenty of resources available to the community to try out things to make life better.

. . .

We still have lots of learning and practicing and aligning to do and always will; it's not utopia, just a different way of organizing around different values. The Earth isn't completely healed, but it's on the way. We are more connected globally than ever, though our production and resiliency knowledge is localized.

.   .   .

I am on a gently sloping hillside in a forest with small well-built cottages around me, scattered through the trees and nestled in the hillsides flowing with the terrain. Everything looks like it belongs and has been there (and will be there) for hundreds of years. Below me is a meadow with children playing and shouting and a community pavilion where neighbors converse while making a shared meal together. Someone is working, taking a video call in a treehouse platform with their interested teenager joining in on the call. A few steps away are children playing below. A few others are making supplies to use and to sell to others in the neighborhood. A large community garden is filled with adults and children working together to tend the plants and care for the animals. Over in the workshop someone is fixing a device, 3D printing parts and using the community's shared robotic assembly system, getting virtual support from the device company's repair support hotline.

.   .   .

I step outside to work in my front garden and I am hearing a host of birds chirping and singing. My grandchildren come to visit and help me harvest and maintain the fruit and vegetables. They love working in the garden, but they also go from yard to yard playing with the neighborhood children out and about. This community is rooted in a strong cultural identity steeped in tradition, thriving green spaces, full of cooperative enterprises, the most sustainable housing, and deep civic engagement by its residents teaching others how to achieve the joy and virtuous cycles they have built.

. . .

As the morning star shines brightly upon Unci Maka (mother earth), the tiyospaye (family) begins our morning too. First, a drink of water (mni wiconi) as it is our first medicine. Next we azilya (smudge) with wachanga (sweetgrass) to invite all positive in, now wacekiya (pray) as a family together, connect ourselves to our relatives, our environment, our spirits. Open the windows and the doorway to the community. Happy to live here with my tiyospaye amongst the Lakota Oyate (people), comfortable with my role now as an elder woman, protected by our akicita (warriors), with leaders chosen Itacan and see our sacred children free to be Lakota. Thinking back (ehanni) to when mornings like this seemed to be a dream, (I am thankful) wopila tanka iciciyapi. What I am witnessing today is what our ancestors prayed for, what our people took action for, and now our children's children will only know this beautiful Lakota way of life.

. . .

I'm walking out of my home without fear—and honestly feel that I'm walking into my second home. The environment is rich with racial and ethnic diversity, with the intersectionality of ability status, sexual orientation, and gender identity. Reparations have occurred and are sustained. We've moved beyond searching for equality but are holding each other accountable for collective liberation. We are not a monolith, but beautiful in our individuality. I'm seeing families of all shapes and sizes, from intergenerational to a collective of "single" friends.

. . .

There is a street vendor selling breakfast tacos to a group of teenagers and you can smell the eggs and bacon wafting from their cart. People are playing music sitting on their porch. I can't quite tell what song it is, but it's bass and some in English, some in Spanish. The lot and abandoned houses once on my street thirty years ago are now occupied, one as a multifamily house and the other as a residential center for struggling youth. Friday is no longer a workday so I'm not working today; I'm instead heading to the park where my fifty-plus adult softball league has games. I wave goodbye to my wife who is just sitting down at her pottery wheel on our porch as I take off on my bike. The smells and noise of cars is replaced by the smell of fresh cut grass and neighbors arguing about sports. Waves and hellos to neighbors pepper the route. My old friend grabs me a local beer from the vendor at our field to meet me as I arrive. I can barely remember what it was like before.

. . .

THROUGH TRANSFORMING your work, practicing one day at a time, when you awaken in a beloved economy, what will it feel like to you?

GETTING STARTED

WHEN NEW people and groups joined the co-learning community, we often asked them: What would make this research most useful to you? What would you like to see covered in an article or book about the findings that would most directly support and apply to your work?

Beyond what is already covered in this book, co-learners suggested a write-up that clearly demonstrates the value of applying the seven practices, which they could share with a supervisor, their funders, members of a board of directors, investors, and/or fellow team members. They pointed out that in order to start with the seven practices, one often has to first communicate about them and their benefits to a wide range of collaborators. Co-learners often have to explain why these ways of work aren't merely "feel good" nice-to-haves but rather that transforming one's work in ways that deconsolidate rights to design is smart, strategic, and high-impact.

To support our readers in getting started with the seven practices, we want to share three points that may be useful. First, we share more about the value proposition—the return on investment, as some might say—of the practices. Second, we offer a concrete suggestion for how to start this conversation within your group(s). Last, we touch on a key point of advice co-learners have shared over the years for groups to start strong, stay the course, and tap into the practices' potential for breakout innovation.

The value proposition of the seven practices

As covered in Chapter 2, a primary finding of the research is that the seven practices correlate with achieving breakout innovation and its three elements: boldly imaginative ideas that directly contribute to what makes life good for all involved; realization and widespread adoption of these ideas; and awakening a sense of agency, among everyone involved, to innovate—including taking initiative to improve the current endeavor.

The seven practices achieve this breakout innovation by unlocking a wealth of insight and information. They do so by reversing the tendency in business as usual for only a small subset of people to shape the ideas, agendas, and designs that constitute a group's shared work. The practices instead enable everyone involved to creatively contribute to shaping the work in ways that draw upon a wide range of knowledge and capacities. Our research shows that ways of work emerging from the seven practices also generate multiple other benefits.

De-risking

Tapping into the fuller insights of everyone involved is a powerful strategy for what some sectors refer to as de-risking: identifying risks early on and course-correcting to prevent missteps. Working in ways aligned with the seven practices supports team members to proactively offer unique perspectives on where risk could arise as well as correcting feedback. Beyond identifying what's needed, team members also take initiative in implementing the necessary corrections and new directions. This initiative is tied to the powerful sense of shared ownership sparked by this way of work—especially when groups extend the practices into the structural sharing of decision-making power, returns, risks, and other forms of ownership. We have found that people give their best when they truly have a stake in what is being built together, which includes giving their best in identifying and mitigating risks. Perhaps most importantly, working in ways aligned with the seven practices enables the concept of risk to be reimagined beyond the limited notion of the concept within business as usual. Everyone involved in an effort can help deepen their group's understanding of what may be the greatest risks, who may be disproportionately shouldering these, and what is needed to meaningfully prevent and manage such risks.

Resilience

The forms of shared ownership and responsibility generated by the seven practices also link to another benefit: greater resilience in times of crisis or unexpected change. As we noted in Chapter 2, groups working in ways aligned with the seven practices demonstrated strong resilience during the COVID-19 pandemic, finding imaginative ways with team members, collaborators, clients, and community members to reorient their work and stay afloat. This resilience also shows up as an ability to successfully adapt when circumstances change. The strong, caring relationships that are nurtured through the seven practices inspire teams to give their best and to thrive even when plans are disrupted.

Going farther, faster

While shifting to ways of work aligned with the seven practices can initially feel like slowing down, many examples from the research exemplify what breakout actors often refer to as going slow to go fast. Breakout actors note that putting in initial time to attend to the quality of a group's relationships, shared vision, and systems for operating can result in the work subsequently taking off with unexpected speed and reach. Similarly, even when shifting a group's ways of work requires a front-end investment of time as well as financial resources, many breakout actors report that the value of the ideas and outcomes generated, alongside the missteps prevented, result in significant cost and time savings overall.

WE ASKED breakout actors whether they believed ways of work aligned with the seven practices were worthwhile and, if so, why. Their answers offered a unanimous affirmation. In addition to the above trends, here are the most common themes that emerged, along with phrases breakout actors used to describe what they found to be most valuable:

- **Quality outputs:** increased productivity, faster and better results, better quality products and services, more novel ideas, and stronger and more sustained outcomes.

- **Quality processes:** efficient decision-making, increased competency and brilliance, low levels of attrition and turnover, high-quality candidate pool for recruitment, shared sense of trust, shared responsibility, successful coalition-building, better communication, more compromise, and more win-win situations.

- **Enhanced leadership:** shared leadership, shared rewards, leadership development, self-reflection, and learning new skills.

- **Broad-based buy-in:** community buy-in and investment, increased engagement and participation, people power, broader social networks, and increased social capital.

* **Greater sense of connection:** feelings of coming home, connectedness to the work and one another, community, loyalty, and belonging.

* **Greater sense of well-being and joy:** positive health outcomes, reduced stress and tension, spaciousness of time, better quality of life, sense of satisfaction, working in alignment with values, optimism, altruism, confidence, sense of pride, being yourself, not bound by too many rules, work feels better, playful, adventure, love, generosity, kindness, happiness, peaceful, form of meditation, makes space for humanity in work, shared vulnerability, hope for the future, enchantment, reawakening, and liberation.

Beginning the shift with your team

In transforming how your team works, it is important to keep in mind that a shift is not likely to be effective if it is imposed by a few. It works best if the shift embodies the democratizing spirit of the practices. One way to achieve this is to start with a group-wide reflection process to explore why such a shift could be needed—and what engaging with each of the practices might look like in your group's specific context.

What it looks like to hold this first conversation and start a reflection process varies immensely, due to many factors including the particular power dynamics of a group and the positional power of the person or people initiating the conversation and process. We do not promise or assume that this step will be easy. For the person or people sparking this shift, they will know best how to navigate the risks and challenges of doing so in their specific context, and which approaches will have the best chance at being well received and sustained.

However you might get there, once a group-wide reflection process is underway, it may be helpful to share with your collaborators that a major finding of the research on the seven practices is that the means are the ends: a group's results are a direct reflection of how that group operates. The quality and character of how a team works deeply influence its offerings and impact. For this reason, you could communicate to team members that improving how work feels and flows is an immensely worthwhile aim in itself.

When inviting collaborators to share during an initial reflection process, it can be useful to focus on the concept of balance. For instance, you might consider together: What could it look like to strike a healthy balance with each practice? What feels out of balance currently? What might be a risk or concern if the practice were to tip out of balance, heading too far in one direction? Such reflections invite people to share questions or concerns they may have about departing from business as usual.

Before closing each step in a reflection process, we suggest your group decides together on at least one action step. Rather than the next step being determined by only a few, it can be most effective if everyone involved has not only contributed to co-defining the purpose and possibilities for shifts the group can make but has also co-identified the next right step(s).

Whether your group starts with one small action or a broader plan to consider in-depth systemic shifts, you only need one first step to begin on a path toward fully embodying the seven practices, achieving breakout innovation through transformed ways of work, and contributing to the creation of beloved economies.

Mindset matters

This book focuses on the seven practices as ways of work that a group can do together and how that work as a group can create ripple effects extending to our broader economic systems. Within this shift is change on the part of each individual that may be needed to effectively show up for the work of the group. Entire books could be written on this topic of inner work, as co-learner Katherine Tyler Scott calls it. Although it is beyond the scope of this book to cover the inner work involved for a group's practices to deeply flourish, we feel it is our responsibility to note that a team's practice is only as good as its members' commitment to do such self-work. Each member's commitment to their own inner work informs their mindset and approach to collaborative efforts.

We have learned that simply stating this reality can go a long way—especially when a group names this at the outset of processes to transform work. In business as usual, we are not always invited to reflect on how we may need to grow in order to bring our best selves to shared work. Pointing this out and inviting everyone to do their own reflection helps normalize and spark intentional self-work while fostering a shared commitment to do so. With inner work, just as with the seven practices, it is not about being perfect; there is also no being done. Instead, we need to get started and continue to practice all along the way. When people commit to their own journey of self-reflection and growth, their individual transformation can shape collective action, and the resulting ripple effects are profound. As you get started, we invite you to share your learnings, best practices, and advice with others so that we can continue to build on this work together.

SEVEN PRACTICES AND LIFE'S PRINCIPLES

CO-AUTHORED WITH TOBY HERZLICH, DEBORAH BIDWELL, AND MCCALL LANGFORD

I N THE FINAL phase of our research, we embarked on a multiyear collaboration with the nonprofit Biomimicry for Social Innovation (BSI), to understand if and how the seven practices reflect dynamics of nonhuman living organisms and systems. Over the course of this collaboration, we learned from BSI team members—founder and director Toby Herzlich, biologist Deborah Bidwell, and biomimicry consultant McCall Langford—that there are indeed many examples throughout nature of living organisms having evolved behaviors and strategies similar to those we see in the practices of breakout actors. Together we came to understand how the seven practices specifically parallel what nonhuman living organisms and systems do to adapt and evolve. In this bonus chapter, we share some striking examples of dynamics among organisms in the natural world that mirror the seven practices, as inspiration for reorienting work toward life.

HUMAN CHALLENGES are not functionally different from those faced by nonhuman organisms, which have evolved success strategies in the face of threats over 3.8 billion years of evolution. Life's ways hold lessons for us about how we can adapt and evolve toward more regenerative outcomes by transforming how we work.

As we discussed in Chapter 13, biomimicry is the practice of designing like nature to fit into nature, and seeking ways of being within our human society that are inherently sustainable and regenerative. From filtering water to transporting and distributing resources to complex social collaboration, nature's biodiversity represents a library of tens of millions of regenerative design solutions, time-tested over millions of years. These solutions can inform resilient, life-friendly human design. Until recently—just a few thousand years ago—all humans looked to nature for design advice. Many Indigenous communities remain deeply connected to nature in this way. But many within the loveless economy have ceased to seek nature's advice.

Biomimicry aims to build a bridge back to recalling that we are nature, reconnecting us to our places, ancestry, and the larger community of life. It is a practice that reorients us toward, in the words of Janine Benyus, author of *Biomimicry: Innovation Inspired by Nature*, "[c]reating conditions conducive to life." She asks, "How do we make the act of asking nature's advice a normal part of everyday inventing?"[1]

Biomimicry inventions have been taking root quietly around the world. For example, the original design of the Shinkansen bullet train in Japan generated an unacceptable sonic boom as the train pushed pressure waves ahead of it whenever it exited tunnels at high speeds. Eiji Nakatsu, an engineer on staff at West Japan Railway Company, was an avid bird watcher and knew kingfishers plunge headfirst into water without causing a splash—an adaptive capacity they evolved over millions of years to avoid scaring away the fish they were aiming to catch. The form of the kingfisher's beak inspired the redesign of the train; the front portion was reshaped to penetrate the air the same way the bird's beak penetrates the water, reducing turbulence, eliminating the noisy booms, and increasing the energy efficiency of the train by up to 15 percent.[2]

In another case, David Oakey, an executive design consultant for the commercial flooring company Interface, invented Entropy, a nondirectional carpet tile inspired by the attractive but imprecise "organized chaos" of the forest floor. These carpet tiles do not have to be laid in a specific direction to look good next to one another. The forest-floor-inspired design lessens manufacturing, installation, and replacement waste; decreases installment time; and reduces dye usage due to the fact that dye lots do not need to be as closely matched.[3]

Biomimicry is often applied to technology, architecture, and product design. BSI is a leader among a growing community of people studying the forms, processes, and system dynamics of the natural world for insight on social innovation—such as strategies for leadership, team resiliency, partnership development, and organizational structure. BSI translates and applies well-adapted ecosystem patterns and regenerative strategies seen broadly across nature to promote thriving and resilient human organizations, teams, and social movements. Their research and offerings aim to transform the ways we think, work, and lead in order to build businesses and organizational policies that are more life-friendly—and specifically more equitable, locally attuned, efficient, collaborative, resilient, networked, and co-evolving.

In the realm of social innovation, an example of applying biomimicry is work practices developed by the organization Canopy, a Canadian-based nonprofit dedicated to protecting the world's forests. Canopy's strategy is to work closely with supply chain decision-makers in companies that use virgin forest products, helping them shift from being destroyers of pristine old-growth forests to becoming champions of conservation within their industries. Their work centers on building trusting, long-term partnerships in dynamic corporate contexts. Canopy asked BSI, "How does nature create and maintain cooperative relationships, even in the face of disruption?"

BSI, with research partner Biomimicry 3.8, examined deep patterns within hundreds of examples of cross-species partnership—everything from clownfish and sea anemones (made famous in the movie *Finding Nemo*) to the tiniest of bacteria—and were able to distill nature's lessons in "Four Key Criteria for Enduring Partnerships,"[4] as well as a set of nature-inspired communication strategies. Learning from the nonhuman world has made a big difference to the team at Canopy. Canopy's executive director Nicole Rycroft shares with Toby, "Engaging with biomimicry gave us a framework to deeply examine nature-inspired practices and to institute them into our work, our campaign planning, the structure of our partnerships." Using nature's principles, the Canopy team has shifted the ways they collaborate with partners—inviting them to play a role in the ecosystem, drive systemic change, and help one another thrive.

When it comes to transforming how we work, there is an opportunity to learn deeply from the operating dynamics that sustain the nonhuman living world; this was true for the Canopy team and is true for all groups.

The seven practices reflect successful dynamics within nature. We could share examples as richly varied as life itself that demonstrate how nonhuman species put each practice into action. Below we share a small sampling of what most stood out to us from the many examples the BSI team researched and described. May they help you remember and awaken to the incredible array of mentors and teachers with whom we all share our planet.

Share decision-making power

In natural systems, dynamics of power-sharing are at the heart of what enables living beings to thrive and be resilient. The research conducted by BSI illuminated ways in which distributed decision-making shows up in natural systems. Deborah reports that it is, in fact, a common way that things get done in nature.

As we shared in Chapter 13, we were struck by a decision-making process of the western honeybee: its "waggle dance" in which hundreds of bees dance with each other to arrive at an optimal decision for a hive's new location.

Another striking example of shared decision-making power is the way Canada geese exercise both leadership and responsibility in their migration practices.[5] Seen in their classic V formations, they head south from northern latitudes in the early winter, traveling as far as Mexico and returning north as temperatures warm in the spring. The V formation helps the birds conserve energy for the long haul. Each gets a lift from the air moving over the wings of the goose that is positioned ahead of it, allowing for up to 70 percent more distance to be covered for the same energetic cost than if they flew alone. The formation is led by the strongest flyers, whose responsibility is not only to navigate but also to reduce aerodynamic drag for the rest of the flock. As they fatigue, they release this position, falling back to take advantage of the lifting power of other birds. The geese share power by taking turns and precisely matching the length of time they spend in the more effortful lead position with the more advantageous following positions. This sharing of the lead and the lift is exhibited by other migrating birds as well, including turn-taking behavior in the northern bald ibis.[6] Studies show that the propensity to reciprocate in leading has a strong influence on the cohesion and size of flight formations.

Canada geese also distribute decision-making power with regard to when to depart on the journey. Communication cues made up of vocalizations, movement, and other signals of readiness begin with a few initiators, which arouse others within the large flocks. These signals can be initiated by any goose. The second and third to amplify the movement also prompt neighboring birds in a continuous process of synchronizing and recruiting more interest among the flock until a consensus is reached.

Whether for bees, geese, or humans, sharing decision-making power requires processes that are intricate and conducted with care, which lead to outcomes that are well worth the effort.

Prioritize relationships

Complex living systems like coral reefs or forests run on mutually beneficial relationships between multiple organisms—collaborative webs that are much more than the sum of their parts. While many different kinds of relationships exist in nature, BSI emphasizes that many of these relationships are cooperative and mutually beneficial. Toby sums up some key benefits of co-existing in a mutually supportive way: "These partnerships co-evolve because engaging in relationships conserves energy, expands opportunity, extends one's capabilities, and even enhances the possibility of evolving into a new niche."

Of the many stunning examples of this dynamic in natural systems, an image that has stuck with us is one of wolf pups and ravens playing together. The relationship between the two species is ancient; they have long been associated together in both mythology and fact. The Nordic god Odin is depicted with ravens and wolves alongside his throne, and both Tlingit and Inuit tribes of North America have stories of wolves, ravens, and humans engaged together in hunting. "Ravens' high-flying capabilities and vigilant nature offer extra eyes and ears for the wolves," Toby explains. "Ravens call out to alert the wolves when spotting an injured elk or locating other potential prey on the landscape. Wolves go in for the kill and slice open the carcass. The two hunting partners then share the spoils."

Deborah shares that it's been postulated that wolves evolved to hunt in packs so they could take down bigger prey and still have adequate resources, even with a portion going to ravens. The two species frequently interact at kill sites and in other places. They chase each other, ravens playing with wolf pups near dens or pulling on wolves' tails as they romp together in their shared ecosystem. Biologists believe that this investment in the relationship may allow them to learn to read one another's signals and understand each other's communication.[7]

It seems that for all of us—whether two-legged, four-legged, or winged—nourishing deep relationships with one another enables us to be far more than the sum of our parts when the next great challenge or opportunity arises.

Reckon with history

"While we can't really project the ways that nonhuman nature 'reckons' with history in the ways that human minds make meaning from our past," Toby advises, "we *can* metaphorically assert that nature does not disregard nor disrespect the past." She explains that evolution may seem to be direction-ally future-oriented, but, in fact, it has no sense of the future. "It is the past that gives evolution its mojo."

The BSI team explains that in evolutionary change, the past is the historical platform from which an evolutionary trait may become increasingly specialized; this allows for fur-ther attunement in response to changing opportunities and selective challenges in the environment. Even in the life cycle of a landscape, the process of succession from one set of ini-tial species into a more complex web of organisms (such as a forest ecosystem rebuilding itself after a fire) follows a pattern in which each stage prepares the ground for what is to come.

"Whether in a hailstone or pearl; tree rings, spiraling shells, or coral reefs," says Toby with reverence for these beings and forces, "even [in] the process of natural selection itself, the former becomes the basis for a developmental path. New growth is layered onto old, and even in cases where the inner layers are dead or dormant, they often have a purpose."

Toby's last comment particularly struck us. It resonates with our experiences of this practice in human circles. Even if elements of the past seem long gone, or are painful to re-examine, as we work together to surface relevant histo-ries, these pieces of the past invariably hold a vital purpose for guiding our next steps. The practice of reckoning with history is a profound recognition of the past's purpose in lighting our way forward.

Seek difference

Diversity is essential for an ecosystem's health and survival. BSI points to research showing that it's not simply that healthy ecosystems are biodiverse, but that biodiversity actively makes systems healthier. Richness in the types and numbers of organisms in an ecosystem *drives* the health, stability, and efficiency of that ecosystem's functioning.

This richness makes ecosystems resilient. One of the many examples that BSI shared with us about resilience in action references North America's tallgrass prairies. For many of us, these once-vast grasslands are not something that comes to mind when we think of biodiversity, but the tallgrass prairie is one of the most complex and diverse ecosystems on our planet. It is because of this diversity that its inhabitants thrive despite an environment of extremes. The prairie withstands extreme summer heat and drought, as well as bitterly cold winters buried in snow and blasted by intense, frigid winds. Grazing—historically by an estimated thirty to sixty million bison—and regular wildfires can reduce the grasslands to bare earth. Because of the prairie's diverse seed bank and deep perennial roots—75 to 80 percent of the prairie's biomass is underground—these disruptions unlock new growth. The diverse pool of species allows for a wide variety of potential responses to the dynamic conditions.[8] Through diversity, resilience is built in.

We were struck by a quote that McCall shared with us from the US National Park Service Tallgrass Prairie National Preserve:

> Pristine Kansas prairie isn't one kind of grass, or kind of flower. It's hundreds. Meadow rose and wavy-leafed thistle. Bluestem and sunflower. Leadplant and milkweed. The variety does more than look pretty. It insures against biological calamity. In hot weather, some species wilt—others flourish. When insects and disease strike, some suffer—others thrive. Here's how the prairie bears adversity: diversity.[9]

Whether for human or plant communities, when we function and grow with diversity woven into all levels of our system, we can meet adversity with a wealth of responses and bring forth what's needed to match each unique challenge. In doing so, we course-correct and renew our foundation, so that our system can rebound, balance, and thrive.

Source from multiple ways of knowing

Nonhuman organisms have a huge range of ways that they perceive, process information, make decisions, and know their world—ways that are different from ours. "Their methods have been evolving for nearly four billion years, and ours only 300,000," Toby points out. BSI shared an array of stunning examples with us that left us humbled by the ways our fellow beings can know.

Dogs can hear up to double the frequency range of their human companions and perhaps as much as four times farther. Bees see UV light in hues and detail that we can't even imagine, and pit viper snakes can visually sense heat. Ants and termites maximize cooperation within massive societies through chemical signals that prescribe simple rules for decision-making. Fish navigate using a variety of sensory cues, including reading the geomagnetic field of the planet. Strawberries send warning signals to nearby plants in the meadow when a deer has taken a bite, and those neighboring plants diminish the sweetness of their fruits. And so much more.

The humble slime mold—a single-celled amoeba-like, fungi-like organism with no eyes, ears, neurons, or brain—is particularly awe-inspiring. Slime molds typically live on the forest floor, feeding on bacteria, algae, and fungal spores. When resources get scarce, the one-celled organism sends out a chemical alert signal calling for others to join, and this newly fused colony engages in a quorum sensing process that determines it's time to move together in search of food. Individual cells retain their own decision-making as they fuse into a gelatinous blob. Together they also tap into a new level of knowing that confounds Western science.

"Among the marvels of these brainless superorganisms," explains Toby, "is that they seem to have a collective consciousness that learns, adjusts behaviors, and solves problems." When placed in a new environment, slime molds spread out into a fractal pattern to test opportunities, reinforcing the pathways that lead to something beneficial. One of their most famous feats involved an experiment in which researchers placed oat flakes in a pattern mirroring the arrangement of cities within and around Tokyo. The slime mold spread out to surround the food and then created a network of nutrient tunnels to distribute the nourishment, gradually strengthening tunnels that were most efficient and pruning those that had less value in the system. Within a day, the transport network created by the slime mold was a near replication of the Tokyo subway system map. "These brainless social amoebas," Toby says, "can sketch out in a few hours a subway system that took urban planners a career to develop."[10]

For all our presumptions about cognition, learning, and decision-making, we become baffled as we consider the slime mold, several hundred million years our senior as Earth inhabitants. Toby reflects that, even in terms of learning from our fellow humans, there is much available to expand our understanding when we listen and observe in new ways. This practice enables us to learn far more from the humans and nonhumans with whom we share our days. As Toby says, they "may bring a different way of perceiving and knowing beyond the wavelengths in which we are most comfortable.

Trust there is time

The very ground beneath us can be one of our greatest teachers of trusting there is time. "In the slow time of nature," Jay Griffiths reminds us in the essay "Dwelling on Earth," "it takes about a thousand years for an inch of topsoil to form."[11] This rich layer of soil then "gives and gives and gives... [I]n the most ordinary miracle... [t]he soil is the ground for every harvest, the seedbed for every crop."

The soil reminds us, in building a rich foundational layer beneath us, that there is no substitute for *time*. Time is what enables soil richness to form and take hold. From this layer, so much can spring forth, again and again. And like decomposers and nutrient cyclers in the living soil, when we nourish the foundational grounding of our groups and teams, the quality of our community relationships improves. Our ability to share and sustain connections builds trust, as well as a deepening understanding of one another's unique perspectives and experiences. This investment is not depleted over time by the inevitable strains and ruptures of working together. Instead, when we take time to replenish our foundation along the way, our grounding can become even richer and deeper than when we began.

Prototype early and often

Nature doesn't plan in the way we might think it does. There is no specific destination or outcome that the natural world is consciously evolving toward. Life is a complex adaptive system, in which the elements interact in ways that create emergent behaviors and patterns. This process is unpredictable and does not follow any specific agenda. When sharing what BSI found in its research on dynamics akin to rapid prototyping in nature, however, McCall emphasizes that "natural selection as a whole is a form of prototyping."

The peppered moth, common in the US and Britain, taught scientists a famous lesson about nature's powerful capacity to swiftly iterate, lift up the new iterations that best serve, and change course accordingly.[12] The peppered moth typically has light-colored wings speckled with small dark spots. This camouflage protects them from predatory birds, as they blend in with pale lichen living on the surfaces of trees where they live and hide. As the industrial revolution gained momentum in the early decades of the twentieth century, air pollution was entirely unregulated, and sulfur dioxide killed off much of the lichen, revealing the darker-colored bark beneath. On paler trees, airborne industrial soot also coated and darkened tree surfaces. The large population of light-gray speckled peppered moths quickly became detectable on the darkened soot-covered tree bark and fell victim to predatory birds.

Fortunately for the species, McCall explains to us, "Variation within the moth population included a tiny subset of moths displaying a mutation for darker-colored wings—and this 'iteration' proved to be successful in the new industrialized context." The adaptation of darker wings protected these individuals from predation and spread widely, resulting in a population rebound and a decades-long shift in peppered moth genetics.

When air quality regulations were put in place, sulfur dioxide and soot emissions subsided, lichens recovered, trees regained their preindustrial color, and the darker moths became more easily spotted on the lighter surface of the trees. The proportion of the peppered moth population with the dark-colored trait plummeted. In prototyping terms, McCall explains to us that because moths are short-lived with multiple variation-rich generations possible in a single season, "the population repeatedly 'tries out' a diverse expression of genetics each summer." In response to clearer air and paler tree surfaces when the lighter-colored moth genes were "prototyped" again, this variation soon became advantageous and has lasted through today.

It is important to point out, notes Toby, that the diversity within the population is what allowed for different possibilities to be tried out and honed by natural selection. "Exactly!" Deborah says. "A population without variation—a population of clones—cannot evolve by natural selection. It can still evolve—by mutation, gene flow, or genetic drift—but not by natural selection, since there is no variant in the population that would be more fit for changing conditions than any other."

Indeed, "it is the variation in a population that natural selection can work with," sums up Toby. "Life likes to mix it up."

When we regularly have new cycles of possibilities and iterations to work with, our system can collectively align between the precise iterations that best serve our changing conditions.

FOR MORE information about learning from nature to transform how you work, check out our research collaborators, Biomimicry for Social Innovation, at bio-sis.net.

A WINDOW
INTO THE RESEARCH

T O PROVIDE a window into the many sources of wisdom that flowed through our research process, we share below a timeline of our research activities, and name the people who led and contributed.

Jess Rimington and Joanna Levitt Cea co-led the Beloved Economies learning journey over the course of seven years as an intentionally co-creative endeavor. Toward this aim, they established the research initiative as a fiscally sponsored nonprofit project. They raised philanthropic grant support to resource multiple collaborators over the years, each contributing their own expertise, talents, and insights. Additionally, at times some of the activities were completed on a volunteer basis around other paid work by Cea, Rimington, and a handful of other collaborators. Throughout, a beloved community made this research and its insights possible—from co-learners to research collaborators to grant-making institutions.

What unfolded across our research journey is hard to fully capture within a linear timeline. Many steps were planned in advance; many were responses to what emerged. The more we learned about the practices of breakout actors, the more we were inspired and emboldened to incorporate the practices into the process of research and creating this book.

Phase 1: Refining research scope and questions (2015)

- Conducted literature reviews to understand the roots of business as usual and contemporary trends related to deconsolidating the rights to design (e.g. co-creation, crowdsourcing, lean methodology)

- Identified thirty-five examples of individuals and groups across a variety of fields that work differently from their peers and achieve standout results by:

  - Conducting seventy-five "snowball" style interviews, beginning with an initial group of interviewees from within our personal networks in the fields of social entrepreneurship, philanthropy, impact finance, high technology, social justice movement organizing, and development aid. Each interviewee was asked for recommendations of additional individuals whom we should interview.

  - Completing desk research of approximately two hundred cases.

- Got to know the thirty-five recommended standout organizations and individuals by interviewing them about their mission, motivation for doing so, mechanics and practices of how they go about their work, governance, results, and key challenges.

- Developed our own Beloved Economies definition of a breakout actor by comparing the interviews of the thirty-five recommended standout cases. The qualities that we considered to be "breakout" included validation of the group's work from external parties, the degree to which the group's practices differed from the business-as-usual approaches of its field, and the degree to which staff, volunteers, and those the work is intended to benefit assessed the experience of the work as exceptionally positive.

- Based on our definition of breakout actor, we combed through our interviews with the thirty-five cases and identified twenty organizations or individuals that met the criteria. We began referring to this group as our "co-learning community," which expanded over time as we identified and invited additional breakout actors and subject-matter experts to join the research process.

- Conducted three to five follow-up interviews with each member of the initial group of twenty breakout actors.

Phase 1 research was conducted by Jess Rimington and Joanna Cea, with support from Hudson Brown on research coordination and Kate Gasparro on the literature review of crowdsourcing and co-creation. During Phase 1, Cea and Rimington held positions as visiting scholars with the Global Projects Center at Stanford University, with Dr. Ashby Monk serving as an adviser to the research.

Phase 2: Understanding breakout innovation and identifying initial practices (2016–2018)

Identifying common elements in how breakout actors work

- Facilitated ideation and collaborative synthesis sessions (beginning with an in-person gathering in New Orleans, Louisiana, in May 2016) with the co-learning group members. Collectively, we identified an initial set of elements common to the ways of work of all groups present.

- Broadened the initial co-learning group to sixty members, including additional breakout actors and subject-matter experts, based on recommendations from existing co-learning group members as well as from additional interviewees engaged through a continuation of the snowball process from Phase 1.

Confirming an initial set of five practices linked to breakout innovation

- Conducted virtual prototype testing of an initial list of twelve common elements of breakout actors' approach and work methods. Through individual prototyping sessions with members of the co-learning community as well as group prototyping sessions with co-learners and their recommended invitees, the initial prototype was iteratively refined into a list of five common practices, as well as a definition of breakout innovation.

- Hired a team of independent researchers and evaluators to cross-check the validity of the five identified practices. The researchers assessed ten groups and conducted interviews with multiple stakeholders of each group about the group's ways of work, the experience of being involved in the work, and the results. The evaluators found that the groups most strongly following the five practices were also the groups in which stakeholders described results comprising breakout innovation.

- Published a feature article in *Stanford Social Innovation Review* (*SSIR*) about the five initially identified practices linked to breakout innovation and the findings of the independent research and evaluation described above. Through *SSIR* readers reaching out in response to the article, we learned of additional breakout actors and examples of the practices in action.

- Conducted follow-up interviews and case-study research with existing and recently identified breakout actors to deepen understanding of how they enact the practices.

- Undertook applied research by trying the practices in our own work, specifically applying the practices in our capacities as staff or consultants with five different initiatives.

Phase 2 research was conducted by Jess Rimington and Joanna Cea, with Dylan Rose Schneider, Hafsa Mustafa, Melissa Nelson, and Shelly Helgeson conducting an independent analysis of the five practices through ten case studies. M. Strickland led numerous case studies and follow-up interviews with breakout actors and identified additional members of the co-learning community who contributed pivotal new perspectives and analysis.

Phase 3: Deepening our understanding of the practices and the ripple effects of breakout innovation (2019–2022)

Arriving at a set of seven practices

- Conducted a series of interviews with nineteen members of the co-learning community whose work focuses on building alternatives to the current economy. Interviews explored the groups' motivations for working differently, the results of their work to date, and their analysis of opportunities and pathways for positive economic change.

- Identified two additional practices (the practices of trust there is time and reckon with history) and validated these additional practices with the co-learning community.

- Validated the seven practices through a literature review of practices for more effective work across a variety of fields.

Understanding why the practices unlock breakout innovation

- Conducted a series of three to eight interviews each with thirty-one co-learners about their assessment of what the practices spark and undo.

- Based on the recommendations of our co-learning community, conducted additional desk research, literature review, and interviews with subject-matter experts related to what the practices spark and undo, why the practices unlock breakout innovation and broader economic transformation, how to implement the practices, their value proposition, and links between changing ways of work and creating broader economic change.

- Prototype tested with nineteen co-learners an overall analysis of why and how the practices spark broader economic transformation, in the form of an initial book outline.

- Synthesized 103 interview transcripts to re-ground our analysis in the words of our co-learning community.

- Conducted two follow-up interviews, each with sixteen co-learners engaged in the research since 2015 or 2016, to assess how their work had changed over time, as well as specifically how they had adapted to the COVID-19 pandemic.

Understanding how the seven practices relate to intelligence from the natural world

- Identified that there is a correlation between the seven practices and Life's Principles.

- Biomimicry for Social Innovation (BSI) gathered a "hive mind" of twelve biomimicry professionals to brainstorm together on the question: What insights can nature offer about these practices?

- The BSI team conducted a literature review to identify organisms' behaviors and ecosystem dynamics that reflect the essence of the seven practices.

- The BSI team surveyed the examples to surface larger patterns in natural dynamics related to feedback loops, adaptive cycles, mutualisms, and complex adaptive systems.

Iteratively writing and editing the book manuscript

- Completed a final round of synthesis by coding and identifying themes across 167 interview transcripts collected since 2016 to corroborate all key points of the book manuscript.

- Developed draft sections of the book manuscript and shared with approximately thirty co-learners for their co-creative input.

- Refined our analysis and recommendations by inviting review by ten subject-matter experts, as well as ten "narrative testers"—individuals who reflect target audiences for the book.

Phase 3 research was conducted by Jess Rimington and Joanna Cea, with M. Strickland leading the validation of the seven practices through literature review and offering qualitative research expertise to the final round of synthesis; Sonia Sarkar co-leading interviews with co-learners on what the practices spark and undo; Nairuti Shastry leading on desk research, literature review, and interviews with subject-matter experts on links between changing ways of work and creating broader economic change, as well as follow-up interviews on changes over time with sixteen co-learners, and designing and coordinating the final round of synthesis; Anke Ehlert supporting on desk research, literature review, and research synthesis; and additional research synthesis support from Lauren Ressler and Fiona Teng. Jaclyn Gilstrap led on narrative-testing, with initial support from Ellie Diaz Bahrmasel. Deborah Bidwell, McCall Langford, and Toby Herzlich of Biomimicry for Social Innovation led the research on how the practices relate to intelligence from the natural world.

· · ·

Throughout the phases described above, as we uncovered the seven practices, we strove to embody them within our research and the creation of this book.

ACKNOWLEDGMENTS

Co-learning community

The members of the co-learning community have been our North Star and inspiration. So many went above and beyond what we asked of them, which not only vaulted the research and book to new heights, but also encouraged and supported us to persist and keep believing on the long and winding road of this endeavor. To the co-learning community: We are forever changed, for the better, by what we have learned from each of you and your teams.

Research and book development collaborators

The process of researching and creating this book was profoundly collaborative. To the incredible people with whom we have had the honor to collaboratively bring forth this book: Thank you for your leadership, insight, care, and commitment to integrity in every aspect of this work.

We want to lift up the contributions of the following research and book collaborators—and encourage readers to learn more in the section "A Window into the Research."

Naomi McDougall Jones brought expertise as a writer and storyteller to guide the manuscript's narrative through nine drafts of revisions. At the outset, she led a process of breaking down the initial manuscript into component parts of its argument and guiding us in reconstructing it into a clearer narrative for readers. With each draft, she pushed for continual refinement and sharpening of the book's arguments to create narrative flow for the text and enhance the writing. Naomi also offered ancillary support needed to birth the book: she project-managed throughout the publishing process with steady composure. She also jumped in to handle life logistics to allow us the space and time necessary to work effectively. We quickly lost count of the number of days we felt immense gratitude for the blessing of Naomi's support and the many ways she made this book possible.

Dr. Ashby Monk was one of the first people to recognize the potential of this research and served as academic adviser to this research during our time as visiting scholars at Stanford University's Global Project Center. In the years since, he has continued to provide targeted advising, and abundant encouragement, to this research and the broader Beloved Economies endeavor.

M. Strickland brought experience in qualitative research methods and equity-based human-centered design and contributed to findings across the book. They identified several groups who became vital members of the co-learning community, and they conducted dozens of interviews with breakout actors to understand the nuances of their work. M conducted research and analysis of contemporary books relevant to the seven practices, the history and context of several of the core concepts central to the argument and framing of the book, and the values alignment of individuals whose work is cited in the manuscript. They wrote foundational content for the vignettes about TenSquared and Concordia as well as for several examples in the chapters about the seven practices.

M reviewed multiple manuscript drafts, offering editorial support to cross-check accuracy with primary research findings, enhance values alignment in language choice and framing, and strengthen clarity of the overall argument. They provided methodological direction and supporting leadership for the final round of research synthesis, which encompassed 167 interview transcripts. Their lived experience related to disability justice, queer and trans liberation, and neurodivergence were an essential part of our own team's pathway toward seeking difference. Finally, M played a leading role in articulating the research methods employed, including in crafting the section "A Window into the Research."

Nairuti Shastry brought passion and demonstrated commitment to changing how we work as a pathway to broader economic justice and inclusion; offered expertise in qualitative research methods—in particular, interview analysis and survey methodologies for understanding change over time—and a structural analysis grounded in economic sociology, contemporary trends and movements related to democratizing work, and critical race theory. She played a lead role in deepening the research in the final two years of the project, implementing an expansive range of desk research and literature review, conducting follow-up interviews with co-learning community members, and forging relationships with subject-matter experts across academia and industry who became key advisers to the research. She led the final round of research synthesis, integrating 167 interview transcripts, which included meaning-making in putting core concepts in relationship with one another grounded in the primary research, which worked to validate and add important nuance to the book's arguments. Nairuti reviewed numerous manuscript drafts, offering editorial guidance and support to cross-check alignment with primary research findings, identifying ways to further center voices of marginalized communities—particularly along lines of race, class, and diasporic identities—and highlighting important nuances of what co-learners' experienced, as clarified through the research synthesis process. Nairuti contributed text, framing, and content recommendations on several sections, most notably, the chapters on the seven practices—to enhance their alignment with the research findings and co-learner lived experiences. She also contributed insights on overall research findings and their implications, which were critical in strengthening the book's core argument and structure.

Anke Ehlert brought expertise in socioeconomic research and business; conducted targeted literature review and desk research on several topics to strengthen the book's argument; participated in the final synthesis of interview transcripts; and helped integrate feedback from the co-learning community in drafts of the manuscript.

Fiona Teng brought communications expertise; provided editorial feedback to enhance narrative accessibility; and participated in the final synthesis of interview transcripts.

Lauren Ressler brought expertise as a social justice advocate and campaigner; provided editorial feedback toward refining the manuscript's overall argument and ensuring it reflected a coherent theory of change; participated in the final synthesis of interview transcripts; and compiled information from interviews with PUSH Buffalo and Cooperation Buffalo to inform the vignette and examples of their work.

Dr. Sonia Sarkar brought expertise as a writer, researcher at the doctoral level, and advocate for inclusive economies that support well-being. She played a key role in coordinating and co-conducting interviews with co-learning community members during the final two years of research; she offered insights on choosing interview questions and led virtual "write-shops" for co-learners—the results of which appear in the epilogue of this book. Sonia also contributed editorial recommendations on the near-final draft of the manuscript.

Toby Herzlich, Deborah Bidwell, and McCall Langford of Biomimicry for Social Innovation conducted extensive work to identify and describe examples of our nonhuman fellow beings operating in ways they reflect the dynamics of the seven practices. Furthermore, they consistently went above and beyond to step up as thought partners in surfacing implications of their findings for the book's overall argument; in carefully reviewing and contributing to draft sections; and in sharing warmth, encouragement, and care that buoyed our spirits at multiple times of challenge in our lives and work.

We thank Jenna Sofia for copyediting with such care to do the heavy lift of "untangling the manuscript" while keeping it true to spirit and intent. We thank Crissy Calhoun for impeccable copyedits and going truly above and beyond in enabling the copyedit to be completed amid formidable schedule shifts and challenges. We thank Emily Krieger for initial fact-checking support—and encouragement overall. We thank Carolyn A. Shea for making an additional round of fact-checking happen—despite a tight timeline—on the final version of this manuscript, and doing so with phenomenal care and comprehensiveness.

We thank each of the people who served as narrative testers throughout this research and so thoughtfully shared frank and insightful feedback. We thank Jaclyn Gilstrap for leading this arena of the research—and also for her skillful support on presenting this work through our website. We thank Ellie Diaz Bahrmasel for her contributions in launching narrative testing; Dr. Anastasia Nylund for her brilliant linguistic analysis and insights on framing; and Brent Dixon,

M. Strickland, Milicent Johnson, Rahmin Sarabi, and Scott Shigeoka for their insightful recommendations on framing opportunities.

We thank Amanda Coslor for providing a profoundly nourishing space—in the fullest sense—during the initial months of this research when we worked out of the studio unit beneath her family's home. Amanda's friendship, sage advice, and thoughtful introductions were a blessing to the foundational time of this work.

We thank Stacy Johnson for the many times she came to the rescue with cheer, a can-do spirit, and competence at a truly impressive range of tasks—from coordinating care packages to compiling edits on final manuscript proofs.

We thank Dylan Rose Schneider and Shelly Helgeson for the generosity, effort, and care they put into the process of conducting and transcribing interviews for research published in the 2017 article in Stanford Social Innovation Review (SSIR). We thank Hafsa Mustafa and Dr. Melissa K. Nelson for bringing their substantial expertise in evaluative methods to the process of evaluating each interview, and for their contributions to the findings featured in the SSIR article.

We thank Dr. Kate Gasparro for her support with literature review and in shaping initial research questions. We thank Hudson Brown for his support in write-ups and presentations on the emerging findings.

We thank Maritza Schafer for her support encouraging both our initial efforts to develop a manuscript and our public speaking about the story and examples of the research to date.

This manuscript benefited immensely from thoughtful review by the following: Dr. Bradford Baker, Dr. Caitlin Rosenthal, Dr. Dayna Baumeister, Dr. Fred Block, Jaclyn Gilstrap, Jaime Westendarp, Dr. Jenny Cameron, John Egan, KA McKercher, Larnies Bowen, Mara Zepeda, Mutombo

Mpanya, Rebecca Rozin, and Dr. Tiffany Johnson. We were truly humbled by the care that each of you poured into your feedback and recommendations.

We thank each of our generous test readers who diligently read the manuscript and offered their important feedback.

The following individuals stand out among the many incredible people we interviewed during the initial phase of this research process—for their generosity of spirit, depth of insight, and active support to advance this endeavor: Catriona Fay, Chris Worman, Dennis Whittle, Dori Koll, Emil Tsao, Irma Gonzalez, John Esterle, Kaylynn Sullivan TwoTrees, Mary Anthony, Matt Kolan, Matthew Ridenour, Rajasvini Bhansali, Rebecca Trobe, Robyn Beavers, Russ Gaskin, and Sarah Hennessy.

Personal thanks from Jess and Joanna

From Jess: The number of people who supported me, in profound ways, to bring forth this book are more than I can list in the confines of this section. The beings—human and non-human—who have stepped up to co-create and support the path that led to this book are vast in number, and without you this would not have been possible. I bow deeply to each of you (you know who you are). To my family, both of origin and chosen: Thank you. To those who serve as beloved mentors in my life: Thank you. To those who brought joy and strength during this time period: Thank you. To those who read iterations of this draft, sometimes again and again: Thank you. I thank, also, the spirit of this book that kept us going, whether it came to us through great, old trees, serendipitous moments, or sudden whisperings. I am so grateful.

From Joanna: Thank you to my sister Zoë Levitt. Thank you for your save-the-day support when COVID hit my family in the final months of the book process—and all you did for both my family and this book. I could not have crossed the finish line without you.

Heartfelt gratitude to Analicia Laureano for your encouragement to me and nourishing food and support on the home front during the final three months of birthing this book.

To the members of the first-ever Global Advocacy Team of International Accountability Project (Bernardino, Jamil, Jessica, Mela, Mohamed, Moon, Sokunroth, and Sukhgerel): It was my experience collaborating with—and learning from—each of you that generated the idea in me for this whole endeavor. Thank you for your inspiration and the brave work you continue to do.

To the partners, staff, board, artists in residence, and funding allies of Thousand Currents: My time with Thousand Currents taught me profound lessons about what else is possible for how we work and the economies we build. Thank you for the teachings and welcoming me into the Thousand Currents community. Once a Current, always a Current.

To my whole family: You have supported me in so many ways—from my earliest years to the final days of birthing this book—that have made this endeavor possible. I am deeply humbled by your love and support. May I rise equally to support each of you. To my husband and son: You were part of everything I wrote. Words fall short to express my gratitude for your love and strength throughout this process, and always.

From both of us: A resounding thank you to the entire team at Page Two. Deep gratitude to each of our funding partners, including our solidarity lenders, for your belief in us and for sustaining this endeavor. And a special note of appreciation for the work of adrienne maree brown in providing inspiration and paving the way.

ENDNOTES

Chapter 1: Work Isn't Working

1. Aaron De Smet, Bonnie Dowling, Marino Mugayar-Baldocchi, and Bill Schaninger, "'Great Attrition' or 'Great Attraction'? The choice is yours," *McKinsey Quarterly*, September 8, 2021, https://www.mckinsey.com/business-functions/people-and-organizational-performance/our-insights/great-attrition-or-great-attraction-the-choice-is-yours.

2. De Smet et al., "'Great Attrition' or 'Great Attraction'?"

3. Jeffrey Pfeffer, *Dying for a Paycheck: How Modern Management Harms Employee Health and Company Performance—and What We Can Do About It* (New York: HarperCollins Publishers, 2018), 2.

4. Dylan Walsh, "The Workplace Is Killing People and Nobody Cares," *Stanford Graduate School of Business*, March 15, 2018, https://www.gsb.stanford.edu/insights/workplace-killing-people-nobody-cares.

5. National Highway Traffic Safety Administration, "2020 Fatality Data Show Increased Traffic Fatalities During Pandemic," June 3, 2021, nhtsa.gov/press-releases/2020-fatality-data-show-increased-traffic-fatalities-during-pandemic.

6. Walsh, "The Workplace Is Killing People."

7. Walsh, "The Workplace Is Killing People."

8. Walsh, "The Workplace Is Killing People."

9. Walsh, "The Workplace Is Killing People."

10. US Federal Reserve Board, Division of Consumer and Community Affairs, Consumer and Community Research Section, *Economic*

Well-Being of U.S. Households in 2020 (May 2021), 29, https://www.federalreserve.gov/publications/files/2020-report-economic-well-being-us-households-202105.pdf.

11. Bryce Covert, "8 Hours a Day, 5 Days a Week Is Not Working for Us," *New York Times*, July 20, 2021, https://www.nytimes.com/2021/07/20/opinion/covid-return-to-office.html.

12. US Federal Reserve Board, Division of Consumer and Community Affairs, Consumer and Community Research Section, "Dealing with Unexpected Expenses," *Report on the Economic Well-Being of US Households in 2020* (May 2021), https://www.federalreserve.gov/publications/2021-economic-well-being-of-us-households-in-2020-dealing-with-unexpected-expenses.htm.

13. Kristy Threlkeld, "Employee Burnout Report: COVID-19's Impact and 3 Strategies to Curb It," Indeed/LEAD, March 11, 2021, https://www.indeed.com/lead/preventing-employee-burnout-report.

14. Chris Arsenault, "Only 60 Years of Farming Left If Soil Degradation Continues," *Scientific American*, December 5, 2014, https://www.scientificamerican.com/article/only-60-years-of-farming-left-if-soil-degradation-continues/.

15. Juliet B. Schor, *True Wealth: How and Why Millions of Americans Are Creating a Time-Rich, Ecologically Light, Small-Scale, High-Satisfaction Economy* (New York: Penguin Books, 2011), 4. Our definition of business as usual is inspired by the work of climate justice activists and of economic sociologist Juliet B. Schor; their definitions arose from climate discourse to indicate what might happen if we did not collectively address the crisis of rising emissions. In *True Wealth*, Schor writes, "[business as usual] indicate[s] the continuation of the current economic rules, practices, growth trajectory, and ecological consequences of production and consumption. It especially refers to the large corporate entities that dominate the market and are heavily invested in it."

16. Marjorie Kelly and Ted Howard, *The Making of a Democratic Economy: Building Prosperity for the Many, Not Just the Few* (Oakland, CA: Berrett-Koehler Publishers, 2019), 4–5.

17. Tom Rath and Jim Harter, *Wellbeing: The Five Essential Elements* (New York: Gallup Press, 2010), 6.

18. J.K. Gibson-Graham, Jenny Cameron, and Stephen Healy, *Take Back the Economy: An Ethical Guide for Transforming Our Communities* (Minneapolis: University of Minnesota Press, 2013),

201. This additional form of well-being—spiritual—is suggested in *Take Back the Economy*.

19. Paul Fowler, "The Role of Private Equity in the Decline of a Major Forest Products Company: A Case Study," NYU Stern Center for Sustainable Business, December 2021, https://www.stern.nyu.edu/ sites/default/files/assets/documents/NYU%20Stern%20CSB%20 -%20The%20Role%20of%20Private%20Equity%20in%20the %20Decline%20of%20a%20Major%20Forest%20Products %20Company.pdf.

20. Stacy Mitchell and Marie Donahue, "Report: Dollar Stores Are Targeting Struggling Urban Neighborhoods and Small Towns. One Community Is Showing How to Fight Back," Institute for Local Self-Reliance, December 6, 2018, https:/ ilsr.org/dollar-stores-target-cities-towns-one-fights-back/.

21. Eileen Appelbaum, "How Private Equity Makes You Sicker," *American Prospect*, October 7, 2019, https://prospect.org/health/ how-private-equity-makes-you-sicker/.

22. Marc Edelman, "How Capitalism Underdeveloped Rural America," *Jacobin*, January 26, 2020, https://jacobinmag.com/2020/01/ capitalism-underdeveloped-rural-america-trump-white-workingclass.

23. Robert McClure, "Pledges Forgotten, Local Governments Repurpose Federally Funded Parks," *InvestigateWest*, June 11, 2012, https://www.invw.org/2012/06/11/pledges-forgotten-local-g-1277/.

24. Dedrick Asante-Muhammad, Chuck Collins, Josh Hoxie, and Emanuel Nieves, "The Road to Zero Wealth: How the Racial Wealth Divide Is Hollowing Out America's Middle Class," The Institute for Policy Studies and Prosperity Now, 2017, 6, https://prosperitynow. org/sites/default/files/PDFs/10-2017_Road_to_Zero_Wealth_Slides.

25. Alexandra Bastien, "Income Is How You Get Out of Poverty, Assets Are How You Stay Out," *Shelterforce*, January 22, 2015, https:// shelterforce.org/2015/01/22/income-is-how-you-get-out-of-poverty-assets-are-how-you-stay-out/.

26. Asante-Muhammad et al., "The Road to Zero Wealth," 6.

27. Asante-Muhammad et al., "The Road to Zero Wealth," 9.

28. People with disabilities live in poverty at more than twice the rate of people without disabilities in the US. People with disabilities make up approximately 12 percent of the US working-age population; however, they account for more than half of those living in long-term poverty. Only 32 percent of working-age people

with disabilities are employed compared with 73 percent of those without disabilities. These statistics are drawn from "Highlighting Disability/Poverty Connection, NCD Urges Congress to Alter Federal Policies that Disadvantage People with Disabilities" (press release), National Council on Disability, October 26, 2017, https://ncd.gov/newsroom/2017/disability-poverty-connection-2017-progress-report-release.

29. Heather McCulloch, "Closing the Women's Wealth Gap: What It Is, Why It Matters, and What Can Be Done About It," Closing the Women's Wealth Gap, January 2017, https://womenswealthgap.org/wp-content/uploads/2017/06/Closing-the-Womens-Wealth-Gap-Report-Jan2017.pdf.

30. Ana Hernández Kent and Lowell Ricketts, "Gender Wealth Gap: Families Headed by Women Have Lower Wealth," Federal Reserve Bank of St. Louis, January 12, 2021, https://www.stlouisfed.org/publications/in-the-balance/2021/gender-wealth-gap-families-women-lower-wealth.

31. bell hooks, *All About Love* (New York: William Morrow, 2001), x. We would like to recognize Melissa Lee, a member of the co-learning community advising this research, for reminding us of the work of bell hooks on themes directly related to our research questions and outcomes.

32. hooks, *All About Love*, 71–72.

33. Dr. Wood served as director of the National Task Force on the Black Economic Agenda, jointly co-chaired by Dr. Vivian Henderson and Dr. Edward Irons, prominent African American economists. Dr. Wood reported on their joint work at the 1975 Southern Christian Leadership Conference in Anniston, Alabama.

34. Michael Brown, "A Service Year for the Nation's Young People Would Hasten King's Vision for America," *Huffington Post* (blog), January 18, 2015, https://www.huffpost.com/entry/a-serviceyear-for-the-na_b_6497294. In a blog post on the *Huffington Post* contributor platform, Michael Brown, City Year CEO and co-founder, writes, "Among Dr. King's most compelling visions is that of a Beloved Community: a community in which people of different backgrounds recognize that we are all interconnected and that our individual well-being is inextricably linked to the well-being of others."

35. hooks, *All About Love*, x–xi.

36. Jeffrey Pfeffer, *Dying for a Paycheck: How Modern Management Harms Employee Health and Company Performance—and What We Can Do About It* (New York: HarperCollins Publishers, 2018), 3.

37. We first heard this term in 2019 in a conversation we had with Ellen Friedman, former executive director of the Compton Foundation. She noted that a colleague had used this phrase to describe the cumulative effect on society of the United States' predominant ways of work and pervasive economic injustice. In the years since, the term has become more common.

Chapter 2: Reclaiming Our Rights to Design

1. Metrics of this level of resilience among breakout actors include: few to no layoffs; dissipated financial and other types of risk; more adaptive teams; strong, trusting relationships with collaborators, clients, and suppliers leading to resilient supply chains; and an overall feeling of empowerment from collaborative structures. This phenomenon is affirmed by broader research on the economic resilience of enterprises that embody collectivist approaches, similar to the ways in which breakout actors work. According to an article by Marc Schneiberg, during the Great Recession, counties with more enterprises that had a built-in collaborative structure—such as cooperatives or community banks—suffered fewer job losses, and in the aftermath of the recession, more job growth. Marc Schneiberg, "Organizational Infrastructures for Economic Resilience: Alternatives to Shareholder Value-oriented Corporations and Unemployment Trajectories in the US During the Great Recession," in *Organizational Imaginaries: Tempering Capitalism and Tending to Communities through Cooperatives and Collectivist Democracy*, eds. Katherine K. Chen and Victor T. Chen (Bingley, UK: Emerald Publishing, 2021), 187–228.

2. Rights to design are related to several rights enshrined in the Universal Declaration of Human Rights (http://www.un.org/en/universal-declaration-human-rights/). They also connect to principles of international law, such as the right to participate in society (https://www.humanrights.is/en/human-rights-education-project/human-rights-concepts-ideas-and-fora/substantive-human-rights).

3. Adam Simpson, "Capital Bias vs. Generative Design w/ Marjorie Kelly," September 20, 2017, in *The Next System Podcast*, podcast,

https://thenextsystem.org/learn/stories/episode-6-capital-bias-vs-generative-design-w-marjorie-kelly.

4. Caitlin Rosenthal, *Accounting for Slavery: Masters and Management* (Cambridge, MA: Harvard University Press, 2018), 134.

5. Michael Sainato, "'I'm not a robot': Amazon workers condemn unsafe, grueling conditions at warehouse," *Guardian*, February 5, 2020, https://www.theguardian.com/technology/2020/feb/05/amazon-workers-protest-unsafe-grueling-conditions-warehouse.

6. Vilna Bashi Treitler, *The Ethnic Project: Transforming Racial Fiction into Ethnic Factions* (Stanford, CA: Stanford University Press, 2013), 54.

7. Robert Reich, "Who Benefits from Racism?" (blog), June 16, 2020, https://robertreich.org/post/621130262966878209.

8. Correcting and reinforcing feedback loops are often called negative and positive feedback loops, respectively.

9. Orly Lobel, "NDAs Are Out of Control. Here's What Needs to Change," *Harvard Business Review*, January 30, 2018, https://hbr.org/2018/01/ndas-are-out-of-control-heres-what-needs-to-change.

10. James Surowiecki, *The Wisdom of Crowds: Why the Many Are Smarter than the Few and How Collective Wisdom Shapes Business, Economies, Societies, and Nations* (New York: Anchor Books, 2004), 36.

11. Venkat Ramaswamy and Francis Gouillart, *The Power of Co-Creation: Build It with Them to Boost Growth, Productivity, and Profits* (New York: Free Press, 2010).

12. Joanna Levitt Cea and Jess Rimington, "Creating Breakout Innovation," *Stanford Social Innovation Review*, Summer 2017, https://ssir.org/articles/entry/creating_breakout_innovation.

Chapter 3: The Seven Practices

1. As quoted in Robin Wall Kimmerer, "The Serviceberry: An Economy of Abundance," *Emergence Magazine*, December 10, 2020, https://emergencemagazine.org/essay/the-serviceberry/.

2. J.K. Gibson-Graham, Jenny Cameron, and Stephen Healy, *Take Back the Economy: An Ethical Guide for Transforming Our Communities* (Minneapolis: University of Minnesota Press, 2013), xiii.

3. Nicholas W. Eyrich, Robert E. Quinn, and David P. Fessell, "How One Person Can Change the Conscience of an Organization," *Harvard Business Review*, December 27, 2019, https://hbr.

org/2019/12/how-one-person-can-change-the-conscience-of-
an-organization.

4. S. Fisher Qua and Keith McCandless, "More Magic, Less Mystery:
Sustaining Creative Adaptability with Liberating Structures [Part
1 of 3]," *Medium* (blog), May 14, 2020, https://keithmccandless.
medium.com/more-magic-less-mystery-f9bc2d614e85. According
to S. Fisher Qua and Keith McCandless, who are two contributors
to the popular facilitation toolkit Liberating Structures, this
phenomenon is supported by the natural world. In "More Magic,
Less Mystery," they draw on *At Home in the Universe: The Search for
Laws of Self-Organization and Complexity* by theoretical biologist
Stuart A. Kaufman, who "proposes an 'adjacent possible' theory to
explain biodiversity on earth. [He] suggests that novel combinations
of proteins in DNA open up as you add other new combinations—
life keeps expanding into the adjacent possible. Life *orders itself
for free* in a continuous process of coevolution, enabling and
constraining biodiversity. The boundaries of what is possible *grow*
as you explore them."

5. For a complete list of co-learners, see pages 2–4.

RUNWAY

1. "About RUNWAY," RUNWAY, https://www.runway.family/
runway-overview.

2. "Pioneering Universal Basic Income for Entrepreneurs," *RUNWAY
Magazine*, September 2021, 24–28, https://static1.squarespace.
com/static/5f92023ca9102437ea92d188/t/6139411d3933f311f5
040c59/1631142231261/RUNWAY-Magazine-01-0921-spreads.pdf.

3. "Pioneering Universal Basic Income," *RUNWAY Magazine*, 24–28.

4. "Pioneering Universal Basic Income," *RUNWAY Magazine*, 24–28.

5. "The Runway Project: 2018–2019 Impact Report," RUNWAY, https://
static1.squarespace.com/static/5f92023ca9102437ea92d188/t/5f977
689b4dfb969e9cfe1bb/1603761807613/annual-report-091919.pdf.

6. Widely recognized for her groundbreaking work in economic
disruption, Jessica was a Center for Economic Democracy Fellow,
an RSF Social Finance Integrated Capital Fellow, a Nathan
Cummings Foundation Fellow, a BALLE Local Economy Fellow,
and is a lifelong fellow of the Sanford School of Public Policy at
Duke University and Southern University College of Business, as
well as the Political Power and Social Change Fellow of the HipHop

Archive & Research Institute at Harvard University's Hutchins Center for African & African American Research. Her innovative work has been profiled by NPR, *Next City*, *Essence*, Conscious Company, and F*ast Company*. *New York Times* -bestselling author of *Decolonizing Wealth*, Edgar Villanueva, calls her work the "medicine" modern philanthropy and investment need.

Chapter 4: Share Decision-Making Power

1. Frederic Laloux, *Reinventing Organizations: A Guide to Creating Organizations Inspired by the Next Stage of Human Consciousness* (Brussels, Belgium: Nelson Parker, 2014), 135.
2. Joreen (Jo Freeman), "The Tyranny of Structurelessness," in *Radical Feminism*, eds. Anne Koedt, Ellen Levine, and Anita Rapone (New York: Quadrangle Books, 1973), http://feminist-reprise.org/docs/ RF/TYRANNY_STRUCTURELESSNESS.pdf.
3. Joreen, "The Tyranny of Structurelessness," 297–98.
4. CommunityRule, https://communityrule.info/.
5. Dana Miranda and Rob Watts, "What Is a RAC I Chart? How This Project Management Tool Can Boost Your Productivity," Forbes Advisor, March 25, 2022, https://www.forbes.com/advisor/. business/raci-chart/.
6. "Clarifying Responsibilities with MOCHA," The Management Center, October 28, 2021, https://www.managementcenter.org/ resources/assigning-responsibilities/.
7. Wynton Marsalis and Geoffrey Ward, *Moving to Higher Ground: How Jazz Can Change Your Life* (New York: Random House, 2008), 38–40.
8. Mary B. Anderson, Dayna Brown, and Isabella Jean, *Time to Listen: Hearing People on the Receiving End of International Aid* (Cambridge, MA: CDA Collaborative Learning Projects, 2012), https://www. cdacollaborative.org/publication/time- to-listen-hearing-people-onthe-receiving-end-of-international-aid/.

Heart Research Alliance

1. Heart Research Alliance (website), heartresearchalliance.org/.

Chapter 5: Prioritize Relationships

1. Sarah Jaffe, *Work Won't Love You Back: How Devotion to Our Jobs Keeps Us Exploited, Exhausted, and Alone* (New York: Bold Type Books, 2021), 9.

2. "What Is Radical Candor?" Radical Candor, https://www.radicalcandor.com/.

3. "What We Do," Pathways to Resilience, https://pathwaystoresilience.net/about.

4. Kelly Ryan, "Community Picnic: It's about us," Incourage Community Foundation, August 2, 2016, https://incouragecf.org/news-media/blog-entry/community-picnic-us/.

5. Google, "Guide: Understand team effectiveness," re:Work, https://rework.withgoogle.com/print/guides/5721312655835136/.

6. Interaction Institute for Social Change, interactioninstitute.org/; Change Elemental: changeelemental.org/; Norma Wong. Norma Wong (Norma Ryuko Kawelokū Wong Roshi) is a teacher at the Institute of Zen Studies and Daihonzan Chozen-ji, having trained in Zen for nearly forty years. She serves practice communities in Hawai'i, across the continental US, and in Toronto, Canada. She works as a thought and strategy partner to community and justice activists. (wechooseallofus.sched.com/speaker/norma_wong.1y3eil2v.)

Incourage Community Foundation

1. Hold in Trust is a trademarked phrase of Ki ThoughtBridge. To learn more, please see the Ki ThoughtBridge website at https://www.kithoughtbridge.com/

Chapter 6: Reckon with History

1. Nwamaka Agbo, "What Is Restorative Economics?" https://www.nwamakaagbo.com/restorative-economics.

2. The Inner Work of the Leader is a trademarked phrase of Ki ThoughtBridge. To learn more, please see the Ki ThoughtBridge website at https://www.kithoughtbridge.com/

3. The Emergence Collective, https://www.emergence-collective.net/.

4. Jessica Gordon Nembhard, *Collective Courage: A History of African American Cooperative Economic Thought and Practice* (University Park: Penn State University Press, 2014).

5. bell hooks, *All About Love* (New York: William Morrow, 2001), 234.

TenSquared

1. TenSquared was developed as a collaboration between SAI and the Rapid Results Institute and with funding and support from the Walt Disney Company, it was piloted with dozens of companies in Turkey, Brazil, and China.

2. Social Accountability International, "TenSquared," November 19, 2015, YouTube video, 2:46, https://youtu.be/JoVDiFhlFiU.

3. Other examples of results from TenSquared's program include improving ergonomic setups for workers and reducing absenteeism related to workplace injury by 40 percent in an electronics manufacturing company in Brazil (https://sa-intl.org/resources/tensquared-case-studies/reducing-workplace-injuries-with-ergonomic-innovation-tensquared-case-study/)and reducing evacuation time by 75 percent for workers in an electronics manufacturing company in China (https://sa-intl.org/resources/tensquared-case-studies/improving-emergency-preparedness-tensquared-case-study/).

4. Social Accountability International, "TenSquared Turkey Pilot Final Report," August 2019, 16, https://sa-intl.org/resources/tensquared-case-studies/tensquared-turkey-final-report/.

5. Social Accountability International, "TenSquared."

6. Social Accountability International, "TenSquared."

7. Social Accountability International, "TenSquared."

8. Social Accountability International, "TenSquared."

Chapter 7: Seek Difference

1. David Rock and Heidi Grant, "Why Diverse Teams Are Smarter," *Harvard Business Review*, November 4, 2016, https://hbr.org/2016/11/why-diverse-teams-are-smarter; Aparna Joshi and Brett H. Neely, "A Structural-Emergence Model of Diversity in Teams," *Annual Review of Organizational Psychology and Organizational Behavior* 5, no. 1 (January 2018), 361–85, https://doi.org/10.1146/annurev-orgpsych-041015-062421.

2. Lisa H. Nishii, "The Benefits of Climate for Inclusion for Gender-Diverse Groups," *The Academy of Management Journal* 56, no. 6 (December 2013), 1754–74, https://doi.org/10.5465/amj.2009.0823.

3. KA McKercher, *Beyond Sticky Notes: Co-Design for Real: Mindsets, Methods and Movements* (self-pub., 2020), 152.

4. Edgar Villanueva, *Decolonizing Wealth: Indigenous Wisdom to Heal Divides and Restore Balance* (Oakland, CA: Berrett-Koehler Publishers, 2018), 57.

5. Liberating Structures, https://www.liberatingstructures.com/.

Standing Rock

1. Wikipedia, "Dakota Access Pipeline," last modified May 5, 2022, www.en.wikipedia.org/wiki/Dakota_Access_Pipeline.

Chapter 8: Source from Multiple Ways of Knowing

1. Sinziana Dorobantu and Dennis Flemming, "It's Never Been More Important for Big Companies to Listen to Local Communities," *Harvard Business Review*, November 10, 2017, https://hbr.org/2017/11/its-never-been-more-important-for-big-companies-tolisten-to-local-communities.

2. Lingtao Yu and Mary Zellmer-Bruhn, "What Mindfulness Can Do for a Team," *Harvard Business Review*, May 31, 2019, https://hbr.org/2019/05/what-mindfulness-can-do-for-a-team; Clay Routledge, "Bring the Outdoors into Your Hybrid Work Routine," *Harvard Business Review*, September 16, 2021, https://hbr.org/2021/09/bring-the-outdoors-into-your-hybrid-work-routine.

3. Kenneth Jones and Tema Okun, "White Supremacy Culture," in Dismantling *Racism: A Workbook for Social* (ChangeWork, 2001), reprinted by Minnesota Historical Society Department of Inclusion and Community Engagement, https://www.thc.texas.gov/public/upload/preserve/museums/files/White_Supremacy_Culture.pdf.

4. C. Otto Scharmer, *Theory U: Learning from the Future as it Emerges* (San Francisco, CA: Berrett-Koehler Publishers, 2009).

5. Russ Volckmann, "10/13—Otto Scharmer: Theory U—Leading from the Future as It Emerges," *Fresh Perspective*, Integral Leadership Review, October 13, 2013, http://integralleadershipreview.com/10916-otto-scharmer-theory-u-leading-future-emerges/.

6. Ron Friedman, "Regular Exercise Is Part of Your Job," *Harvard Business Review*, October 3, 2014, https://hbr.org/2014/10/regular-exercise-is-part-of-your-job.

7. Henna Inam, "Lead with Your Body in Mind," *Forbes*, May 13, 2014, https://www.forbes.com/sites/hennainam/2014/05/13/lead-with-your-body-in-mind/?sh=2e28c29549578.

8. Emma Seppälä and Johann Berlin, "Why You Should Tell Your Team to Take a Break and Go Outside," *Harvard Business Review*, June 26, 2017, https://hbr.org/2017/06/why-you-should-tell-your-team-to-take-a-break-and-go-outside.

9. KA McKercher, "What is Co-Design," in *Beyond Sticky Notes: Co-Design for Real: Mindsets, Methods and Movements* (self-pub., 2020), accessed at https://www.beyondstickynotes.com/what-is-codesign.

10. Palena Neale, "'Serious' Leaders Need Self-Care, Too," *Harvard Business Review*, October 22, 2020, https://hbr.org/2020/10/serious-leaders-need-self-care-too.

Creative Reaction Lab

1. Creative Reaction Lab, "Redesigners for Justice: the leaders we need for an equitable future," *Medium* (blog), September 23, 2019, https://medium.com/equal-space/redesigners-for-justice-theleaders-we-need-for-an-equitable-future-d3a73459ba60.

Chapter 9: Trust There Is Time

1. Tema Okun, "Sense of Urgency," White Supremacy Culture, https://www.whitesupremacyculture.info/urgency.html.
2. Juliet B. Schor, *The Overworked American: The Unexpected Decline of Leisure* (New York: Basic Books, 1993), 50.
3. Schor, *The Overworked American*, 50.
4. Okun, "Sense of Urgency."
5. Ayana Young, "Transcript: Dr. Bayo Akomolafe on Slowing Down in Urgent Times," January 22, 2020, in *for the wild*, podcast, 1:29:15, https://forthewild.world/podcast-transcripts/https/forthewildworld/listen/bayo-akomolafe-on-slowing-down-in-urgent-times.
6. Ayana Young, "Transcript: Dr. Bayo Akomolafe."

Chapter 10: Prototype Early and Often

1. Eric Ries, *The Lean Startup: How Today's Entrepreneurs Use Continuous Innovation to Create Radically Successful Businesses* (New York: Random House, 2011).
2. KA McKercher, *Beyond Sticky Notes: Co-Design for Real: Mindsets, methods, and movements* (self-pub., 2020), 34.
3. Kenneth Jones and Tema Okun, "White Supremacy Culture," in *Dismantling Racism: A Workbook for Social Change Groups* (ChangeWork, 2001), accessed via Minnesota Historical Society Department of Inclusion and Community Engagement, https://www.thc.texas.gov/public/upload/preserve/museums/files/White_Supremacy_Culture.pdf
4. "Philanthropist MacKenzie Scott graces INPEACE with a $5 Million Gift for Education in Indigenous Communities," INPEACE, February 25, 2022, https://inpeace.org/philanthropist-mackenzie-

scott-graces-inpeace-with-a-5-million-gift-for-education-in-indigenous-communities/.

Chapter 11: They May Try to Stop You

1. In a sample of twenty-seven breakout actors, each of whom we followed for at least five years, six encountered backlash. The primary forms of backlash experienced were: firing staff who led the breakout work (one breakout actor); denial or retraction of funding needed to support the breakout work (one breakout actor); a change in leadership in which new leadership rolled back the changes made and reinstated business-as-usual ways of work (three breakout actors); threats and attempted legal action against individuals leading the breakout work (one breakout actor).

2. Joanna Cea and Jess Rimington, "Designing with the Beneficiary: An Essential Strategy to Optimize Impact," *Innovations: Technology,Governance, Globalization* 11, no. 3–4 (Summer–Fall 2017): 98–111, https://doi.org/10.1162/inov_a_00259.

3. Heather Cox Richardson, "April 7, 2022," *Letters from an American* (newsletter), https://heathercoxrichardson.substack.com/p/april-7-2021.

4. Richardson, "April 7, 2022."

5. Matthew Wills, "A Critical Look at Gilded Age Philanthropy," *JSTOR Daily*, May 5, 2016, https://daily.jstor.org/gilded-age-philanthropy/.

6. Kevin D. Williamson, "Why Not Fewer Voters?" *National Review*, April 6, 2021.nationalreview.com/2021/04/why-not-fewer-voters/?taid=606d835e99742000014749f2.

7. Mike Solon and Bill Greene, "The Filibuster Helps Nobody, and That Means You," *Wall Street Journal*, June 20, 2021, https://www.wsj.com/articles/the-filibuster-helps-nobody-and-that-means-you-11624226249.

8. Thomas Hobbes, *Leviathan: Or The Matter, Forme & Power of a Commonwealth, Ecclesiasticall and Civill* (Cambridge, UK: Cambridge University Press, 1904), accessed via Google Books, https://www.google.ca/books/edition/Leviathan/-UA5AQAAMAAJ?hl.

9. Hobbes, *Leviathan*, 95–96.

10. "Garrett Hardin," Southern Poverty Law Center, https://www.splcenter.org/fighting-hate/extremist-files/individual/garrett-hardin.

11. E.P. Thompson, *Customs in Common* (London: Penguin Books,1993), 107. Quoted in Simon Fairlie, "A Short History of Enclosure in Britain," *The Land: An occasional magazine about land rights* 7 (Summer 2009), https://www.thelandmagazine.org.uk/articles/short-history-enclosure-britain.

12. Simon Fairlie, "A Short History of Enclosure in Britain," *The Land: An occasional magazine about land rights* 7 (Summer 2009), https://www.thelandmagazine.org.uk/articles/short-history-enclosure-britain.

13. Rebecca Solnit, *A Paradise Built in Hell* (New York: Penguin Books, 2009).

14. Dr. Riane Eisler's groundbreaking research discusses partnership systems versus domination systems. Domination systems are "a system of top-down rankings ultimately backed up by fear or force—man over man, man over woman, race over race, religion over religion, and man over nature," whereas "the configuration of the partnership system consists of... mutually supporting core components, such a more democratic and egalitarian structure in the family, economy, and state or tribe." In domination systems, there is a "devaluation by both men and women of anything stereotypically considered 'feminine,' including care." Riane Eisler, *The Chalice and the Blade: Our History, Our Future* (New York: HarperCollins, 1987), 13.

15. Robin Wall Kimmerer, "The Serviceberry: An Economy of Abundance," *Emergence Magazine*, December 10, 2020, https://emergencemagazine.org/essay/the-serviceberry/.

16. Prior to colonization, "America was a quilt of Native commons, each governed by the land-use rules of a specific human society." Allan Greer, "Commons and Enclosure in the Colonization of North America," *The American Historical Review* 117, no. 2 (April 2012), 365–86, https://doi.org/10.1086/ahr.117.2.365.

17. Jessica Gordon Nembhard, *Collective Courage: A History of African American Cooperative Economic Thought and Practice* (University Park: Penn State University Press, 2014).

18. "Our Vision," Zebras Unite Co-op, https://zebrasunite.coop/our-vision; "Zebra's Fix What Unicorns Break," *Medium* (blog), March 8, 2017, https://medium.com/zebras-unite/zebrasfix-c467e55f9d96.

19. "Almost overnight, peasant revolts ceased being local affairs and became large-scale threats to the feudal order. After 1347 these uprisings were synchronized—they were system-wide responses to an epochal crisis, a fundamental breakdown in feudalism's logic of power, production and nature." Jason W. Moore and Raj Patel, *A History of the World in Seven Cheap Things: A Guide to Capitalism, Nature, and the Future of the Planet* (Oakland: University of California Press, 2018), 12.

20. Jason W. Moore and Raj Patel, "Unearthing the Capitalocene: Towards a Reparations Ecology," Resilience, January 4, 2018, https://www.resilience.org/stories/2018-01-04/unearthing-the-capitalocene-towards-a-reparations-ecology/.

21. Moore and Patel, "Unearthing the Capitalocene."

22. Robin Wall Kimmerer, "Corn Tastes Better on the Honor System," *Emergence Magazine*, https://emergencemagazine.org/feature/corn-tastes-better/.

23. Fairlie, "A Short History of Enclosure in Britain."

24. Matthew Desmond, "In order to understand the brutality of American capitalism, you have to start on the plantation," in *The 1619 Project*, *The New York Times Magazine*, August 14, 2019, https://www.nytimes.com/interactive/2019/08/14/magazine/slaverycapitalism.html.

25. Tiya Miles, "Municipal Bonds: How Slavery Built Wall Street," in *The 1619 Project*, *The New York Times Magazine*, August 18, 2019, 40. Accessed via https://pulitzercenter.org/sites/default/files/inline-images/sRbkkE4IduC2XGTmp5SM5C0mOCyDZ4saROooccRM5t4NjkCgcj.pdf.

26. Fairlie, "A Short History of Enclosure in Britain."

27. Mary Watkins, *Mutual Accompaniment and the Creation of the Commons* (New Haven, CT: Yale University Press, 2019), 291.

28. Fairlie, "A Short History of Enclosure in Britain."

29. *Global Analysis 2020*, Front Line Defenders, February 9, 2021, https://www.frontlinedefenders.org/en/resource-publication/global-analysis-2020.

30. *Miners Shot Down*, directed by Rehad Desai (2014), documentary film, 84 min., https://minersshotdown.co.za/.

31. Jonathan Watts, "Berta Cáceres, Honduran human rights and environment activist, murdered," *Guardian*, March 4, 2016, https://www.theguardian.com/world/2016/mar/03/honduras-berta-caceres-murder-enivronment-activist-human-rights.

32. Jim Yong Kim, Joyce V. Mullen, Alec Irwin, and John Gershman, eds., *Dying for Growth: Global Inequality and the Health of the Poor* (Monroe, ME: Common Courage Press, 2000), 26.

PUSH Buffalo

1. Supportive housing is a strategy of community development that integrates affordable housing with intensive coordinated health and social services to enable people most vulnerable to displacement and homelessness—including seniors, people living with disabilities, and low-income families—to stay and thrive in their communities. Ehren Dohler, Peggy Bailey, Douglas Rice, and Hannah Katch, "Supportive Housing Helps Vulnerable People Live and Thrive in Community," Center on Budget and Policy Priorities, May 31, 2016, https://www.cbpp.org/research/housing/supportive-housing-helps-vulnerable-people-live-and-thrive-in-the-community.

Chapter 12: Practicing Beloved Economies

1. WRMCA recognizes Wisconsin Rapids Recreation Complex project," *Wisconsin Rapids City Times*, April 29, 2021, https://wrcitytimes.com/2021/04/29/wrmca-recognizes-wisconsin-rapids-recreation-complexproject/; "Wisconsin Rapids Regional Aquatics Center," *Athletic Business*, https://www.athleticbusiness.com/project-galleries/aquatic-design-portfolio/E6zOVr6l93/wisconsin-rapids-regional-aquatics-center-wisconsin-rapids-wi.

2. J.K. Gibson-Graham and Kelly Dombroski, eds., *The Handbook of Diverse Economies* (Cheltenham, UK: Edward Elgar Publishing, 2020), 197.

3. "Organically Grown Company Pioneers Groundbreaking Ownership Structure to Maintain Mission & Independence in Perpetuity," RSF Social Finance (press release), July 9, 2018, https://rsfsocialfinance.org/2018/07/09/organically-grown-company-pioneers-groundbreaking-ownershipstructure-to-maintain-mission-independence-in-perpetuity/. Bruce Campbell explains, "As investor counsel, Blue Dot helped to tailor investment and governance documents that elevated the influence of noninvestor stakeholders and dramatically limited conventional minority investment rights."

4. Dr. Wood adds, "It is when a nation makes it possible for every citizen to have a right to the earnings of capital as well as the earnings from labor."

5. "The good and just society is neither the thesis of capitalism nor the antithesis of communism, but a socially conscious democracy which reconciles the truths of individualism and collectivism." Dr. Martin Luther King Jr., *Where Do We Go from Here: Chaos or Community?* (Boston: Beacon Press, 2010), 197, originally published in 1967, accessed via https://www.google.ca/books/edition/ Where_Do_We_Go_from_Here/ka4TcURYXy4C?hl.

6. "Pioneering Universal Basic Income for Entrepreneurs," *RUNWAY Magazine*, September 2021, 24–28, https://static1.squarespace. com/static/5f92023ca9102437ea92d188/t/6139411d3933f311f5 040c59/1631142231261/RUNWAY-Magazine-01-0921-spreads.pdf.

7. John Ikerd, "The Case for Community Food Utilities," *Metro Caring* (blog), October 15, 2020, https://www.metrocaring.org/ blog/2020/10/15/guest-blog-the-case-for-community-food-utilities.

Thunder Valley Community Development Corporation

1. "Community Development Corporations (CDCs)," Community-Wealth.org, https://community-wealth.org/sector/ community-development-corporations-cdcs.

2. "Social Enterprise," Thunder Valley Community Development Corporation, https://www.thundervalley.org/initiatives/social-enterprise.

3. "Social Enterprise," Thunder Valley Community Development Corporation.

4. "Housing & Home Ownership," Thunder Valley Community Development Corporation, https://www.thundervalley.org/ initiatives/housing-and-home-ownership.

5. "Housing & Home Ownership," Thunder Valley Community Development Corporation.

Chapter 13: Reorienting Work toward Life

1. Dayna Baumeister, *The Biomimicry Resource Handbook: A Seed Bank of Best Practices* (self-pub., 2014).

2. Thomas D. Seeley and P. Kirk Visscher, "Group decision making in nest-site selection by honey bees," *Apidologie* 35, no. 2 (March–April 2004), 101–16, https://doi.org/10.1051/apido:2004004.

3. When applying biomimicry to our ways of work, it is important to look into the deep patterns exhibited across many species ways of collaborating, organizing, and adapting to ensure resilience that show up over and over again as success strategies. Toby Herzlich has emphasized to us that it would be a mistake to emulate the strategies of a single nonhuman species because, for instance, we are not ants, bees, or geese.

4. "A Conversation with Author Janine Benyus," The Buzz, Biomimicry 3.8, October 12, 2016, https://biomimicry.net/the-buzz/resources/conversation-author-janine-benyus/.

5. Ayana Young, "Transcript: Dr. Bayo Akomolafe on Slowing Down in Urgent Times," January 22, 2020, in *for the wild*, podcast, 1:29:15, https://forthewild.world/podcasttranscripts/https/forthewildworld/listen/bayo-akomolafe-on-slowing-down-in-urgent-times-155.

6. Arturo Escobar, *Designs for the Pluriverse: Radical Interdependence, Autonomy, and the Making of Worlds* (Durham, NC: Duke University Press, 2018).

7. Robin Wall Kimmerer, "Corn Tastes Better on the Honor System," *Emergence Magazine*, https://emergencemagazine.org/feature/corn-tastes-better/.

8. Ayana Young, "Transcript: Dr. Bayo Akomolafe on Slowing Down in Urgent Times."

9. Charles Eisenstein, "Transcript: The Wound of Separation," January 29, 2019, YouTube video, 6:15, https://charleseisenstein.org/video/the-wound-of-separation/.

10. Charles Eisenstein, "Transcript: The Wound of Separation."

11. Karen Barad, *Meeting the Universe Halfway: Quantum Physics and the Entanglement of Matter and Meaning* (Durham, NC: Duke University Press, 2007).

Epilogue

1. Excerpts are drawn from the writings of co-learning community members Andrew Delmonte, Antionette D. Carroll, Brian McLaren, Bryana DiFonzo, Ed Whitfield, Enoch Elwell, Jessica Norwood, John Ikerd, Katherine Tyler Scott, Lynn Cuny, Maurice BP-Weeks, and Rahwa Ghirmatzion.

Seven Practices and Life's Principles

1. Janine M. Benyus, "A Biomimicry Primer," *Biomimicry 3.8 Resource Handbook*, 2011, https://biomimicry.net/b38files/A_Biomimicry_Primer_Janine_Benyus.pdf.

2. Janine Benyus, "Biomimicry in action," TEDGlobal, July 2009, video, 17:23, https://www.ted.com/talks/janine_benyus_biomimicry_in_action?language=en.

3. Biomimicry Institute, "Entropy: Non-directional Carpet Tiles," http://toolbox.biomimicry.org/wp-content/uploads/2016/03/CS_Interface_TBI_Toolbox-2.pdf.

4. Dayna Baumeister, "Key Criteria for Building Enduring Partnerships," Synapse, October 16, 2017, https://synapse.bio/blog/2017/10/16/key-criteria-for-building-enduring-partnerships.

5. Tanveer Naseer, "Migrating Geese—A Lesson in Leadership and Collaboration," *Tanveer Naseer Leadership* (blog), n.d., https://www.tanveernaseer.com/migrating-geese-a-lesson-in-leadership-and-collaboration/.

6. Bernhard Voelkl, Steven J. Portugal, Markus Unsöld, James R. Usherwood, Alan M.Wilson, and Johannes Fritz, "Matching times of leading and following suggest cooperation through direct reciprocity during V-formation flight in ibis," *Proceedings of the National Academy of Sciences* 112, no. 7 (February 2, 2015), 2115–20, https://doi.org/10.1073/pnas.1413589112.

7. John A. Vucetich, Rolf O. Peterson, and Thomas A. Waite, "Raven scavenging favours group foraging in wolves," *Animal Behaviour* 67, no. 6 (June 2004), 1117–26, http://doi.org/10.1016/j.anbehav.2003.06.018.

8. Eric W. Seabloom, "Compensation and the Stability of Restored Grassland Communities," *Ecological Applications* 17, no. 7 (October 2007), 1876–85, https://doi.org/10.1890/06-0409.1; David Tilman, Johannes Knops, David Wedin, Peter Reich, Mark Ritchie, and Evan Siemann, "The influence of functional diversity and composition on ecosystem processes," *Science* 277, no. 5330 (1997), 1300–1302, https://doi.org/10.1126/science.277.5330.1300.

9. Anon., "Tallgrass Prairie: Basic Information," National Park Service, https://www.nps.gov/tapr/planyourvisit/basicinfo.htm.

10. Brian Resnick, "Trump doesn't have a science adviser. This slime mold is available," *Vox*, April 5, 2018, https://www.vox.com/science-andhealth/2018/3/6/17072380/slime-mold-intelligence-hampshire-college.

11. Jay Griffiths, "Dwelling on Earth," *Emergence Magazine*, October 3, 2019, https://emergencemagazine.org/essay/dwelling-on-earth/.

12. Gwyneth Dickey Zakaib, "The peppered moth's dark genetic past revealed," *Nature*, April 14, 2011, https://doi.org/10.1038/news.2011.238.